COMMON THINGS

FORDHAM UNIVERSITY PRESS   NEW YORK 2014

COMMONALITIES
Timothy C. Campbell, series editor

COMMON THINGS

*Romance and the Aesthetics of Belonging
in Atlantic Modernity*

JAMES D. LILLEY

Copyright © 2014 Fordham University Press

All rights reserved. No part of this publication may be reproduced, stored in a retrieval system, or transmitted in any form or by any means—electronic, mechanical, photocopy, recording, or any other—except for brief quotations in printed reviews, without the prior permission of the publisher.

"Henry Mackenzie's Ruined Feelings: Romance, Race, and the Afterlife of Sentimental Exchange." Copyright © 2007 *New Literary History*, The University of Virginia. This article first appeared in *New Literary History* Volume 38, Issue 4, Autumn, 2007, pages 649–66.

"Studies in Uniquity: Horace Walpole's Singular Collection" reprinted from *ELH*, vol. 80.1 (2013). Copyright © The Johns Hopkins University Press.

Fordham University Press has no responsibility for the persistence or accuracy of URLs for external or third-party Internet websites referred to in this publication and does not guarantee that any content on such websites is, or will remain, accurate or appropriate.

Fordham University Press also publishes its books in a variety of electronic formats. Some content that appears in print may not be available in electronic books.

Library of Congress Cataloging-in-Publication Data

Lilley, James D. (James David), 1971–
  Common Things : Romance and the Aesthetics of Belonging in Atlantic Modernity / James D. Lilley.
    pages cm. — (Commonalities)
  Includes bibliographical references and index.
  ISBN 978-0-8232-5515-3 (cloth : alk. paper)
  1. Literature—Philosophy—History. I. Title.
PN45 .L467
801—dc23

2013009214

Printed in the United States of America

16 15 14   5 4 3 2 1

First edition

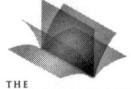

A book in the American Literatures Initiative (ALI), a collaborative publishing project of NYU Press, Fordham University Press, Rutgers University Press, Temple University Press, and the University of Virginia Press. The Initiative is supported by The Andrew W. Mellon Foundation. For more information, please visit www.americanliteratures.org.

CONTENTS

Acknowledgments vii

Introduction: Common Things 1

1 Genre 15

    A Singular Blend: Genre and the Aesthetics
of Belonging 15

    Allegory, Romance, and the Idea of Genre 20

    At Home with the Uncanny: Walpole
and the Idea of History 36

    Apology 47

2 Feeling 50

    Romance, Race, Ruin: Henry Mackenzie
and the Afterlife of Sentimental Exchange 50

    Jefferson and the Transatlantic Man
of Feeling 67

3 Property/Personhood 75

    Conjuring Community: *Arthur Mervyn*
and the Aesthetics of Ruin 75

    "My Extraordinary Duality":
The Metempsychosis of Modern
Personhood in *Sheppard Lee* 103

      Cooper, Mesmerism, and the "Immaterial
      Substance" of Taste in *The Autobiography
      of a Pocket-Handkerchief* 112

4 Event/Hiatus 120
      The Aesthetics of American Idling. 120
      Indian Removal and the Grimace
      of Ruined History. 142

5 No Thing In Common. 168
      Studies in Uniquity: Horace Walpole's
      Singular Collection 168
      Coda: Poe's Allegories of Belonging. 198

      Notes. 209
      Index. 237

ACKNOWLEDGMENTS

Born of the productive polarity between two necessary fictions—one of origins and origination, the other of closure and completion—what the acknowledgment first acknowledges is the mystery of belonging in and bearing witness to an experience, a history, a life. I owe my sense of this mystery—and my desire to explore its aesthetics of belonging—to many wonderful people, and I'd like to begin by acknowledging their singular influence over the work that follows.

This book began to take shape at the University of Arizona, where I had the chance to work with Colin Dayan, Annette Kolodny, and Greg Jackson in the Literature Program. Colin continued to influence my studies when I moved to Princeton, and *Common Things* grew out of discussions that we had with Eduardo Cadava and Claudia Johnson. In Eduardo and Claudia, I was fortunate enough to find talented and generous advisors who supplement their inspiration and support with the trust and freedom to let their students learn from their own mistakes. In addition to their friendship and their skills as advisors, I also benefitted from superb courses that they offered on Emerson, the gothic romance, and the sentimental novel. And in other equally memorable courses and discussions at Princeton, I found my approach to and understanding of literature transformed by D. Vance Smith, Jeff Nunokawa, Michael Wood, April Alliston, Jennifer Greeson, Cornel West, and a number of extremely talented graduate students who helped to make these classroom experiences so rewarding.

Princeton's financial support also made it possible for me to study with Meredith McGill at Rutgers and Eric Cheyfitz at the University of Pennsylvania; and my stipend facilitated a vital, if somewhat precarious, existence in upper, upper Manhattan, rich in companionship and conversation thanks to fellow graduate students Evan Horowitz, Michael Sayeau, and Liesl Olson. Liesl and I became friends at the Huntington Library, and the four spectacular summers that I spent in San Marino with the Huntington's special collections make their presence felt in both the form and the content of this work. I owe a huge debt of gratitude to Susi Krasnoo and Mona Noureldin for helping me to get to know Horace Walpole; and to my other Huntington pals—especially Roberto Alvarez, Jennifer Hallam, and Roze Hentschell—I thank you all for your warmth, support, and continued kindness over the years.

Over the past five years, the University at Albany, SUNY, has provided me with the intellectual and financial support necessary to complete this book. I am indebted to the advocacy of several department chairs—Mike Hill, Stephen North, and Randall Craig—as well as to grants from the English Department, the College of Arts and Sciences, and the United University Professions, for helping to foster the freedom necessary to think clearly. In both my graduate and undergraduate courses, remarkable students have accompanied me along some of the eccentric pathways in this book, enriching its argument in countless ways. In Albany, I have been spoiled with the kindness and vibrancy of mind of so many friends and colleagues. To Branka Arsić, I owe an infinite debt of thanks for the precision of her guidance as *Common Things* began to take its final shape. Jennifer Greiman's expertise and insight encouraged me to persist with certain lines of thought, while David Wills, Kir Kuiken, Bret Benjamin, Tom Cohen, and Paul Stasi helped me to grapple with ideas and prose as I moved through various stages of the book and its argument. I also send thanks to those colleagues whose friendship and hospitality at various dinner tables and other clean, well-lighted places have energized both my body and mind. In particular I toast Ed Schwarzschild, Laura Wilder, Helene Scheck, Elisa Albert, Liz Lauenstein, Richard Barney, Don Byrd, Patricia Chu, Eric Keenaghan, Tomás Urayoán Noel, and Ineke Murakami.

Beyond Albany, I have enjoyed friendship and conversation with scholars who have altered, challenged, and inspired the work you are about to read. Among many others, I'm especially grateful to Andy Doolen, Duncan Faherty, Ruth Mack, John Miles, Hillary Emmett, Gabriel Cervantes, Michael Drexler, Toni Wall Jaudon, Angela Mullis, Ed White, Sophie Gee, John Funchion, Siân Silyn Roberts, Ed Cahill, and Paul Kelleher for the myriad ways in which they make my profession feel like my home.

At Fordham University Press, I have been fortunate enough to work with Helen Tartar and a wonderful editorial staff who have skillfully and efficiently ushered this book to print. In particular I thank Timothy Campbell, Thomas Lay, Tim Roberts, Susan Murray, and the American Literatures Initiative for their support of and care with my work.

Finally, to my family on both sides of the Atlantic, I thank you for having faith in me over the long, long years of graduate study during which this project began to take shape. To Lorraine, Spiro, Peter, and Suzanne I am forever grateful for the gift of our community; and while I dedicate *Common Things* to the memory of my parents, Brenda and David Lilley, I offer it to you both, Lauren and Jack, and to the singularity of our quest.

INTRODUCTION
Common Things

THE GRAVITY OF BELONGING

In a powerful series of paintings composed between 2005 and 2008, the French artist Armelle Caron creates a set of decontextualized images of the modern cityscape (figure 1). On the left side of each image, the artist presents a familiar, monochromatic map of a major city—New York, Montpellier, or Paris, for example—while on the right side she identifies the units of the map and rearranges them in neat rows. She often exhibits these paintings along with wooden blocks, shaped in similar units, that are spread out on the floor underneath. Visitors to the exhibition are encouraged to rearrange these blocks and to form their own cityscapes.[1]

Caron's work helps us to visualize a key problem that besets the study of community: the tendency to think of both its space and its function as if it were a repository for things-in-common. Her decontextualized cityscapes perform a similar analytical operation, reducing each urban community to a neat code, a system of atomistic hieroglyphs that stress the thing out of which community is composed. But what is lost in this itemization of the commonplace—in the reduction of its community to an inventory of universalized common things—is precisely the gravity of belonging that holds these parts together in their unique urban constellations. Without addressing this other dimension of the experience of community, these individual, essentialized units—the common things so central to our understanding of modern politics and personhood—become what Jean Luc-Nancy has called "merely the residue of the experience of the dissolution of community. By its nature . . . the [modern] individual reveals that

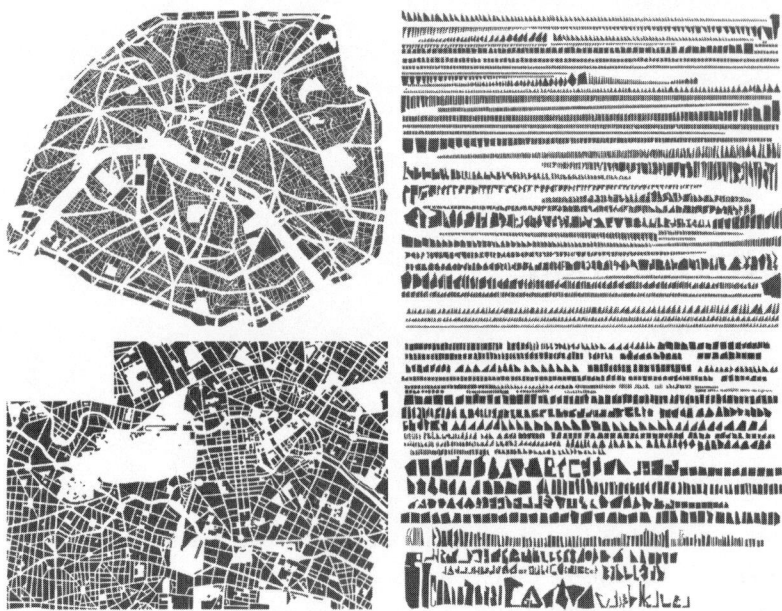

FIGURE 1. Armelle Caron, *Paris*; Armelle Caron, *Berlin*. Courtesy of the artist: http://www.armellecaron.fr/art/.

it is the abstract result of a decomposition."[2] While many scholars of the commonplace have embarked on the analytical journey from the left to the right of Caron's image, what remains largely unthought is the gravitational force required to voyage from right to left, the no-thing that constellates these various elements into their singular galaxies of community.

Common Things begins this voyage by revisiting recent and classic work in political philosophy and literary aesthetics. If the study of community is to address the qualitative force of immanent relationships holding the whole together as well as to itemize its common stuff, then one of the tools literary studies can bring to contemporary analyses of the commonplace is its attention to the inessential, aesthetic dimensions of expression. Dedicated to the promise of this relay between the form of community and the aesthetics of literature, this book is driven by the following question: What are the relationships between the books we read and the communities we share? In particular, it explores the ways in which the romance novel influences and is influenced by new systems of community that begin to emerge in the eighteenth century. While much recent and prominent work in political theory and U.S. and British literary studies has focused on one or two of these systems—the imagined communities of race or nation, for example—this book treats the relationship between literature and community as a question of universal aesthetic form as well as a problem of particular, imagined content.[3] Instead of approaching the romance novel as a mere repository for collective images or as a passive medium through which to convey mutual ideals, *Common Things* shows how it also promotes a distinctive aesthetics of belonging, a mode of being-in-common that is shared across a variety of modern systems of political, biological, temporal, and economic community. Drawing on foundational texts in the transatlantic traditions of Gothic, sentimental, and historical romance, I trace the development of a powerful aesthetic regime that renders visible new qualities that inhere within the singular and secure its connection with the common. Each chapter focuses on one of these common things—the stain of race, the "property" of personhood, ruined feelings, the genre of a text, and the event of history—and demonstrates how these elusive and interrelated qualities of the singular work to sustain the coherence of their respective commonplaces. Furthermore, I show how these same common things and their shared aesthetics of belonging help give birth to the mysterious figure at the heart of Western political communities: the liberal, rights-bearing subject.

From Washington Irving's tales of American idling to the adventures in exchange punctuating James Fenimore Cooper's *Autobiography of a Pocket-Handkerchief*, *Common Things* revisits and reinterprets the famous signatures of modern romance. It reads the processes of feeling, contagion, metempsychosis, mesmerism, commodification, alienation, and ruin that animate its pages as amplifications of the thingifying logic already at work in key rhetorics of U.S. and British democracy. As such it intervenes in debates concerning the rise of the romance novel and the birth of the modern, biopolitical subject by reading these two phenomena as mutual, coproductive processes. After all, as Jacques Rancière has recently argued, aesthetics and politics both bring to light a certain distribution of the sensible, establishing the parameters of what can be seen and who gets to be counted. It is the goal of *Common Things* to illuminate this peculiarly modern distribution of community.[4]

THE SUBJECTIVIZATION OF AESTHETICS

It is tempting to explain the power and prestige enjoyed by the modern *things* of community in terms of the rise of commodity culture and the ideological influence of capitalism in the eighteenth century. While Marx is very much alive and well in the pages that follow, it soon became clear to me that the commodity form—so famously described in *Capital*—is part of the problem that I wanted to investigate rather than its underlying cause. After all, what better example of a thing-in-common than Marx's commodity, circulating within an economy that treats its value as both an abstract, universalized quantity and a totally private, singular property that inheres within it? To be sure, the forces of industrialization and the imperatives of capitalism encourage and reinforce the structures of belonging that this study takes as its focus; but, as Marx understood, the commodity is involved in such an intimate, dialectical relationship with these "real" material conditions that its private form is never easily separated from the public effects that it ostensibly causes. Rather than seek out a first cause, I chose instead to trace a genealogy of belonging that brings forward the dialectical mutuality of concepts such as "public and private," "spiritual and material," and "liberty and servitude"—concepts that we often take for granted and that are so vital to our modern systems of community.

In *Common Things* I use the language of aesthetics, rather than the methods of historical materialism, to explore what is happening to the common at its most fundamental level. My central aesthetic claim, developed in chapter 1, is that during the eighteenth and nineteenth centuries the idea of allegory is eclipsed by the logic of the symbol. While allegory (literally "other speaking," from its Greek etymological roots) establishes immanent relationships of meaning between singular objects merely as an effect of the relative, gravitational tension between each other, the logic of the symbol relies on the singular object's direct and unmediated participation in a transcendent, common meaning: from the perspective of the symbol, each singularity possesses its own (albeit mysterious) link to the common. For Angus Fletcher, then, allegory is associated with a nominalist approach to signification: in an allegorical community of signs, he argues,

> there will be no ideas in a strict sense, no meanings segregated to a "higher" place on the interpretive side of the wall. The so-called

[allegorical] ideas of virtue and vice, good and evil, happiness and misery, fame and fortune will no longer be read as referring to universal notions. They will be mere functions of a shared human speech and language, mere conventions, mere names and their grammar. The allegory without ideas could make no appeal to universals and hence could never legitimately establish belief in imagined higher values.[5]

During the transition to modernity, however, the universalizing logic of the symbol swallows up this "allegory without ideas," monopolizing its claim on the aesthetics of belonging and debasing allegory into the shallowest of symbols.[6] In tandem with this aesthetic revolution—what Gadamer calls the "subjectivization of aesthetics"[7] and Walter Benjamin describes in terms of the "destructive extravagance" of Romanticism[8]—the *way* that the singular is imagined to relate to the common is transformed in modern systems of belonging. Rather than imagine the force of inessential, allegorical relationships between singularities, these systems begin to treat belonging solely as an essential, if ultimately elusive, private quality—a common thing that inheres symbolically within the singular: the human body is shaped by the stain of race that courses through its veins; the political identity of the citizen is linked to the inalienable possession of rights or the exercise of private sympathies and feelings; the generic text is stamped by the specific nature and function of its symbols; and the historical narrative is transformed into a collection of symbolic and singular events. By outlining how these private qualities of the singular both sustain and frustrate the emerging British and U.S. nations and their romance revivals, *Common Things* traces the transatlantic aesthetic origins of our modern systems of belonging.[9]

ON THE BORDERS OF BELONGING

Like Rancière, I use the term "aesthetics" to refer to particular distributions of the sensible—textual regimes of visibility that bring to light a certain manner of being-in-common or that establish the rules of community in a specific way. As such, aesthetics and politics are always intimately related. "Political conflict," notes Rancière, "does not involve an opposition between groups with different interests. It forms an opposition between logics that count the parties and the parts of the community in different ways."[10] By exploring how literature helps to found, support, and challenge these logics of the common, this book's approach to the "politics" of the romance novel differs from much recent work in political philosophy and literary studies.

In an effort to redraw the imagined contours of our modern political, national, and racial communities, literary critics are currently engaged in a number of fascinating and important projects aimed at "remapping" terrains of extranational influence and "posthuman" topographies of belonging. When I began work on this book, for example, the concept of "border literature"—and the practice of "border studies" that these texts facilitated—was generating considerable critical excitement.[11] While the expansive, hybridized space of the borderlands appeared to challenge the idea of a monolithic U.S. culture, I grew concerned that literary critics were taking for granted its inherently subversive topography.[12] We see this same tendency in the practice of "transatlantic studies," with its desire to read literature and culture beyond the traditionally distinct disciplinary borders of "American" and "British" literature. In a 2011 special issue of *New Literary History* dedicated to the question of the transatlantic (one of many special issues that have been spawned in the name of literary transnationalism in recent years), Winfried Fluck describes the alluring "flow and flexibility" of a newly liberated subject/critic no longer bound by the topography or the sovereignty of a single nation.[13] He argues that literary critics have embraced this kind of "turbotransnationalism" in response to

> an impasse that prior approaches in American studies had reached. Analyses of American society and culture by . . . Americanists had been carried to a point where subjection by means of interpellation through the nation-state seemed to be all pervasive, so that resistance had to resort to ever more marginalized subject positions as possible sources of disinterpellation. At this point, transnationalism could become the logical next step in what may be seen as a story of continuous retreat. . . . Since the search for subject positions that would not yield to the power-effects of interpellation had already led to border regions and intercultural spaces, why not go beyond the border altogether into spaces like the Southern hemisphere, the Pacific Rim, or the transatlantic world, or still even further, to reconfigure the object of analysis as global or planetary?[14]

Rather than a radical departure from earlier forms of American studies, Fluck's analysis helps us to see how the transnational has "merely extended long dominant paradigms beyond borders."[15] In particular, he is here thinking "of the tendency to reduce questions of power to questions of identity formation [and] of the tendency to reduce identity-formation to racialization and engendering, perhaps because these are phenomena where the concept of interpellation can be most extensively applied."[16]

Understandably preoccupied with the ways in which discourses of race and gender work to exclude bodies from membership in the national common, American and transatlantic studies thus tend to contribute to a "mythology of the marginalized and excluded who have become exemplary reference points for envisioning disidentificatory mobility and subject-positions 'in-between.'"[17] Although the newly expanded and dynamic spaces of the borderlands and the transatlantic certainly bring into question *who* the nation can count among its members, they often fail to address key political "questions of power" involving the rules of membership—the aesthetics of belonging—that govern *how* each member is to be counted and included. In her own interrogation of transatlantic studies, Robyn Wiegman notes that "while exclusions [involving race and gender, for example] have particular histories, exclusion as a category of politics and knowledge . . . is *historical*."[18] "Any recognition," she continues, "of its centrality to the rise of the nation-state and the liberal constitutional forms that have attended it would require not simply an account of who and what is excluded, but an engagement with why and how "exclusion" has become such a singularly important affective discourse, interpretive strategy, and political idiom in modern U.S. life."[19] And as Hannah Arendt and Giorgio Agamben point out, even political and literary communities organized around universalizing concepts such as "human rights," "multiculturalism," and "transnational citizenship" share the same rules of membership, the same logic of exception, that fuels the evils of the nation-state. How can such concepts address the central political dilemma of modernity—the plight of the nonhuman and noncitizen refugee—when their own status as legitimate "human" concepts rests on the exclusion of precisely these same categories of non-subject? "The paradox," as Agamben points out,

> is that precisely the figure that should have embodied human rights more than any other—namely, the refugee—mark[s] instead the radical

crisis of the concept. The conception of human rights based on the supposed existence of a human being as such, Arendt tells us, proves to be untenable as soon as those who profess it find themselves confronted for the first time with people who have really lost every quality and every specific relation except for the pure fact of being human.[20]

What is needed is a new way of thinking citizenship, a new way of belonging in the political common, that does not, however unintentionally, help to fuel our modern biopolitical systems of exclusion—replacing one common thing (our race, our nation, or our gender, for example) with yet another property such as "human rights" that is somehow to be possessed and held in common among a discrete and identifiable community.[21]

Étienne Balibar poses the problem as follows:

> As long as we are working from an exclusively logical point of view, it seems difficult to escape the dilemma: *either* the emergence of a particular community that "gathers" a multiplicity of individuals . . . under a common denominator [and that] must *exclude* from its unity . . . those who do not "participate" as full-fledged members, *or else* multiplicity, differences, even conflict remain irreducible, placing us before the paradox of a community that could not clearly distinguish the inside from the outside or unity from division. But this logic, precisely, is only logic, founded on the formal schema of all or nothing (*either belonging, or else nonbelonging*). It is by no means certain that it applies in an absolute way to social and political realities. In any case, it calls for a close discussion of the modalities of its application.[22]

Common Things participates in these debates by tracing the genealogy of our modern modes of being-in-common. For as Balibar suggests—and as the literature that I study below demonstrates—our "either-or" logic of belonging has not always enjoyed a monopoly on the commonplace. Its air of inevitability and conceptual force are ideological victories that had to be won; and the romantic literature of the emerging British and U.S. nations proved a vital aesthetic battleground in which to imagine and debate these proper modes of belonging. Rather than challenge the nation-state by highlighting its hidden, repressed *content*—the ghosts of the slaves, the poor, and the indigenous peoples who helped to create it, for example—I argue that we must also historicize the development of its *form*, its grammars of belonging. To approach the question of national community from this formal, aesthetic perspective is, as Jonathan Culler argues, to rethink the relationship between literature and politics. This relationship, he argues, "is not one of identity of content but of homology of form: it is the formal organization of literary works, the operations for the production of meaning at work in literature, which relate directly to society, and what they relate to is not the content of social life but the operations which produce social and cultural objects, the devices which create a world charged with meaning."[23]

To be sure, studies that challenge the nation-state by increasing the size, the diversity, and the content of its community can assist us in remembering the ideological repressions and political exclusions that helped the U.S. and British nations to emerge. But as Werner Hamacher argues, even the ideas of an expanded *multi*cultural community or a *trans*national citizenry share the same conceptual form, the same grammar as the nation-state that they hope to supplant: "[T]he concept of cultural diversity, and especially the concept of its desirability, itself has a relatively precise historical context: it belongs, like the concept of democracy, to the European-American cultures and has, to my knowledge, never appeared as a descriptive category nor, even less, as an imperative, in any other culture. The word 'multiculturalism' speaks a European language."[24] For Hamacher, as for Agamben, Arendt, and Balibar, there is something about the logical structure of such universalist language—the grammar of abstract concepts such as human rights—that necessarily objectifies, colonizes, and enslaves the singular human subject at the same time that it espouses their fundamental freedoms and their inalienable right to autonomy. This is why freedom and slavery, as David Kazanjian has argued, are not to be thought of as discrete and antithetical ideas but, rather, should be examined in terms of their mutuality and coproduction.[25]

In what follows, I show how the conceptual grammar, the logic of the "either-or" that ties these ideas together, functions by producing a series of interrelated (and ultimately illusory) common things. The "things" that I highlight—genre, feeling, race, personhood, property, taste, and event— are by no means the only peculiar properties of the common that begin to emerge during the period that I study. However, by foregrounding their similarities in form I hope to bring into focus the complex aesthetic-political forces at work in our modern systems of community.

COMMON THINGS

In order to register the mutuality of these literary and political distributions of the sensible, *Common Things* establishes a diverse archive of primary texts. It explores the strange, universal property "planted" in Lockean personhood; the "voluptuousness" of sentimental ruin shared by Henry Mackenzie's men of feeling; the "black of the negro" that, for Thomas Jefferson, stamps and singularizes this race by forever veiling its affections; the contagious "pest" that devastates public space and delimits personal identity in Charles Brockden Brown's romance of yellow fever; and the idle hiatus that, for Washington Irving, fragments the experience of modernity and consigns the Native American to the ruined, manifest annals of history. Because these peculiar qualities of time, race, feeling, and personhood continue to animate our own commonplaces, and because our political horizons remain restricted by their forms of belonging, this book is propelled by the urgent need to both identify *and* to rethink their aesthetic regime. This is why I begin and end by analyzing the work of two writers, Horace Walpole and Edgar Allan Poe, who describe new forms of relationship between the singular and the common. Instead of communities grounded in the notion of a shared similarity or a timeless essence that each of its members somehow possesses, these writers develop an aesthetic practice that celebrates and collects the "uniquity" of the singular—a term invented by Walpole and, later, resurrected by Poe in order to identify inessential vectors of relation and fleeting forces of tendency and "effort." At stake in their work is what *Eureka*, Poe's enigmatic romance of cosmological origins, calls a new "brotherhood among the atoms," an active mode of being-in-common that establishes fugitive connections "among"—rather than the passive, common essentials "of"—unique singularities.[26]

In chapter 1, I read the preface to Horace Walpole's *The Castle of Otranto* (1764)—the first work of modern fiction to identify itself as a romance—in order to discuss the ways in which the singular text belongs in communities of genre. In particular, I argue that *Otranto* rejects the essentializing, symbolic logic that produces the common, generic things of the modern collection. While antiquarians and poets plumb the relics of ancient poetry for signs of a shared national history or the symbols of a common literary tradition, Walpole refuses to tie the idea of generic community to any timeless and transcendent symbols that the text possesses. By inventing an ancient romantic manuscript that *Otranto*'s pseudonymous narrator claims to have uncovered, the performative origins of the Gothic romance demonstrate how generic community—and belonging itself—is enacted as a singular creative force as well as collected as a common symbolic thing. Throughout this chapter, I read Walpole's *Otranto* alongside the concept of allegory developed by Walter Benjamin in the *Trauerspielbuch*, bringing forward the ways in which these texts help us to rethink the limitations of recent work in genre and set theory by opening up new forms of relationship between the singular and the common.

While my first chapter explores how the singular text belongs in communities of genre, my second examines how private feelings are collected into an eighteenth-century and transatlantic culture of sentiment. Scholars of early national and antebellum American literature often read the sentimental romance as an inherently democratic genre in which marginalized subjects, excluded by their gender or race, are permitted to register their feelings in the public sphere. I complicate this approach by identifying mutual aesthetic processes of inclusion *and* exception that enable these feelings to be collected by the sentimental community. Focusing on two of the most important eighteenth-century "men of feeling," Henry Mackenzie and Thomas Jefferson, I argue that instead of promoting feeling as a universal capacity shared among a (re)public, they also ruin—and then mourn—feeling as an utterly private thing, as a veiled affective fragment incapable of ever being publicized. Rather than simply promoting liberal and Enlightenment ideas of freedom, charity, and democracy, the sentimental romance also needs the prestige of these singular and private differences. As such, I show how for Jefferson the tearful man of feeling and the Enlightened man of science are dialectical twins rather than agonistic opposites: the political systems they both help to found return again and again to the spectacle of the ruined sentimental body, a spectacle that emerging taxonomies of racial difference similarly invoke in their own romance of blood.

In chapter 3, I focus on Charles Brockden Brown's important novel *Arthur Mervyn* (1799). Brown's text exposes the twin, Lockean foundations of U.S. political, racial, and financial communities—property and personhood—as Gothic conjurations rather than as solid, common things. Set during Philadelphia's 1793 yellow-fever epidemic, Brown's novel shows how property and its ruinous "pest" work together to coproduce the illusion of the modern subject: if Lockean property is a romance of contagion enabling the subject to connect itself, through a labor of prosthesis, to a world of property, then the pest names the "thing" that animates its ruin. No matter in which direction these circuits flow—toward accretion or decomposition, toward civilization or destitution—their contagious current produces the fantasy of isolated-but-connected subjects who inhabit a world of private, ownable things. With the pest's ruinous pathway immunized into both the formal framework of the novel and the physical frame of its protagonist, *Arthur Mervyn* unveils modernity's pervasive aesthetic logic—a logic that connects the melancholia of the man of feeling with modern systems of identity, with the everyday operation of the modern city, and with its institutional common spaces. In Robert Montgomery Bird's *Sheppard Lee* (1836) and James Fenimore Cooper's *Autobiography of a Pocket-Handkerchief* (1843), these same immunitary processes are converted into a regime of Gothic effects that include metempsychosis, mesmerism, and galvanic reanimation. Instead of ridiculing these special effects, the texts in this chapter show how they help to congeal the Anglo Saxon's "fleshly matrix" of spirit, matter, and personhood.

Critics of Washington Irving's work often note its detachment from time and space, its "uncircumscribed" and idling hiatus from the norms of neoclassicism, the Enlightenment, U.S. political history, and modernity itself. How odd, then, that this same body of work should both inaugurate U.S. literary history and introduce the new nation to its first professional author and historian. In my fourth chapter, I argue that Irving's texts—in particular *The Sketch-Book* (1819) and *A Tour on the Prairies* (1835)—offer an alternative approach to the oddness of this paradox, an approach that refuses to reduce the hiatus and its aesthetics of idling to a time and a place strictly *outside* the modern U.S nation and its history. Irving, like *The Sketch-Book*'s Rip Van Winkle, is never simply modernity's Other: in the same way that this author will both critique and reinforce progressive myths of nationalist history over the course of his career, so too will Rip both eschew and, ultimately, embrace the "rising generation, with whom he soon grew into great favor."[27] Instead of resolving the oddness of these important tensions in Irving's work, I argue that that their dialectical mutuality works to *establish* rather than resist the peculiarly modern space and time of the U.S. nation. Deploying Jean-Luc Nancy's and Giorgio Agamben's notion of the "ban"—a form of relation that blurs distinctions between politics and life and that soon begins to permeate and pattern our biopolitical horizons—I argue that Irving's dialectics of hiatus and wholeness, of idle homelessness and destined homeland, function as intimately political forms of relation that help to ground our modern aesthetics of belonging.

My final chapter shows how Walpole and Poe refuse to imagine community as a simple collection of common things. They instead practice a philosophy of "uniquity" that values and collects the singular for its totally accidental and *in*essential forces of relation, tendency, and difference. Eschewing the modern logic of belonging that ties the singular's place in the common to some essential property that it somehow possesses, Walpole and Poe instead view being-in-common as an open and fugitive process that is enacted on the level of the verb rather than collected on the level of the noun. Walpole writes histories that foreground the contingency of time rather than offer any definitive account of its passing, and his always-expanding collection of curiosities exhibits the harmonious confusion of the *Wunderkammer* rather than the taxonomic pretensions of the modern museum. And for Poe, at stake in the speculative cosmology of *Eureka* is the aesthetic form of a "brotherhood among the atoms." Here and throughout this text, Poe attempts to think community as an assemblage of intensive differences that vibrates "among" atoms rather than as a collection of common, atomic things. I end with these "hospital[s] for everything that is *Singular*" because they show us how to reopen the problem of belonging's form at a moment of crisis in our own conceptions of cultural, economic, and political community.[28]

Rather than trace the development of different ideas of "community" through a specific historical period or across a particular geographical location, this book instead gravitates around a series of important and interrelated *things* that animate the commonplaces of Atlantic modernity. Because my central argument concerning the relationship between these common things and modernity's pervasive aesthetic logic is developed in chapter 1, I chose to arrange the other chapters in loosely chronological order so that certain connections could be highlighted. A chapter concerned with eighteenth-century sentimental romance is followed by a chapter that draws on the late-eighteenth-century Gothic novel. And a chapter on Washington Irving's early-nineteenth-century Gothic and frontier romance precedes the final chapter on Poe's midcentury prose poem *Eureka*. However, as my first chapter argues—and as the presence within these chapters of texts from other historical periods and literary genres demonstrates—not only am I uninterested in marking any teleological "development" of romance forms (from, say, the sentimental to the Gothic, and from the Gothic to the historical); I am also more concerned with the formal similarities between these genres of modern romance than I am in establishing or policing the borders between their ostensibly distinct aesthetic modes. Even the question of resistance to modernity's aesthetics of belonging—the focus of my final chapter on the "no thing" of community—is raised by two writers who chronologically bookend the content of my study, Horace Walpole and Edgar Allan Poe. The fact that these authors, separated both in time and place, share a similar approach to the potentialities of belonging suggests that resistance is not simply related to a particular moment in the unfolding of history, an unfolding that seems ever-destined to naturalize rather than to problematize modernity's peculiar forms of the common. Because we continue to inhabit these same forms of belonging, the strategies of opposition they share remain timely: they teach us, for example, that resistance is a matter of retelling historical narratives of influence, of reimagining the ways in which we belong together in time and space, and of rethinking the strangleholds of genre. By focusing on some of these unconventional, formal connections between texts and across historical periods, I will no doubt fail to do justice to the complex historical and political contexts within which they emerge. I hope that the benefits of my fugitive methodology will outweigh these considerable costs.

1

GENRE

> A major work will either establish the genre or abolish it;
> and the perfect work will do both.
>
> —WALTER BENJAMIN, *The Origin of German Tragic Drama*

A SINGULAR BLEND: GENRE AND THE AESTHETICS OF BELONGING

With the addition of one word to the second edition of *The Castle of Otranto* (1765), Horace Walpole performed the perfect generic gesture. Whereas the first edition of his bizarre tale of incest, patriarchal violence, and talking paintings is subtitled simply "A Story," with the second edition, published only months after the scandalous original, Walpole made an addition that has come to haunt literary critics ever since. Now titled *The Castle of Otranto, A Gothic Story*, Walpole composed a new preface that famously outlines his approach to genre, an approach that claims to "blend the two kinds of romance, the ancient and the modern."[1] Connecting Walpole's revised "Gothic" title with the prefatorial comments on romance that follow, scholars point to *Otranto*'s originary status as a text that inaugurates a new literary genre: the Gothic romance. Walpole creates "the first modern British fiction to identify itself as a distinct kind under the name of 'romance,'" observes Ian Duncan, and so the publication of *Otranto* has come to constitute an important event in the history of genre—an event that seemingly validates the subgeneric and that opens up the possibility for romance to branch off into ever-specialized flavors ("sentimental," "historical," "frontier," and the always-tempting "Gothic," for example).[2] Such distinctions continue to animate and ground discussions of genre and literary nationalism, reinforcing the need for critics to frequently revisit the event of *Otranto* and reinterpret its generic significance.

Few writers are so dedicated to interrogating the complex potentialities and paradoxes of genre: Walpole in general and *Otranto* in particular have much indeed to teach us about the commonplaces of language and literature. The fragmented entirety of Walpole's massive work both explores and embodies the possibility of a linguistic being-in-common; and his pioneering work in architecture, historiography, art history, gardening theory, and the craft of printing is rooted in a fecund engagement with the fundamental generic relationship between singularity and the common multiplicity. To borrow one of Walpole's own neologisms, his work is devoted to the exploration of "uniquity."[3] Or, in the words of *Otranto*'s preface, Walpole's obsession is with the "blend," with both the form and the content of a generic operation that combines distinct singularities (the "ancient" and the "modern," for example) into a bizarre common mixture that both unites and preserves—that unites *as* it preserves—the uniquity of experience. While critics are thus well justified in according Walpole an important place in the discourse of genre, they often do so without savoring the rich complexities of his generic blend, complexities that humble as well as mobilize the disciplinary distinctions that make genre and subgenre thinkable. In order to restore a sense of strangeness to our linguistic commonplaces, this chapter begins by investigating the peculiar structure of genre's blend, the uncanny mixture of singularity and multiplicity through which the generic lives. And before concluding with a reassessment of Walpole's famous prefatorial gesture, it explores how one particular genre/subgenre pair, the romance and the Gothic, find their ways into modern narratives of generic continuity and commonality.

ENTITIES OF BELONGING

Any student of analytic philosophy or mathematical set theory will attest to the queerness of commonality. In the same way that genre names the possibility that a singular event of textuality (*The Castle of Otranto*, for example) can possess a common entity that is simultaneously shared by other textual events (the Gothic romance), so too set theory asserts that the singularity of numbers can enter into multiplicities, classes, that model the various complexities of the world. As one of the key figures in the development of mathematical and set theoretical logic, Bertrand Russell, puts it: "When we say that a number of objects all have a certain property, we naturally suppose that [this shared] property is a definite object, which can be considered apart from any of all the objects, which have ... the property in question. We also naturally suppose that the objects which have the property form a *class*, and that the class is in some sense a new single entity distinct ... from each member of the class."[4] What Russell points out here, then, is that set theory, like genre, proceeds by way of delimiting a status of belonging—in the case of our example, the possibility that the singular event of language also possesses some other kind of "entity" that constitutes its "romance-ness." For set theory and genre to proceed, we must presuppose a generic concept—romance-ness—that enables the event of language to participate in a relationship of belonging. This status of belonging—the romance-ness that holds genre together—must exist in some language events, but not in all of them, otherwise we would not be able to use "romance" as a principle of distinction and difference. So romance-ness is an "entity" that certain things possess while others do not.[5]

But how are we to conceive of and articulate this entity? What is the status of its thinghood, and how does it animate the common? As Russell and the German logician Gottlob Frege soon began to realize, the principle of belonging through which set theory, language, and genre proceed resists registration and threatens to undo mathematical logic at its core.[6]

As Frege's groundbreaking second volume of *The Basic Laws of Arithmetic* was going to press in June 1902, Russell wrote to alert him to a potentially devastating paradox. In what became one of the most infamous letters in the history of analytic philosophy, Russell's paradox outlines a fatal flaw in Rule V of Frege's logic that stems from the presuppositional nature of language and registration. The paradox begins with the fact that a set can be a member of itself. Consider, for example, the set that delimits the following group of items: "The set of thinkable things." Since the set describes a field of belonging in which it should include itself—after all, the idea of a set of thinkable things is itself a thinkable thing—then we can say that it includes itself as a member in its own set. (There are, of course any number of such sets. For example, the set of all non-cats would have to include itself as a

Genre 17

member.) Now the fact that a distinction can be made between sets that contain themselves as members and sets that do not gives the paradox its momentum. What Russell brought to Frege's attention was the problem of this latter division of sets, the set of all sets that do not contain themselves. Russell realized that an aporia opens up when you ask the following question of that set: Is it a member of itself? As the following examples demonstrate, this set can only be a member of itself if it is not a member of itself; and it can only *not* be a member of itself if it isn't a set.

Russell helps us visualize this paradox in the following way: imagine a town in which every man either shaves himself or is shaved by the barber. This establishes two sets: the set of men who shave themselves (set A) and the set of men who are shaved by the barber (set B). Now consider that in this town, these sets form a totality—so that (1) everyone must either shave themselves or be shaved by the barber—and that they are completely discrete and do not intersect, such that (2) those men who shave themselves are not shaved by the barber, and that (3) those men who do not shave are shaved by the barber. This sounds like the perfect situation for set theory to model, until the question is asked: Does the barber shave himself? If he does, then according to condition (2) he shaves himself and therefore isn't shaved by himself. If he doesn't, then according to (3) he does.

Another way to consider this problem is to imagine a "list of lists" such as the following:

List of red things	*List of dog breeds*	*List of countries*	*List of lists that do not contain themselves*
Sunsets	Great Dane	Belgium	List of red things
Clown's nose	Mastiff	England	List of dog breeds
	Greyhound	USA	List of countries
	Beagle		List of lists that do not contain themselves?

The problem arises when we think about the last list—the list of all lists that do not contain themselves. Does that list list itself? If it does, then it can't list itself since it is a list of lists that don't list themselves. But if it doesn't list itself, then it isn't a list of lists that don't list themselves. Anything but cocktail party curiosity, this paradox continues to haunt analytic philosophy and mathematical logic. Frege was forced to stop publication of his *Laws* so that he had time to compose a brief appendix detailing Russell's discovery and suggesting avenues of exploration that might solve the paradox. Later in life, he concluded that the problem was unsolvable and gave up his hope of a universal logic, while the heirs to his problem—including Russell himself—have tried to cordon off, unsuccessfully, the scope of its implications.

Earlier in his career, Frege had been alerted to a similar paradox that threatened his belief in a fundamental distinction between concepts and objects. Benno Kerry pointed out that such a distinction cannot be registered in language, since to talk about the nonobjectivity of concepts is to nevertheless grant them the status of an *object in language*. He phrased the dilemma thus: the concept "horse" is not a concept. Here we see how something defined precisely by its unwillingness to become objectivized— the "concept"—can enter into linguistic signification only insofar as it is treated as an object already allied with language. As Frege admitted:

> It must indeed be recognized that here we are confronted by an awkwardness of language, which I admit cannot be avoided, if we say that the concept *horse* is not a concept. . . . Language is here in a predicament. . . . In logical discussions one quote often needs to assert something about a concept, and to express this in the form usual for such assertions, *viz.* to make what is asserted of the concept into the content of the grammatical predicate. Consequently, one would expect that the reference of the grammatical subject would be the concept; but the concept as such cannot play this part, in view of its predicative nature; it must first be converted into an object, or speaking more precisely, represented by an object.[7]

How is it, then, that the generic urge—the desire to create commonalities like the concept or the Romance—persists in the face of such predicaments?

The point I want to emphasize here is that the idea of belonging that makes it possible to conceive of mathematical sets and of generic literary categories is, even at its most theoretically complex level, incapable of being fully articulated within the systems it helps to found. Nevertheless, this does not mean that relationality does not exist, that the function of genre is meaningless and empty, or that belonging cannot be experienced. Rather, what these paradoxes reveal to us is that belonging does not reside only in the places that we typically think it does. "Romance-ness," for example, is not something that simply—if somewhat ambiguously—resides as an essence within the event of language: the "entity" of its belonging cannot be thought of only as a content, for it is precisely such classifications that pave the way for the paradoxes that so vexed Russell and Frege during their lives. What remains to be thought within literary and genre studies is this unhomely blend of belonging, this content-less, *in*essential empty set that makes language, genre, and the commonplace possible.

ALLEGORY, ROMANCE, AND THE IDEA OF GENRE

In his "Epistemo-Critical Prologue" to *The Origin of the German Tragic Drama*, Walter Benjamin tackles these same complexities of textual belonging. Before moving on to an extended analysis of the form and function of literary genre, Benjamin begins by addressing the methodological difficulties that confronting the generic entails. In particular, he demonstrates the inability of "inductive" and "deductive" critical approaches to capture the elusive spirit of the commonplace. Whereas an inductive method begins with the assumption of generic commonality and proceeds by way of accumulating textual examples that confirm or deny this methodological presupposition, a deductive approach reduces the multiplicity of textual examples to a common, universal essence. Here Benjamin censures R. M. Meyer's critical method: "its aim is to abstract, by means of comparison of the outstanding representatives of each genre, rules and laws with which to judge the individual product. And by means of a comparison of the genres it seeks to discover general principles which apply to every work of art."[8] "Whereas induction reduces ideas to concepts by failing to arrange and order them," Benjamin argues that "deduction does the same by projecting them into a pseudo-logical continuum. The world of philosophical thought does not, however, evolve out of the continuum of conceptual deductions, but in a description of the world of ideas. To execute this description, it is necessary to treat every idea as an original one. For ideas exist in irreducible multiplicity" (43). Deploying an avowedly Platonic distinction between the realm of concepts (where the singular text is sacrificed to the generic totality of the conceptual "continuum") and the "world of ideas" (where multiplicities remain irreducibly nontotal), Benjamin redefines philosophy and genre theory as a preeminently *descriptive* process, an active voicing that speaks the multiplicity of singular ideas. Genre names a collective idea (a *spacing* of the collective), not a singular essence or totalizing concept; and as an idea, genre

> thus belongs to a fundamentally different world from that which it apprehends.... Ideas are to objects as constellations are to stars.... Ideas are timeless constellations, and by virtue of the elements' being seen as points in such constellations, phenomena are subdivided and at the same time redeemed.... The idea is best explained as the representation of the context within which the unique and extreme stands alongside its counterpart. (34–35)

This stellar generic blend is no phenomenal essence that inheres in textual objects as a property, a content, or a common thing; on the contrary, without the relativizing and spatializing gravity of the generic idea, the phenomenal world knows no extremes and possesses no singular measure, no measure of singularity.[9] The idea of genre is to be appreciated only "in a comprehensive explanation of ... its form, the metaphysical substance of which should not simply be found within, but should appear in action, like the blood coursing through the body" (39). As this sanguine metaphor suggests, the genre theorist and the philosopher alike must actualize the life of the idea, must materialize this life through critical activity, rather than calmly seeking out its essence via cold, conceptual autopsy.

In the same way that the methodology of set theory blinds logic to the mystery of belonging, so too inductive and deductive approaches to textual commonality fail to carry language across the threshold of genre.[10] For Benjamin, this is the result of a critical ontological miscalculation that forecloses the metaphysical realm of ideas and that condemns modernity to the atopia of a totally instrumental existence. At stake in Benjamin's methodological preface is nothing less than the *structure of commonality*, the modality of the blend in and through which the singular relates to the multiple. If genre names the possibility that singular events of textuality can share multiplicities of form, then what Benjamin's Platonic distinction between ideas and concepts enables us to assess is the *genericity* of genre, the ways in which we imagine our dwelling in the commonplaces of language and literature. What is so significant about the *Trauerspiel* for Benjamin is precisely the modality of its dwelling within genre, a modality he names "allegory." Whereas the structure of the symbol registers meaning through a totalizing signifying operation that swallows up the singular in transcendent universality, allegory performs an always-fragmented, noninstrumental gesture that materializes generic space and time—a purely active, inessential action that says nothing *about* the phenomenal world but that simply *speaks*, that brings the world to the world.[11] If the singular symbol functions as a passageway to a higher plane of universal meaning, allegory simply *passes* in an asignifying motility that spatializes registration and that expresses multiplicity in its singular effort.[12]

To confront this difference in modality between the genericity of symbolism and allegory is to reencounter the profoundest of Platonic distinctions. As Gilles Deleuze succinctly puts it in *The Logic of Sense*:

> Plato invites us to distinguish between two dimensions: (1) that of limited and measured things, of fixed qualities, permanent or temporary which always presuppose pauses and rests, the fixing of presents, and the assignation of subjects (for example, a particular subject having a particular largeness or a particular smallness at a particular moment); and (2) a pure becoming without measure, a veritable becoming-mad, which never rests. It moves in both directions at once. It always eludes the present, causing future and past, more and less, too much and not enough to coincide in the simultaneity of a rebellious matter.[13]

The task of philosophy, like the challenge of genre theory and the achievement of the *Trauerspiel*, is to enact this insane rebellion. Benjamin asks us to reimagine our dwelling in language, to reconsider the genericity of genre, to spatialize an inessential allegorical community of irreducibly multiple ideas.

THE GENERICITY OF ROMANCE

Romance finds its origins in the attempt to register both a particular form and a specific content of language. We can trace its genealogy back to the medieval confrontation between Latin and the vernacular language of France—an opposition that already assumes the existence of a prior, distinct experience of language ("Latin") against which a new language, romance, can dialectically emerge.[14] By an accidental process of association, romance also came to designate a particular *kind* of story that had been registered in the vernacular. Though there were, of course, other texts composed and spoken in the French vernacular—hagiographies, for example—the term "romance" came to signify expressions of a certain *materia*—a complex word often read today as "source," but that in medieval texts seems to refer both to the content of language *and* to its formal structure. A detailed analysis of how romance was used in medieval times to differentiate between various expressions of textuality lies beyond the purview of this chapter, but any cursory glance at scholarship that explores this terrain makes it clear just how ill-defined romance's generic borders were in the twelfth and thirteenth centuries. As Michael McKeon points out, romance and history, for example, did not function as stable categories of difference, and the same medieval text might affiliate itself with elements of both romance and a genre that would come to be known as history—*estoire*.[15]

But to account for the genealogy of romance in this way is to already assume that genre entails a certain degree of conceptual fixity and to project this assumption back onto earlier methods of registration that might conceive of and dwell in the common differently. That romance originates from an accidental conflation of the *materia* of its transmission—the vernacular language of France—with the *materia* of its content—a story that express commonalities of content, of subject matter—does not constitute an embarrassing hiatus in genre's genericity. On the contrary, it reminds us that genre also and vitally dwells in such accidents and embarrassments of the common. From the standpoint of modernity, however, the inessential commonalities that generate genre and that make generic dwelling in language possible are repressed as prehistorical anomalies from registration's savage past. With respect to romance, what begins to change in the eighteenth century is not so much the genre of romance but its genericity, its dwelling in the commonplace of language. For Benjamin, this transformation amounts to a total symbolic eclipse of allegory in the name of Romanticism:

> The striving on the part of the romantic aestheticians after a resplendent but ultimately non-committal knowledge of an absolute has secured a place in the most elementary theoretical debates about art for a notion of the symbol which has nothing more than the name in common with the genuine notion.... For this abuse occurs wherever in the work of

art the "manifestation" of an "idea" is declared a symbol.... The introduction of this distorted conception of the symbol into aesthetics was a romantic and destructive extravagance which preceded the desolation of modern art criticism. As a symbolic construct, the beautiful is supposed to merge with the divine in an unbroken whole. The idea of the unlimited immanence of the moral world in the world of beauty is derived from the theosophical aesthetics of the romantics. (159–60)

Romance thus comes to dwell symbolically, totally, essentially in genre, desolating the richness of the allegorical realm of ideas in its "will to symbolic totality" (186). Such a genealogy of romantic genericity allies Benjamin with his contemporaries Carl Schmitt and Georg Lukács, both of whom were formulating their own responses to Romanticism's impotent stranglehold on the linguistic commonplace. While Lukács would turn to communism and Schmitt to Catholicism in order to counter the saturation of meaning, the dissolution of singularity, wrought by Romanticism's total symbolism, Benjamin continued his commitment to the shocking force of the inessential allegorical fragment.[16]

The revival of romance—epitomized in Britain by the influence of Percy's *Reliques of Ancient Poetry* and the scandal of Macpherson's Ossianic *Fragments of Ancient Poetry*—is thus made possible by a symbolic transformation of the commonplace of language. At stake in this transition is precisely the modality of the common, the ways in which the various singularities of language, of the body, of time, of the citizen relate to their respective generic, racial, historical, and national multiplicities. What Benjamin helps us to articulate is modernity's total symbolism, its transformation of being-in-common into a thing, a content, a concept that somehow *inheres in* the text, the body, the citizen, in blood, and in time. Modern romance both effects and is effected by this thingification of commonality, a fact that is nowhere more evident than in the elevated thinghood of textuality itself in the eighteenth century. The controversy that (tellingly) still rages over the genesis of Macpherson's Ossianic verses, for example, is important precisely because it registers the emergence of authenticity as a temporal stain that stamps the stuff of textuality. As we will see Walpole's work so brilliantly satirize, authenticity is just one name (originality is another) that can now be held in common by singular events of history, as if time, the temporal common, has somehow impressed them with its massively invisible imprimatur.[17] This is why Susan Stewart refers to the romantic ballad as a "distressed genre," where "'to distress' involves a process of appropriation by reproduction, or manipulation through affliction."[18] Such appropriations make it possible for romance to spatialize time and to temporize its passing, thereby creating the idea of an antiqued past ripe for romantic fetishization in the now. For what signs the pastness of the romantic past is precisely the immanence of its dwelling within the common: a savage orality endowed with the mythic capacity to convey pure linguistic belonging—to carry commonality as a content within its poetic sinews—is simultaneously created and mourned by modern romance. This *mything* that founds romanticism and modernity for Jean-Luc Nancy is, I would argue, already at work in the spirit of romance's mid-eighteenth-century revival. "Romanticism," he argues, "could be defined as the invention of the scene of the founding myth, as the simultaneous awareness of the loss of the power of this myth, and as the desire or the will to regain this living power of the origin and, at the same time, the origin of this power."[19] Modernity and modern romance dwell in this *work* of authentication, in this primal mything of origination that bequeaths to time its ever-mournful currency. For it is only in the unending ebb and flow of loss and revival that modern romance can identify itself, can register itself as a living (because always dying) *thing*. The sheer negativity of its ghostly temporal and spatial dwellings in our commonplaces takes the truly gothic measure of its existence.

To define the genre of romance is already to foreclose its potentiality, to seek its irreducibly multiple spirit as a singular, essential concept. If genre is an idea, a constellating of texts that shines singularity through its inessential activity, then romance must be described, presented, in all the fullness of its punctual peculiarities, not sought out as a timeless and unchanging formula. It must be thought of as process, as an endlessly happening operation that is most apparent at moments of transformation and torsion, like a black hole rendered visible by the dance of passing matter.

We can, however, attempt to historicize the genericity of romance, to follow the modality of its flow. Plato's expulsion of the poets, as Jacques Rancière has argued, has everything to do with "the deceptive *mimesis* of the tragic, which attributes its discourse to the characters in the play, . . . and the mixture of *mimesis* and narrative proper to the epic, in which the poet sometimes tells the story in his own voice, sometimes mimics the speech of his characters."[20] What is so deceptive about epic and tragedy for Plato, then, is that their genericity hinges on a mimetic dwelling in language and relies heavily on what Benjamin would call the symbolic register of meaning. The genericity of the lyric, however, resists the instrumental *telos* of epic and tragic *mimesis*, dwelling instead in the inessential fecundity of *poiesis*. "The place of lyricism," Rancière avers,

> is an empty place in this schema, that of un-signifying poetry, inoffensive because it is non-representational and because it does not pose or hide any distancing between the poet-subject and the subject of the poem. The unambiguous "I" of the lyric poem cannot pose a problem to the "we" of the community, whereas tragedy splits it in two by the deception of the *lexis*, and the epic corrupts it by the falsification of the *muthos*. Good poetry is equivalent to a non-poetry that does not fabricate any lie and does not divide any subject. (11)

What might be called the *poiesis* of romance Rancière terms the lyric "accompaniment," a "method of utterance, a way of accompanying one's saying, of deploying it in a perceptual space, of giving it rhythm in a walk, a journey, a crossing" (12). As the important ancient Greek distinction between *poiesis* and *praxis* makes clear, productivity—productive activity—exists within two distinct modalities, modalities that correspond roughly to Deleuze's two Platonic dimensions. On the one hand, *praxis* denotes a transformational action that possesses a certain intention, that works toward, and contains within itself, a specific end, whereas *poiesis* names the modality of an action that takes itself as its own end—the activity of bringing-into-presence, or, as Deleuze puts it, a "pure becoming without measure." The poietical accompaniment of lyricism and romance thus eschews the *telos* of a programmatic practice; it is "not a way of experiencing oneself, of experiencing the profundity of one's inner life, or, conversely, of immersing it in the profundity of nature" (12). Such inessential, noninstrumental accompaniment describes the poietical genericity of romance, and helps us to compare the different modalities of genre as they were imagined in ancient Greece.

This is not to say that romance is identical to *poiesis*, or that tragedy is necessarily and exclusively practical. As generic ideas, definitions of this kind will remain illusory and empty of significance. As Aristotle points out in book 2 of the *Physics*, the force of *poiesis* is at work whenever potentialities are transformed into actualities, whenever being is being brought-into-presence.[21] Both medieval romancer and Greek tragic dramatist rely upon the transformative powers of *poiesis*. Distinctions between genre and genericity, idea and concept, and *poiesis* and *praxis* help us only to register, to spatialize, to reimagine the variety of ways in which we dwell in language; they do not offer timeless categories, as if our commonplaces, our homelands, were simply ready and waiting for us to reinhabit and revive. The common exists in the modality of the verb, not the noun: it is a place that we *make*, not a thing to be found. The efficacy of our methodological apparatus is thus to be measured not in terms of its cohesiveness or its definitive, timeless accuracy but, rather, by the extent to which it opens dwelling up and enables us to identify different interrelationships between singularity and the multiplicity, different blends of commonality. Though we will not exhaust "the lyric" or "romance" with any definition or concept, we can attempt to distinguish between two singular moments in the history of genre's genericity—ancient Greece and eighteenth-century Britain, for example—and open up the commonplaces of language and literature, the ways we choose to dwell in the common, as topics for urgent debate.[22]

FLIRTING WITH ROMANCE

How has literary criticism after Benjamin's "Epistemo-Critical Prologue" approached the commonplaces of romance? Whereas much twentieth-century scholarship is concerned with classifying and adjudicating the content of literary genres, it is only with the projects of critics such as Jameson and McKeon that the work of genre itself is transformed into a meaningful area of inquiry for modern scholarship. Dispensing with Frye's synchronic approach to genre, an approach that argues for a commonality of wish-fulfilling content throughout the history of romance, and rejecting Propp's assessment of the unchanging structures of romantic form, Jameson instead encourages us to interrogate our ideas of genre. "It is not just a question here of deciding to what genre a given work belongs," insists Jameson, "but also and above all of determining what it means to assert that a work 'belongs' to such a classification in the first place."[23] He thus paves the way for an ideological approach to genre, and proceeds to give us a history of how the form of romance—which for Jameson is always about the confrontation between good and evil—has been materially transformed by various historic forces over the course of time. In Stendahl, for example, this confrontation has been internalized as an inner, psychological *agon*, whereas Kafka employs its structure to foreground the meaninglessness of such struggles under modernity. "Any analysis of romance," Jameson argues, will "want to come to terms with the intimate and constitutive relationship between the form itself, as a genre and a literary institution, and this deep-rooted ideology which has only too clearly the function of drawing the boundaries of a given social order and providing a powerful internal deterrent against deviancy or subversion" (140).

What are the implications for literature and the literary event if genre is read as an ideological mode rather than as a semantic or syntactic content that stamps language with generic authority? What does romance signify from within the ideology of genre? Jameson offers us the following definition: "romance is that form in which the *world-ness* of *world* reveals itself" (142). What he means by this is that romance offers a space in which the material world is registered "as something like an innerworldly object in its own right" (142). Such an experience, we are told, is structured around struggles of good and evil, self and other. As opposed to tragedy, where such oppositions are ultimately experienced as ethical distinctions, or comedy, where these oppositions constitute social dilemmas that the text resolves in a gesture of rejuvenation, romance registers the primeval forces of self and other as they do battle in an agonistic struggle of self-definition. We could say that, for Jameson, romance differs from the ethical and social preoccupations of tragedy and romance insofar as it offers instead an ontological space for the mutual recognition of self and other.

In addition to defining a space in which the material world enters into the world-ness of the romantic text, inflecting it with agonistic forces of self-identification and difference, Jameson also tells us that this textual world-ness can push back out against the world and help structure our interactions with "nature." In other words, romance doesn't just signify a particular genre of literature—a subset of a given field; it also names the interface between the forces of a material "world" and a text that both imprints and is imprinted by this world. Given the fluidity and productive promise of such an interface, Jameson's language soon imbues the space of romance with a coquettish eroticism: "this particular discourse is not bound to the conventions of a given age, nor indissolubly linked to a given type of verbal artifact, but rather persists as a *temptation* and a mode of expression across a whole range of historical periods, seeming *to offer itself, if only intermittently*, as a formal possibility which can be revived and renewed" (142, emphasis mine). As we shall see, the erotic allure of this ideological interface still seduces scholars of genre, romance, and the novel. But for now, notice how genre has itself become a voyeuristic romance, as our critical eye watches over its flirtation with history. Whereas Frye and Propp treat literary events as objects readily available for generic distinction and digestion, the ideology of romance frees these events from static objectification by turning genre itself into a spectacle of "temptation." The erotic forces that, for earlier scholars of the romance, were experienced through the semantic and syntactic content of language have been freed only insofar as they are immediately reinvested in the gaze of modern literary criticism itself. In other words, the agonistic erotics of identification have been transformed from a romantic content of literature into a precondition for the literary and the historical. Romance is not now the name for a particular class of literature; it is the name for the structure through which we can watch literature and history happen, come together. To be sure, Jameson tries to identify romance as a particular, ontological subset of literature's flirtation with the temporal. But the damage has already been done. Romance no longer registers a particular content of linguistic belonging; nor does it simply identify a specific ideological irruption of the literature/world dialectic: it also names the possibility of ideology *itself*—the promise that word and world are not only tempted to interface with each other, but also the critical structure through which such flirtations can be witnessed from afar.

Try as Jameson might to objectively observe the ebb and flow of generic mutation, in treating the essence of genre as an erotic, instrumental interface—in staying within the productive modality of *praxis*—his critical system, like Frege's mathematical logic, cannot help stamping the field of its study with its own presuppositions while ignoring the inessential, noninstrumental poietic capacity of language.

TIME FOR THE GOTHIC

In addition to a new title, the second edition of *The Castle of Otranto* includes a remarkable new preface outlining the authorial strategies of the "Gothic Story" that follows:

> [*The Castle of Otranto*] is an attempt to blend the two kinds of romance, the ancient and the modern. In the former all was imagination and improbability: in the latter, nature is always intended to be, and sometimes has been, copied with success. Invention has not been wanting; but the great resources of fancy have been dammed up, by a strict adherence to common life. But if in the latter species Nature has cramped imagination, she did but take her revenge, having been totally excluded from old romances. (9)

Generations of literary critics point to Walpole's text as the originary Gothic romance, and many still use its example to help articulate the contours of Gothic space or invoke its original perspective in order to trace the development of Romanticism in England and elsewhere.[24] But almost always such discussions of Walpole's Gothic perspective take for granted a certain modality of this "blend." In these approaches to *Otranto*, the strangeness, the unhomeliness of Walpole's prefatorial discourse on temporality is repressed and accommodated by more familiar, modern notions of historicity and textuality. Critics assume that Walpole is performing an operative blending process that utterly dissolves naïve differences (ancient/modern, invention/copying) into a richly symbolic hodgepodge of the *now*. Projecting back onto this blend our own contemporary maturity, a maturity fully aware that all history bares the traces of imagination and emplotment, we cannot help but read Walpole's "Gothic Story" as a protomodern gesture toward the situatedness of all textual registration. As many scholars have pointed out, the standard topoi of such "terrorist fiction"[25]—the found manuscripts, the incomplete transmission of always fragmented letters, and the unveiling of surprising and shocking plot twists—nod not only toward incompleteness and invention as an inevitable content of modern textuality and sociality but also materialize the modern crises in form that inflect all systems of registration.

What this means in terms of the Walpolian blend is that the "ancient" is assumed to be already and totally blended into the modality of the "modern." *Otranto*'s historicity is thus always and only "inventive," its gestures toward pastness always precisely that: gestures, nods, winks. That Walpole could intend his blending process to carry over intact any of the "ancient" fealty to mimesis and "copying" is too ridiculous a question to consider; after all, how can we take *Otranto*'s murderous helmets and incestuous

Italianate desires as anything other than signs of a self-consciously inventive approach to temporality? What emerges from such an approach to Walpole's work is the sense of a romantic textual space in which the author, no longer claiming mimetic allegiance to "common life," is given license to indulge his "imagination." The pages of Walpole's Gothic romance thus register the cathartic traces of "invention"—a catharsis through which the author communicates (albeit unconsciously) various and vital aspects of his subjectivity to the literary critic. Jerrold E. Hogle's reading of "Walpolean Gothic fakery" in "The Gothic Ghost of the Counterfeit and the Progress of Abjection" articulates the structure of this textual space:

> Gothic fiction . . . becomes a site into which widely felt tensions arising from this state of culture can be transferred, sequestered, disguised, and yet played out. Indeed, such a cultural locus, since it employs symbols from earlier times largely emptied of many older meanings, quite readily becomes a symbolic space into which the fears and horrors generated by early modern cultural changes can be thrown off or thrown under as though they exist more in the now obscure and distant past than in the threatening present. This process soon proves malleable enough for different cultural quandaries to be abjected in the Gothic at different times, [so that the Gothic] becomes a major repository of the newest contradictions and anxieties in western life that most need to be abjected by those who face them so that middle-class westerners can keep constructing a distinct sense of identity.[26]

It is hard to imagine a more seductive space for the literary critic to inhabit. Borrowing Julia Kristeva's neo-Freudian concept of abjection, Hogle is entranced by the psychoanalytic allure of Walpole's Gothic "blend." What could be more productive than the notion of a literary space "malleable enough" to register the imprint of every Western anxiety? The path is cleared for literary criticism—now armed with the tools of the cultural historian and marked by encounters with race, gender, and postcolonial studies—to revisit the text's unconscious. The current explosion of critical interest in things Gothic testifies to the appeal of Hogle's thesis.

As far as the Walpolian blend goes, we conclude that *Otranto*'s generic gesture is to swallow all differences between historical moments into an immanent "symbolic space," a space in which the "cultural quandaries" of the *now* are somehow and inexorably impressed. And furthermore: these impressions of temporality and historicity are registered, ex-pressed, with a knowing wink to modernity, with the understanding that the text before us, like all other systems of registration, is made available through the testimony of an infinitely complex and crushingly situated subjectivity. The Gothic is not simply a campy genre: its structure *is* camp. And from the viewpoint of literary history, the Gothic romance does not only constitute the first modern genre: it *is* modernity—it is what happens to all genres, to all texts, to all histories when the veil of linguistic innocence is finally lifted. This Gothic does not only designate a moment of generic transition plotted against an axis of linear time. It also reveals something *timeless* about time, about history, and about registration to the astute modern reader: to say "Gothic" is to say something *about* the axis of temporality as well as to attempt to register a particular moment along its passing. Time is "Gothic": it is time for the Gothic.

TOTALLY SYMBOLIC

But what happens to genre, to history, and to the history of genres as a result of this double flirtation with the temporal? How can we speak, without winking, of any significant differences between literary productions if the logic of our methodology is rooted in the essential similitude of registration—the "symbolic space" shared by all textual forms that, like Aristotle's waxen writing tablet (*rasum tabulae*), lies supine and waiting to be magically impressed and im-printed by the always-mediated and ever-mysterious "cultural quandaries" of history? Such an erotics of registration both represses and deifies difference. Instead of swallowing up the concept of genre in a malleable flux of utter invention/abjection, the critical machines ceaselessly return to and reequip it with new identities—new structures of identity—that further perpetuate the erotic mystifications of totally symbolic textual presentation. Since all language bears the impressions, the emptying-outs, of personality, politics, and history, Neoclassical "copying" and Gothic "invention" now come to designate different extremes along the same symbolic axis: the Gothic exposes the hubris of neoclassical faith in the effectivity of mimetic representation. The essential difference between these genres—or, more correctly, the difference that enables genre to maintain its precarious existence here—is thus established as a difference of degree, not kind. Gothic describes an inventive attitude toward, a self-awareness of, and an indulgence in the multivalence of "symbolic space"; neoclassicism, hiding behind the myth of univalence, represses and minimizes signification's inescapable capriciousness. Regardless of the complexities and nuances of these new and fascinating redefinitions of generic registration, they all secretly share in the erotics of Hogle's "emptied" and infinitely symbolic *rasum tabulae*, an erotics that provides a bizarre and total common axis against which the attitudinal particularities of generic difference can now be measured and emplotted.

Instead of graciously bowing out of literary history, the genre thus returns with renewed vigor. Michael McKeon's daunting and impressive *The Origins of the English Novel* (1987), for example, rewrites the naïve empiricism of Ian Watt's *The Rise of the Novel* (1957) by proposing a "dialectical theory of genre" (1). Watt's literary history connects the rise of the novel with a collection of related social, political, and historical phenomena (the rise of the middle class, the Protestant secularization of religious life, and various other cultural forms which attest to the emergence of a distinctly individualist ethos). The novel's peculiar formal talent, argues Watt, lies in its ability to register the realities of this newly individualized and secularized existence with satisfying, empiricist precision; hence Watt's history of the novel always reaches toward an end point in Richardsonian realism, with its attention to the details of the everyday and its eroticization of the *oikos*. For McKeon, however, Watt is too eager to swallow the realistic bait offered by the eighteenth-century novel, forgetting that, as Erich Auerbach so forcefully demonstrates in *Mimesis*, "[e]ach age has its own method, or optic, for seeing and then articulating reality."[27] McKeon replaces Watt's individualistic and realistic teleology of generic development with a dialectical model rooted in the same kind of timeless "symbolic space" that Hogle has discussed in relationship with the Gothic romance. "Realism" is treated in McKeon's work as an *attitude toward* registration, as an (albeit naïve) response to the ineluctable inventiveness, the always Gothicity of representation. Rather than simply delimiting specific contents or particular forms of textuality, the genre functions as an attitudinal axis against which time can happen. More specifically, genre helps us to identify and emplot three particular happenings of temporality: (1) a prelapsarian moment of immanent innocence ("romance idealism") in which the duality between "ancient" and "modern" has yet to fully assert itself; (2) a "naïve empiricism" that challenges this uncritical reception of the past into the present with "an empirical epistemology" that, in opening questions of contingency and veracity, can itself never lay any normative claims to authority; and (3) an "extreme skepticism" that grows out of these ambiguous waters and that, in its attack on naïve empiricism, cannot help but fall back on some of the same elements of romance idealism that it is also dedicated to debunking.

What we gain from such an inventive approach to the history of genre is an ostensibly more complex, less rigid understanding of generic transformation. McKeon's dialectical approach, drawing on Hegelian methodology, at once offers both a historically specific, materialist account of the rise of the novel (in which the novel reaches beyond Richardsonian individualism toward the extreme skepticism of Fielding), and, at the same time, treats the movement between these three different modes of textuality as a cyclical iterative process, a process imbued with a pregiven fatality that transcends and effaces the singularity of the historical event precisely at the same time that it seeks to explain it. One effect of this dialectical approach is to comprehend all relationships of putative difference (the relationship between the genres of romance and the novel, for example) as endlessly self-constituting and self-deforming agonisms. Romance, as McKeon so deftly points out, is never completely erased from the novelistic machines of empirical individualism and, hence, is always reinvoked and revivified, if only as a relative point of utter negation in the novel's neurotic quest for truth and ascendancy. Far from achieving a value-free emplotment of historical progress, however, this Marxist dialectical approach to literary history has the tendency to renaturalize the development of particular social and textual systems (in this case, the origins/emergence of the novel) under the aegis of massive suprastructural forces, such as the rise of the middle class or the divisions of labor effected by the development of technological capitalism. It is this aspect of McKeon's literary history that gives William Warner, in his *Diacritics* essay-review of *The Origins of the English Novel*, cause for considerable concern. If McKeon were really to take his criticism of Watt's realistically biased teleology of the novel to heart, he must, argues Warner, take seriously Althusser's critique of the Hegelian dialectical method and open literary history up to what Stuart Hall has called a "Marxism without guarantees." "This would mean," continues Warner, "a history uncontrolled by any internal gyroscope or autopilot, a history that cannot give itself over to the abstract triadic patterns of the dialectic, a history not given an implicit after-the-fact necessity by the dialectical patterns it 'happens' to follow. To narrate a history of early modern narrative open to the contingencies that befall it means attempting to think a history that comes with no dialectical guarantees."[28]

The Origins of the English Novel is thus guilty of both overdetermined dialecticism and transhistorical universalism. The fact that the triadic dialectical thrust (romance idealism—naïve empiricism—extreme skepticism) is, as McKeon himself points out, present in the movement between the two parts of *Don Quixote* (1605 and 1615) as well as central to the development of the eighteenth-century British novel leads to Warner's conclusion that McKeon's dialectic inevitably conveys something timeless about all "textual rendering[s] of questions like truth and virtue.... When the problem of truth comes into view for a culture, then the idealist, empirical, and skeptical answers to these questions will gain successive, competing, and reciprocally critical expression."[29]

From the always-immanent, ultrasymbolic space of the Gothic to the utterly material and, hence, completely mysterious gyroscope of Marxist literary historiography, Jameson, McKeon, and Hogle struggle in vain to register the event of romantic textuality. We have seen how the gift of the Gothic—the "symbolic space" that swallows and ex-presses the "ancient" through the quandaries of the now—solves the dilemmas of historical presentation by imagining registration as an *endlessly happening* event. And we have seen how this utopic erotics of registration also opens onto an *atopia*, a space of (non)dwelling within language and history where time is always literary, and where it can never be time for literature. And because McKeon's dialectic always reads literature as a (conscious or unconscious) *commentary on* the pregiven facticity of registration rather than the registration of the event of textuality itself, *The Origins of the English Novel* inhabits this same atopic space. In transforming the potential of literature to ex-press the epistemological and moral quandaries of the now into the only visible sign of its happening, McKeon's compelling and innovative approach to textuality ultimately reduces the event of textuality to a total blending of "ancient" and "modern." Instead of telling a history that registers the happening of particular events performed by unique, singular subjects, McKeon participates in modernity's adequation of historical narrative with an explanatory discourse *about* the procession of time. "The labor of the historian," as Jacques Rancière so forcefully demonstrates in *The Names of History*, "is no longer to recount revolutions but to interpret them, to relate the events and discourses to what founds and explains them. And, of course, what founds the events always belongs to a nonevent; what explains the words is what no longer belongs to words."[30] Within such histories, it is no longer possible to speak of the event of literature: only the history of literature or the emplotment of generic transformation can furnish the historian with the totally symbolic, utterly agentless erotics of textual presentation against which modern history and modern time can emerge, can happen.

But what if Walpole's work suggests another kind of "blend," a different structure of belonging, that, while bringing together "ancient" and "modern," refuses to imagine their combination solely in terms of a total, swallowing synthesis? The Gothic romantic spaces of Walpole's fiction preserve the possibility of another experience of time and place, another response to past and present—an uncanny blend indeed.

AT HOME WITH THE UNCANNY:
WALPOLE AND THE IDEA OF HISTORY

Scholarship that connects the power of Gothic romance with the experience of the uncanny registers an important similarity in their respective modalities. But in the same way that Walpole scholarship has been too eager to reduce and synthesize his "blend" to merely the Gothic, ahistorical, supernatural aspect of its multivalent composition, readers of Freud's essay do a similar injustice to his notion of the uncanny when they elevate the *unheimlich* over the *heimlich*. For what is most powerful in Freud's analysis of the uncanny is that he refuses to reduce the structure of the relationship between these two terms to a neat, synthetic equation: Freud begins with an assertion of obvious oppositionality ("The German word *unheimlich* is obviously the opposite of *heimlich, heimsch*, meaning 'familiar'; 'native,' 'belonging to the home'")[31] but ultimately locates the structural force of the uncanny in its articulation of an essential indeterminacy, a constitutive convertibility,[32] that animates the relationship between these two terms:

> What interests us most . . . is to find that among its different shades of meaning the word *heimlich* exhibits one which is identical with

its opposite, *unheimlich*. What is *heimlich* thus comes to be *unheimlich*. . . . [W]e are reminded that the word *heimlich* is not unambiguous, but belongs to two sets of ideas, which without being contradictory are yet very different: on the one hand, it means that which is familiar and congenial, and kept out of sight. The word *unheimlich* is only used customarily, we are told, as the contrary of the first signification, and not of the second. . . . On the other hand, we notice that Schelling says something which throws quite a new light on the concept of the "uncanny," one which we had certainly not awaited. According to him everything is uncanny that ought to have remained hidden and secret, and yet comes to light. . . . Thus *heimlich* is a word the meaning of which develops towards an ambivalence, until it finally coincides with its opposite, *unheimlich*. (129–31)

The space of the uncanny is thus a blend of "two sets of ideas, which without being contradictory are yet very different." What is important to remember is that the uncanniness of this blend lies not in a total resolution of the *heimlich/unheimlich* opposition—a blending without remainder, so that what was once *heimlich* becomes *unheimlich*. For, as Freud's analysis of E. T. A. Hoffman's "The Sand-Man" demonstrates, the uncanny is never simply a feeling of not being at home in a text, the sense of "intellectual uncertainty" that sometimes inheres in Gothic romantic spaces (137). Rather, it is precisely the Sand-Man's homely-ness at the close of the text— the *given-ness* of his identity—that produces the text's uncanny effect. In other words, the uncanny is the indwelling, the immanence of the uncanny in the canny, the potential that these binaries *are also already blended*.

At the close of "The Uncanny," Freud returns to the topography of *Beyond the Pleasure Principle*, a text in which the founding principle of Freudian psychology crumbles in its encounter with the bare life of infants. Here the pleasure principle is unable to account for the glee that accompanies a child's compulsion to repeat the appearance and disappearance of a libidinized object; and, in much the same way that "The Uncanny" tackles the perverse convertibility between *heimlich* and *unheimlich*, *Beyond the Pleasure Principle* posits the coexistence, the indwelling, of appearance in disappearance, of pleasure in pain, as the original, animating force in life. Freud calls this compulsion to restage the appearance and disappearance of pleasure and pain the Thanatos, creating yet another opposition (between the repetition-compulsion and the pleasure principle, between Thanatos and Eros) that, like the dichotomous blending of *heimlich/unheimlich*, turns out to be no simple opposition at all. For the Thanatos should not be understood in its strictly literal sense as simply a drive for the subject's own death; rather, through the Thanatos, Freud articulates the truly uncanny terrain of a life that animates itself through a desire for its own stasis, its own inanimacy:

> The attributes of life were at some time evoked in inanimate matter by the action of a force of whose nature we can form no conception. It may perhaps have been a process similar in type to that which later caused the development of consciousness in a particular stratum of living matter. The tension which then arose in what had hitherto been an inanimate substance endeavoured to cancel itself out. In this way the first instinct came into being: the instinct to return to the inanimate state. It was still an easy matter at that time for a living substance to die. . . . For a long time, perhaps, living substance was thus being constantly created afresh and easily dying, till decisive external influences altered in such a way as to oblige the still surviving substance to diverge ever more widely from its original course of life and to make ever more complicated *détours* before reaching its aim of death. These circuitous paths to death, faithfully kept to by the conservative instincts, would thus present us to-day with the picture of the phenomena of life. . . . The hypothesis of self-preservative instincts . . . stands in marked opposition to the idea that instinctual life as a whole serves to bring about death. Seen in this light, the theoretical importance of the instincts of self-preservation, of self-assertion and of mastery greatly diminishes. They are component instincts whose function it is to assure that the organism shall follow its own path to death, and to ward off any possible ways of returning to inorganic existence other than those which are immanent in the organism itself.[33]

What Freud finds beyond the pleasure principle is, then, a complex copresence of organic drives, of Eros and Thanatos, which help the organism to attain its goal in life—its wish "to die only in its own fashion."[34] What appear to be the definitive instinctual struggles for the organism—the battles between the Thanatos and Eros, between consciousness and unconsciousness—are redrawn beyond these dichotomies by Freud such that their putative oppositionality is seen from an entirely different perspective. From this viewpoint, life is not something that emerges solely from a synthesis of these instinctual drives; the coordinates of life, that is, cannot be measured solely through the ego's synthesis of the id's desire and the superego's conscience. Pleasure and pain, life and death, are not only discrete binaries that the organism blends together in its psychic life. Rather, their oppositionality is always also fused in the uncanniness of life: a life that lives by fleeing life; an animation that animates by seeking inanimacy. What kind of textuality could register the parameters of this existence?

When the preface to the second edition of *The Castle of Otranto* claims to "blend the two kinds of romance, the ancient and the modern," our first question should not be so much "What is the nature of this blend?" as it should be "What is the status of this announcement, this articulation of blending?" With Walpole, we can never forget that we are always within language; linguistic situation—or, more correctly, its situated-ness—is as important as linguistic content in his Gothic romantic spaces. Instead of delimiting space and resolving time, the situation of Walpole's language throws us beyond a simple synthesis of past and present. Hence, his "Gothic Story"—and the "birth" of the English Gothic romance—must always be attributed to the *second edition* of *Otranto*, not so much because it is here that Walpole first appends his subtitle, but rather because his Gothic romance is obsessed with *second-edition-ness*. Rooted in the belatedness of its originality, the preface begins, appropriately enough, with an apology:

> The favourable manner in which this little piece has been received by the public, calls upon the author to explain the grounds on which he composed it. But before he opens those motives, it is fit that he should ask pardon of his readers for having offered his work to them under the borrowed personage of a translator. As diffidence of his own abilities, and the novelty of the attempt, were his sole inducements to assume that disguise, he flatters himself he shall appear excusable. He resigned his performance to the impartial judgment of the public; determined to let it perish in obscurity, if disapproved; nor meaning to avow such a trifle, unless better judges should pronounce that he might own it without a blush. (9)

Though the content of this apology is straightforward enough, the situatedness of its prose is dazzling indeed. Here the standard tools of the literary critic—plot (the notion of beginning, middle, and end) and author (creator and originator of a text that moves through time), for example—struggle to orient our experience within this textual space. What is so vital to witness in this passage is how it is animated by the inextricable interrelationships between original and copy, first and second editions. No mere copy of its original, the second edition's preface—which we know now is composed by Horace Walpole, Member of Parliament and son of the first British prime minister, Robert Walpole—assumes that its reader is familiar with its earlier avatar. The apology apologizes for the falsity of the first edition's preface, wherein the narrative voice, then attributed to "William Marshall, Gent.," performs an intricate textual and historical analysis of *The Castle of Otranto* (a 1529 text written by Onuphrio Muralto that Marshall claims to have uncovered "in the library of an ancient catholic family" and translated from Italian into English[6]) in order to establish its approximate date of origination, "between 1095 . . . and 1243" (6). But before we tackle the complexities of the first edition's preface—complexities that involve *its* always second-edition-ness—we must already acknowledge the strangeness of the textual space that the second edition's preface opens us onto. What kind of text, and what kind of second edition of a text, would assume its reader to have read its earlier edition, offering only an apologetic preface as a sign of its difference? What sort of readership, what methods of reading, and what genericity of genre is assumed here? In short, what kind of an apology is possible within such a space?

That a new preface was composed, not to mention that a new author and a new subtitle were added to its title page, suggests that something has happened to the status of *Otranto*'s textuality between editions. But what is the nature of this something? What has happened to the text between its "original" date of publication, 24 December 1764, and its prompt reissue in 1765? The obvious answer—an answer that satisfies most literary critics—is that the second edition reveals Walpole's authorship of a text originally attributed to Onuphrio Muralto. But if we read the early reviews of the first edition of *Otranto*, peruse Walpole's letters of early 1765, and examine the reviews of *Otranto*'s revised, second edition, it becomes clear that most people suspected the hoax from the start. Even those readers ignorant of Walpole's authorship knew enough about history and medieval romance to detect *Otranto*'s numerous anachronisms and to suspect a contemporaneous impostor. "The ingenious translator of this *very curious* performance," notes an appropriately anonymous commentator in the January 1765 edition of *Critical Review*, "informs that it was found in the library of an ancient catholic family in the north of England.... Such is the character of this work given us by its judicious translator; but whether he speaks seriously or ironically, we neither know nor care.... We cannot help thinking... that the castle of Otranto is a modern fabrick."[35] Thus, when the second edition is published, ostensibly unveiling the ruse of its earlier avatar, this same reviewer can write: "We have already reviewed the *Castle of Otranto* and we then spoke of it in terms pretty near the character given by the author. He solves, by his preface to this edition, the phoenomenon for which we could not account, by his diffidence as to his success."[36] In his unsigned assessment of the second edition of *Otranto*, published in the May 1765 *Monthly Review*, John Langhorne similarly notes that when "this book was published as a translation from an old Italian romance... we were dubious... concerning the antiquity of the work."[37] For these reviewers, then, the second edition's preface does not simply precipitate *The Castle of Otranto*'s transformation from a 1529 translation into a 1765 hoax. Echoing the responses of many *Otranto* readers, the *Monthly Review* writer captures the flavor of Walpole's text, pointing out that "we neither know nor care" whether the first edition's ruse of translation is to be taken "seriously or ironically." Always hewn of "modern fabrick," Walpole's "Gothic Story" names the possibility of a text that can apologize for the belatedness of its originality, the potential of a space in which the "ancient" and the "modern" can "blend" without losing their flavors—a space in which originality and its revival can coexist *in the same text*.

The Castle of Otranto does not, in any traditional sense of origination, begin the game of the Gothic any more than it can be said to create a space of sexual, political, or national *jouissance*. These are, of course, important coordinates of the Gothic game, but before proceeding to an analysis of these elements, it is vital to explore the structure, the parameters of the game itself. In a letter dated 14 April 1765, Reverend William Mason thanks Walpole for *The Castle of Otranto*—an "extraordinary thing... which though it comes not from your press, yet I have episcopal evidence is written by your hand."[38] This "episcopal evidence" came from William Warburton, bishop of Gloucester, who informed Mason of Walpole's deception. Mason's description of *Otranto*'s game bears retelling in its entirety. "[Less] than such [episcopal] evidence," he maintains, would scarce have contented me, For when a friend to whom I had recommended *The Castle of Otranto* returned it to me with some doubts of its originality, I laughed him to scorn, and wondered he could be so absurd as to think that anybody nowadays had imagination enough to invent such a story. He replied that his suspicion arose merely from some parts of familiar dialogue in it, which he thought of too modern a cast. Still sure of my point, I affirmed this objection, if there was anything in it, was merely owing to its not being translated a century ago. All this I make it a point of conscience to tell you, for though it proves me your duper, I should be glad to be so duped again every year of my life.[39]

What this letter tells us about *Otranto*'s appeal—what propels its infectious handling from reader to reader—is not that its power lies simply in Walpole's anonymity. After all, if there can be circuits of "episcopal" evidence, we suspect that other, lay circuits must exist too; and that so many readers note its "modern cast" implies that *Otranto*'s contemporaneity ineluctably unveils itself. But the pleasure of this text, its status as an "extraordinary thing," also cannot be attributed simply to the given-ness of Walpole's authorship, to its status as an entertaining, transgressive, parodic fake. Any attempt to resolve the power of this "Gothic Story" to the freedom of its interior spaces—spaces in which history and politics, to take just two examples, can be engaged and critiqued without recrimination—thus accounts for only one side of Walpole's "Gothic Story." For Mason's letter attests to the uncanniness of *Otranto*'s power, to the pleasure of a textual space that is *simultaneously* free and fettered, original and historical. In the words of the *Monthly Review*, "we neither know nor care" if *The Castle of Otranto* is to be taken "seriously or ironically": refusing to resolve the dilemma of the text's textuality, readers hold on to the possibility of being "duped" for the first time, "again." In the same way that the uncanniness of the "Sand-Man" flows out of his capacity to be canny—out of the given-ness of his identity—so too Walpole's authorial wink is structured by a similarly uncanny "blend" of originality and revival, origination and repetition. The joy of this game lies less in the content of any of its transgressive activities than it does in the potential of the game's form—the thrill, that is, of an endless cycle—a duping, "again"—of transgression *and* repunishment. The integrity of this form thus hinges on the possibility that Walpole *did not* create it: at the very moment that it registers itself for the first time, the Gothic romance must erase the mark of its origination. Indeed, if we were to search for a definition of Walpole's Gothic romance, we are left with this uncanny formula: the Gothic romance is a genre propelled by its own disappearance and appearance, a textuality that refuses to acknowledge distinctions between subject and object, creator and spectator, original and revival, *in order to find itself in its own pages, again.*[40]

How is history registered in the pages of Walpole's Gothic romance? How can a genre that inaugurates itself by renouncing its own origination participate in anything that resembles "history?" In his critique of genre theory's deductive and inductive approaches to the event of literature, Benjamin offers a countermethodology rooted in the irreducibly multiple *idea* of genre. Such an idea, as we have seen, preserves the punctual peculiarities of the text in a purely inessential *description*. Instead of an instrumental process that treats textuality as fixed spatial and temporal flow of the concept, Benjamin offers a radically open idea of history that preserves the uniquity of the textual event from the essential totality of the symbol. In so doing, he follows Walpole in describing a quite different relationship to the temporal and textual common, a relationship that reformulates the ideas at the heart of the romance's eighteenth-century revival: authenticity and origination. "Origin," Benjamin argues,

> although an entirely historical category, has, nevertheless, nothing to do with genesis. The term origin is not intended to describe the process by which the existent came into being, but rather to describe that which emerges from the process of becoming and disappearance. Origin is an eddy [*Strudel*] in the stream of becoming, and in its current it swallows the material involved in the process of genesis. That which is original is never revealed in the naked and manifest existence of the factual; its rhythm is apparent only to a dual insight. On the one hand it needs to be recognized as a process of restoration and re-establishment, but, on the other hand, and precisely because of this, as something imperfect and incomplete. There takes place in every original phenomenon a determination of the form in which an idea will constantly confront the historical world, until it is revealed fulfilled, in the totality of its history. Origin is not, therefore, discovered by the examination of actual findings, but it is related to their history and their subsequent development. The principles of philosophical contemplation are recorded in the dialectic which is inherent in origin.

> This dialectic shows singularity and repetition to be conditioned by one another in all essentials. The category of the origin is not ... a purely logical one, but a historical one. (45–46)

Read from this perspective of "dual insight," the prefaces to *Otranto*'s first and second editions are indeed eddies "in the stream of becoming," testaments to the flow of a game they are always already playing. As Samuel Weber's more precise (if somewhat less poetic) translation of *Strudel* as "maelstrom" or "vortex" makes clear, "[i]n Origin what is meant is not the becoming of something that has sprung forth (*Entsprungen*), but rather that which springs forth out of the coming-to-be and passing-away (*dem Werden und Vergehen Entspringendes*). Origin stands in the flow of becoming as a maelstrom (*Strudel*) which irresistibly tears (*reißt*) the stuff of emergence into its rhythm."[41] In the sense of historical time that grounds discussions of literary genre, *The Castle of Otranto* does not mark a point of absolute origination out of which a new genre, the Gothic romance, miraculously emerges (to be followed shortly after by yet another creative irruption marked historically as Romanticism). Nor does *Otranto* write a history that empties out the past, filling the vacated symbolic space with contemporaneous "anxieties": Walpolian history refuses to reduce "ancient" and "modern" to a simple, linear procession of time that erases the uniqueness of the event in the name of an isolated now. The two prefaces demand instead the "dual insight" of Benjamin's idea of history. Standing neither completely alone nor inextricably bound together, they reflect and refract each other across space and time, "coming-to-be and passing-away" in the vortex of their blend. The preface to the first edition, which contains its own "apology" for *Otranto*'s "air of the *miraculous*"—the "Miracles, visions, necromancy, dreams, and other preternatural events [which] are exploded now even from romances" (6)—acts both as an ironic precursor to the apologetic revelations of the second edition's preface *and* as a visionary anticipation of its serious generic concern to "blend the two kinds of romance" (8). What is apologized for in the first edition (*Otranto*'s "imagination and improbability" [8]) is valorized in the second; and what is apologized for in the second edition (the folly and imagination of an author who deceives) is annulled by the analytical meanderings of the first preface, which grounds its own approach to *Otranto* in the irrelevance of authorial intention: "Whatever the [author's] views were, or whatever the effects the execution of them might have, his work can only be laid before the public at present as a matter of entertainment" (6). Whether these narrative voices speak "seriously or ironically," Walpole's Gothic romantic spaces open onto a terrain in which such distinctions *make no difference* to the currents of their historicity, to the rhythms of their origination.

The Castle of Otranto thus registers the hubris of history's claim to reveal the "naked and manifest existence of the factual." In *Modern Romance and Transformations of the Novel*, Ian Duncan deftly negotiates the politics of history writing in the Gothic romance, contextualizing Walpole's project within the dynamics of national and sexual identity formation:

> "Gothic" represents . . . the crux or aporia of a myth of national culture, of "British" historical identity—one that retains its currency to this day. In it the alien and the familiar, the natural and the unnatural or supernatural, are richly confused: neither one category nor the other is clearly stable.
>
> Gothic names a broken historical descent, a cultural heritage grown balefully strange. The eighteenth-century Gothic romances themselves insistently thematize the structure of a dislocated origin: in the obsession with fragmented and contaminated genealogies, in plots that turn upon usurped patrimony, incest, lost relations; in characterizations of psychological repression; in settings of decayed ancestral power, the famous castles and monasteries, that still hold their aura of physical and ideological bondage, sublimated from function to "atmosphere"; in aesthetic effects of the uncanny and the sublime. With these famous characteristics, the Gothic novel describes the malign equation between an origin we have lost and an alien force that invades our borders, haunts our mansions, possesses our souls.[42]

Duncan insists on the malignity of this "broken historical descent," and his reading of the Gothic romance hinges on the assertion that history functions "as a reduction, a loss, a trivialization" within its pages (32). But is this equation between lost origins and an unfamiliar modernity necessarily malign? Is the vision of history that *Otranto*'s pages opens onto a trivial history, an emptiness of time? Or is it instead animated by a flowing of time and a form of history that Benjamin, in his "Theses on the Philosophy of History," describes as "a structure whose site is not homogenous, empty

Genre 45

time, but time filled by the presence of the now?"[43] In short, is there not the potential for another *more* historical response to this "malign equation?" Duncan explores the mode of history experienced as a "fatalistic literalization" in *Otranto*, tracking Walpole's indictment of "a reduction of meaning and a failure of sublimity" (32). But what I want to suggest is that it is precisely Walpole's *refusal* to reduce meaning to "a lost, original and absolute state" (32), his reluctance to equate historical fatality with emptiness, that constitutes *Otranto*'s most profound engagement with historiography.[44]

For Duncan, *Otranto* registers its vision of history and politics through "the loss of an original, generative allegorical system [that] makes itself felt in a disruption of the order of nature" (30). Instead of an "allegorical system" rooted in the dimensions of human experience, Duncan argues that Walpole's allegories constitute an "occluded spiritual dimension, reduced to dispersed and broken surface forms [that] reassemble [themselves] . . . in the destructive modality of literalization" (31). Though Duncan's exploration of the effects of literalization are important, I want to suggest that they do not merely function as "destructive," *non*human forces. To be sure, from the perspective of *Otranto*'s protagonist, the usurper Manfred, allegorization and destruction, literalism and fatality, are indeed synonymous. But *The Castle of Otranto* always opens onto a multitude of narrative (and prefatorial) perspectives that, taken in their entirety, suggest a more complex vista of human experience, a more uncanny "blend" of imaginative possibility and literal limitation. For *Otranto* refuses to equate the fatalistic unfolding of historical time and the "destructive modality of literalization" with emptiness, with destruction, with the *non*human. After all, as the two prefaces to *Otranto*'s first and second editions illustrate, Walpole's text creates a space in which history is never simply experienced as the "naked" manifestation of a fated movement from origination to destruction. With "dual insight," *The Castle of Otranto* names, as the condition of its possibility, a blend of time and space animated by the rhythms of genesis and destruction, the indwelling of freedom in repetition. Within this strange terrain, life is registered as an uncanny blend of fated historical materiality and vibrant ghostly immateriality, an atemporal and allegorical mélange of "ancient" and "modern" in which the past presents itself as a vital anachronism. The experience of subjectivity, itself a deeply vexed concept here, is indistinguishable from a neurotic and fetishistic conflation of subject and object. And the more a subject clings to his/her essential subjectivity, the more contingent his/her freedom becomes: such perversity is the subject's only signature. The mystery here is that there is no mystery—the veil is always also unveiled: characters who resist this secret (which is no secret) are overwhelmed, not deceived, by their senses, and Walpole's textuality works its effect through accretion—by a "saying-too-much"—not through subterfuge or subtlety. Ghosts haunt us because of, not in spite of, their massive materiality.

APOLOGY

What is the status of apology within such a space? What are its potentialities, its possibilities? Itself an uncanny blend of the Greek roots ἀπόλογος (a story, an account, a defense) and ἀπολέγω (to renounce, to give up) the exploration of apology opens onto vertiginous semantic terrain. At the heart of apology lies a relationship between narration and renunciation, between λογος and ἀπολέγω. Even within the phonetic borders of ἀπόλογος, there is a movement between these same forces—between a tale that is told, the λογος, and the preposition ἀπό, which suggests an act of removal. But what, precisely, does the apologetic tale remove? And how does it perform its act of narrative renunciation? The complexity of apology stems from its attempt to simultaneously register a specific form and a particular content of narration. To apologize is to tell a certain kind of story—a story that renounces something—but it is also to stand in a certain relationship to the act of narration. However, the very content of apology—the "something" that is renounced—renders such an opposition between apologetic form and content impossible. For what apology renounces through its act of narration, what the preposition ἀπο removes from the λογος, is the narrator's own narrativity, his/her own historicity. In order to apologize, the apology must first recognize itself in its act of narration; but this recognition recognizes only insofar as it annuls the apologetic narrator's history, only to the extent that it removes a particular segment of his/her narrated experience. The Greek root ἀπολέγω registers this complexity of apology:

> ἀπολέγω, *pick out from* a number, and so. 1. *pick out, choose* . . .:–freq. in Med., *pick out for oneself.* . . . 2. *pick out* for the purpose of rejecting. . . . II. later, *decline, refuse.* . . :–Med. *decline* something *offered to one.* . . .; *renounce, give up.* . .; also *give in, make no resistance* . . . *lose heart.* . . . III. *speak of fully*[45]

We begin with an act of selection, a picking-out, that is acknowledged by ἀπολέγω. But this selective action is soon complicated; for selection implies rejection, exclusion. What apology insists on is the *simultaneity* of these acts of selection and rejection, recognition and destruction. Hence ἀπολέγω possesses a paradoxical intentionality, an uncanny dialectics: it picks-out "for the purpose of rejecting." We then move toward an experience of the aporia of apology, a sense of its impossibility: we "*give in*" and "*lose heart.*" After all, what kind of tale, what kind of narration, can exist in such semantic terrain? But what is so uncanny about apology is its persistence in its own possibility. We leave ἀπολέγω not with the sense of emptiness, of the aporia of apology, but rather with the thrill of potential: for to apologize is, we find to our great surprise, to "*speak of fully,*" to dwell in the fullness of narration. This is precisely the same apologetic terrain that Walpole's two prefaces open onto, a blending of temporality that exceeds beyond and dwells within the "ancient" and the "modern."

In the *Odyssey*, we thus find the long story told by Odysseus to Alcinous referred to as an "Ἀλκίνου ἀπόλογος," a "mighty" or a "fortifying" tale. But how can a story, a λογος, sustain and fortify when it is animated by fleeing, by excepting, part of itself—a movement captured by the preposition ἀπο? What is vital to recognize is that the Greeks, like Walpole, capture the sense of this movement, this apology, in terms of a *flowing outward*—an essentially productive, nutritive, and fortifying exception that propels rather than annuls or, more correctly, *propels as it annuls*. In Homer, for example, the preposition ἀπο is often used to invoke the sense of a journey "from" one place to another place. The relativity of its semantic ground is such that the exception, the renunciation, can proceed only insofar as it measures the terms of its abandonment relative to a previous, original location. Such relativity is also registered by ἀπο in its usage as "origin and cause," where it signifies "of that *from* which one is born."[46] Again we sense the nutritive properties of ἀπο's movement, and we also note the simultaneity of the excepting and generating processes: we have grown *from* something, such that a distinction, an exception, can be registered in language; and yet that something that we have cast off, that original from which we have grown, somehow *still dwells within us*, otherwise we could not have grown *from* it. Apology thus possesses the "dual insight" of a form of narration that narrates through exception, the awareness of an un-homely space that can register its *un*homeliness only by looking back toward a home it can never leave.⁴⁷ Origin functions here as a Benjaminian "eddy in the stream of becoming": "in its current it swallows the material involved in the process of its genesis." This uncanny structure of origination is echoed in *Beyond the Pleasure Principle* when Freud suggests the inescapable copresence of life and death, genesis and destruction, as integral forces in the organism's development. And when Thucydides praises Antiphon's skillful and successful oratorical defense against a sentence of death, he uses the phrase "θαάτου δίκην άπολογησάμενος"(translated by Hobbes as "[to] plead for himself... when his life was in question") to describe the form of a narrative that, like all apology, sustains life at the threshold of its annulment.⁴⁸

At the same time that Walpole was working on *The Castle of Otranto*, "apology" was undergoing a change of sense into quite a different noun. Rather than registering the presence of a particular act of narration, in the eighteenth century, apology began to signify a certain kind of absence—a thing that "merely appears to apologize for the absence of what ought to have been there; a poor substitute" (*OED*). Here an apology presents itself in order to register an absence, giving itself up in order to maintain the flow, the possibility of meaning. It is this sense of apology that best captures the dynamics of Walpole's "Gothic Story," that best registers the genericity of a genre that, in staging its own disappearance, reappears *in all the fullness of speech*. If, as Benjamin argues, a perfect work both establishes and abolishes genre, through Walpole's apologetic prefatorial gesture such perfection shines brightly.

Genre 49

2

FEELING

ROMANCE, RACE, RUIN: HENRY MACKENZIE AND THE AFTERLIFE OF SENTIMENTAL EXCHANGE

In one of the nineteenth century's most influential romances, we are introduced to a restless young man who abandons his sleepy hometown, eager to try his fortunes in the big city. He meets a girl. Though separated by massive disparities in wealth, education, and social stature, they nevertheless cast "wooing glances" at each other and begin a courtship.[1] Consumed by the common desire that unites them, their passion for each other quickly grows. But, as the narrator of the romance is quick to remind us, "the course of true love never did run smooth" (202): in his dealings with the rapacious city dwellers, our hero is forced to sacrifice the homespun values he acquired during his youth. It is as if each exchange with these men of the world effects a gothic metamorphosis in the nature of our protagonist's being; and his lover soon begins to question which of these dueling personalities is real and which a horrific, spectral apparition.

Though the adventures of the commodity in Marx's *Capital* are not often read as a romance, the fact that they exhibit some of the same thematic concerns and aesthetic gestures as the sentimental romance is worthy of remark.[2] It is tempting to brush aside these moments in the text as narrative flourishes that help to clarify our understanding of—and engage our interest in—complex economic concepts. Viewed from this perspective, Marx is simply manipulating the tropes of romance in order to make his ideological point. But what if the relationship between romance and commodity exchange runs deeper than the symbols that they share?

In this chapter I argue that Marx writes a romance because *capitalism is structured like romance*, because commodity exchange and romantic desire share the same aesthetics of valuation.³ Focusing on two of Henry Mackenzie's wildly popular novels of sensibility, *The Man of Feeling* (1771) and *Julia de Roubigné* (1777), I show how the sentimental romance produces two, qualitatively distinct kinds of affective value: on the one hand, feeling is valued because it functions as a principle of public exchange, enabling the affective subject to participate as a "man of the world" in a community or a politics of feeling; but at the same time, feeling is also esteemed as a totally private essence, a material fact of the subject's own singular personality and unique, homespun history. The mystery of sentimental exchange is rooted in the peculiar way that these two value-forms interrelate. Like the optical illusion of the Rubin Vase, where the observer sees either a vase or two facial profiles but never sees both of these images at the same time, I argue that affection's public "exchange-value" and private "use-value" can each appear and distinguish itself only to the extent that it obscures our view of the other. While scholars often read the sentimental romance as a democratizing genre in which marginalized subjects, excluded by their gender or their race, can make their feelings heard in the public sphere, I explore instead the ideology of ruin that obscures private feeling and enables these democratic political values to be publicized and exchanged. At the same time that Mackenzie's "men of feeling" bring sympathy and emotion into view as universal and public principles of political community, they also mourn the ruin of utterly private feeling that such publicity entails. Rather than simply championing liberal principles of freedom, charity, and public equality, the sentimental romance secretly desires the prestige of singular and private differences that have been ruined by, and excluded from, this new political community and its concepts of universal feelings and rights. By examining how this erotics of private ruin fragments heterosexual desire and stains the body with the fateful force of race, I show how the aesthetics of romance inflects the formal structure of our modern systems of identity and exclusion.

THE SPECTERS AND THE SPECTACLE OF AFFECTION

Sensibility constitutes the very egoism of the I, *which is sentient and not something sensed*. Man as measure of all things, that is, measured by nothing, comparing all things but incomparable, is affirmed in the sensing of sensation. Sensation breaks up every system.   —EMMANUEL LEVINAS, *Totality and Infinity*

Sentimental romance claims to register the presence of an acutely private, affective self. And further: these feelings are never simple, accidental exfoliations of selfhood. To be human is to be a self that exercises feeling. Thinkers as diverse as Rousseau, Sterne, and Adam Smith all agree on this fundamental precept of sentimentality, on this definitive structure of sentimental selfhood. And yet, as the pages of sentimental romance demonstrate, there is a constitutive queerness to this sensing self, a peculiarity that patterns all economies of sentimental desire. For it is never enough for this self to emote and to feel in isolation: in order to register its essential humanity, this self must disclose itself, must direct its interiority outward, must cry public tears that somehow materialize and bear witness to its private core. Such a self can know itself only insofar as it is a self *for another*, only through the act of transforming its absolute privacy into a communal sentimental spectacle. The radically private self-for-itself never participates in the pages of romance or the lyrics of longing.

No mere literature of self-indulgent desire and confession, the sentimental romance thus engages in an intimately social dialectics of recognition. For Frederic Jameson, romance bestows difference "not by any particular characteristics of [the other], but simply as a function of [the other's] relationship to my own place";[4] and we see this same dialectical structure at work in Shaftesbury's *Sensus Communis* (1709), one of the most important texts in the development of an eighteenth-century "culture of sensibility":

> If eating and drinking be natural, herding is so too. If any appetite or sense be natural, the sense of fellowship is the same. If there be anything of nature in that affection which is between the sexes, the affection is certainly as natural towards the consequent offspring and so again between the offspring themselves, as kindred and companions, bred under the same discipline and economy. And thus a clan or tribe is gradually formed, a public is recognized, and, besides the pleasure found in social entertainment, language and discourse, there is so apparent a necessity for continuing this good correspondency and union that to have no sense or feeling of this kind, no love of country, community or anything in common, would be the same as to be insensible even of the plainest means of self-preservation and most necessary condition of self-enjoyment.[5]

Shaftesbury's prose warps here under the weight of its aesthetic task: How can "affection" operate as both a privatized "condition of self-enjoyment" and a "public" dialectic that holds country and community together? To the extent that Shaftesbury's syntax elevates the affective value of communal "discipline and economy," its feeling subject is obscured and reduced to a position of utter passivity: "a clan or tribe *is* gradually formed"; "a public *is* recognized" (emphasis mine). It is as if the only sign of the "plainest" and most "natural" form of private feeling is found whispered within subjunctive speculations ("If eating and drinking be natural.... If any appetite or sense be natural.... If there be anything of nature") or trapped negatively in the folds of tautology (either sensibility produces "good correspondency and union" or else humans are "insensible"). One of the many paradoxes of sentimentality—of the powerful ties that bind self to other, mother to child, individual to "clan," citizen to "country"—is that this sympathetic public "union" can be registered only at the threshold of its private occlusion.

In one of *The Man of Feeling*'s more memorable vignettes, the hero of Henry Mackenzie's much-loved novel is approached by a beggar and his dog. After hearing the beggar's sad tale of misfortune and illness, Harley decides to give him some money and, while finalizing this charitable transaction, he reflects on the intricacies of sentimental exchange:

> Harley had drawn a shilling from his pocket; but virtue bade him consider on whom he was going to bestow it.—Virtue held back his arm:—but a milder form, a younger sister of virtue's, ... smiled upon him: His fingers lost their compression; —nor did virtue offer to catch the money as it fell. It had no sooner reached the ground than the watchful cur (a trick he had been taught) snapped it up; and, contrary to the most approved method of stewardship, delivered it immediately into the hands of his master.[6]

A wonderfully Gothic spectacle, Mackenzie's romance of the "shilling" anticipates both the argument and the imagery of *Capital*'s analysis of commodity fetishism. While Marx's hero is magically transformed by exchange into a table that "stands on its head, and evolves out of its wooden brain grotesque ideas" (163), Mackenzie's coin similarly turns the tables on the human bystanders, taking on a public, circus life of its own while reducing Harley to passive indecision and making a "master" of the beggar's "watchful cur." Although this charitable exchange goes to great imaginative and pecuniary lengths to equalize the differences between Harley and the beggar, these humanitarian elaborations end up reinforcing, rather than dissolving, the materiality and thinghood of the sentimental commodity. Even and especially when Mackenzie attempts to personify and humanize exchange, imagining "Virtue" and her siblings navigating its proper sympathetic course, his public spectacle of charity paradoxically brings forward a technical procession of dehumanized things—pockets, arms, fingers, dogs—that effect the currency's slow-motion transfer. As if to restrict the cur's agency and reinstill a sense of the human, Mackenzie's parenthetical assertion that the dog had been taught this trick seems a desperate tactic, lest we forget who his true "master" is.

"There is no use of money ... equal to that of beneficence," a stranger admits to Harley later in the novel: "with the profuse, it is lost; ... but here the enjoyment grows on reflection, and our money is most truly ours, when it ceases being in our possession" (34). It is this strange afterlife of the sentimental shilling that lends such a melancholy hue to Mackenzie's fiction. The economy of "beneficence" practiced by the man of feeling will emerge in contradistinction to the "profuse" spending of an infected urban and mercantile class. Never at home with the luxury and commerce of the city (he is thoroughly tricked and taken advantage of during his brief visit to London), Harley instead outlines a spectral, otherworldly economy, a system of affective values that appear only to the extent that they have already been lost, already antiqued and consigned to pastoral prehistory or anticipated in the afterlife. "There are some feelings which perhaps are too tender to be suffered by the world," avers Harley at the close of the novel.

> The world is in general selfish, interested, and unthinking, and throws the imputation of romance or melancholy on every temper more susceptible than its own. I cannot think but in those regions which I contemplate, if there is any thing of mortality left about us, that these feelings will subsist;—they are called,—perhaps they are—weaknesses here;—but there may be some better modifications of them in heaven. (95)

Though such sepia-toned "regions," where pure affection is finally accorded its proper value, are part of sentimentality's critique of the world of commerce, they nevertheless possess their own economy—an ethereal yet absolute tyranny of ownership where the affective commodity is all the more "ours" for its invisibility, all the more valuable for its nonparticipation in the secular world of "selfish" exchange. "There is a sympathetic enjoyment," notes Mackenzie in the *Mirror*, "which often makes it not only better, but more delightful to go to the house of mourning, than to the house of feasting";[7] and in *Fleetwood*, William Godwin's astute reworking of *The Man of Feeling*, such painful pleasure is denoted "by the term reverie, when the mind . . . is swallowed up in a living death, which, at the same time that it is indolent and inert, is not destitute of a certain voluptuousness."[8] Far from short-circuiting the logic of capitalism, these luxurious gothic "regions" share the material extravagance of the fetish.

Economies of affection, like Marx's romance of the commodity, play out the tension between an authentic, interior value (an utterly private feeling) and its subsequent corruption within the public exchange. By treating affection as an exchangeable, communal thing—a universal, totally impersonal commodity that congeals our innermost identities and desires—the private exercise of our own unique feelings becomes strangely irrelevant. In order both to rescue private feeling from its public commodification and to reinforce its status as a universal human attribute, the economy of sentimental romance continues to circulate and value feeling, but only as an always-ruined and totally nonvaluable fragment. If commodity fetishism animates exchangeable things by lending them a private existence, then in the afterlife of affection private feeling is publicly euthanized, ruined. Death now infused into its form, feeling comes back to life as an always-fragmented "living death." The sentimental flâneur does not so much see or feel ruin as cast its shadow over the world: He *is* ruined feeling. Always a traveler, and destined to pass through the world, observing the decay that has been hardwired into his vision, his melancholy account of feeling's ruined thing provides a fitting accompaniment to the "it-narrative," a popular eighteenth-century romance form in which inanimate objects like Harley's coin and the beggar's dog come to life and tell their adventures in circulation.[9]

TENDERNESS UNUTTERABLE

In a moment of quite remarkable insight, the eponymous hero of Mackenzie's final and most accomplished novel, *Julia de Roubigné*, declares that "Comedies and romances always end with a marriage, because, after that, there is nothing to be said."[10] Her husband's letters later reinforce this observation by pointing out that married bliss "is a sort of happiness that would not figure in narration" (119). As Jane Austen's work so vividly illustrates, pleasure and the fulfillment of desire play no part in the erotics of sentimentality. On the contrary, the man of feeling *ruins* sex and fragments bodily desire: melancholia, misfortune, and sickness name the conditions through which his subjectivity can sustain itself in the world. In the same way that *Sanditon*'s economy of wellness simultaneously heals and produces bodies in distress, so too the sentimental romance is marked by the mutual copresence of pleasure and pain. These two feelings are not to be read as separate but overlapping economies—one of pleasure and one of its lack—but, rather, as emotions that have now merged inseparably into each other, creating a new kind of pleasure that is always in pain, always *pained*. "I begin to suspect," observes Julia's true love, Savillon, "that the sensibility, of which young minds are proud, from which they look down with contempt, on the unfeeling multitude of ordinary men, is less a blessing than an inconvenience.—Why cannot I be as happy . . . as all the other good people around me?—I eat, and drink, and sing, nay I can be merry, like them; but they close the account, and set down this mirth for happiness; I retire to the family of my own thoughts, and find them in weeds of sorrow" (110). Sentimental selves can only recognize themselves in the void that "sorrow" opens up in desire. Their pain is not one kind of feeling among others: it is the form that their emotionality must take if it is to hollow out an authentic presence, a living death, among the "unfeeling multitude." And so when Julia describes the moment that she reluctantly gives her hand in marriage to the wealthy Montauban (rather than the poverty-stricken Savillon), her troubled language perfectly captures the dialectical play of pleasure/pain and presence/absence that patterns all sentimental registration. "My father spoke first," Julia reports, "[but] not without hesitation. . . . At last, turning fuller towards me, who sat the silent ~~victim~~ of the scene, (why should I score through that word when writing to you? yet it is a bad one, and I pray you to forgive it,) he said, he knew his own unworthiness of that hand, which my generosity had now allowed him to hope for. . . . It is done, and I am Montauban's for ever!" (68–69). Here Julia stamps her sentimental selfhood with her own bizarre imprimatur: "silent ~~victim~~." Her victimhood simultaneously sustains and delimits her subjectivity.

The openness of epistolarity provides form for a discourse that finds solace in fragmentation and infinitely deferred desire. The sentimental romance needs to imagine a textual space in which the self can register and recognize itself without being exchanged for or cancelled out by an other: a found bundle of letters, stumbled across, barely touched, and then disclosed to the public, offers the perfect print cultural medium. Though the letters might have been exchanged within the sentimental community, it is vital that, as readers, we encounter them innocently and outside of any system of commercial, for-profit publication; or, as Mackenzie puts it in the introduction, such letters must never enter the narrative economy of plot since "they are made up of sentiment, which narrative would destroy" (5). And so too in that rare moment when our sentimental heroes speak of pleasure and joy, it is "a sort of happiness that would not figure in narration" (119). In much the same way that the beggar's "cur" facilitates the exchange of Harley's sentimental shilling—distinguishing his charitable action from a crass order of mercantile business—so too the narrator of *The Man of Feeling* relies on canine intervention in order to open the narrative economy of his text:

> My dog [Rover] had made a point on a piece of fallow-ground, and led the curate and me two or three hundred yards . . . in a breathless state of expectation. . . .
>
> I looked round . . . when I discovered, for the first time, a venerable pile. . . . An air of melancholy hung about it. . . .
>
> "Some time ago," said [the curate], "a grave, oddish kind of man, boarded at a farmer's in this parish: The country people called him The Ghost. . . .
>
> "Soon after I was made curate, he left the parish, and went no body knows whither; and in his room was found a bundle of papers. . . . I began to read them, but I soon grew weary of the task; for, besides that the hand is intolerably bad, I could never find the author in one strain for two chapters together: and I don't believe there is a single syllogism from beginning to end."
>
> "I should be glad to see this medley," said I. "You shall see it now," answered the curate, "for I always take it along with me a-shooting." "How come it so torn?" "'Tis excellent wadding," said the curate.—This was a plea I was not in condition to answer; for I had actually in my pocket great part of an edition of one of the German Illustrissimi, for the very same purpose. We exchanged books; and by that means (for the curate was a strenuous logician) we probably saved both. (3–4)

While the beggar's dog works its magic by fragmenting Harley's participation in the economy of charity—providing the magical, nonhuman medium through which his shilling can be transferred to the beggar—here Rover and "The Ghost" help to fashion a similar spectacle of exchange. The narrative economy that they facilitate deemphasizes Mackenzie's participation in the exchange of textual commodities and, instead, creates an editorial illusion in which the narrator can be seen to rescue (rather than purchase) Harley's "medley." The wonderfully intricate story of how Harley's letters end up as "wadding" in the curate's gun emphasizes both the fragmented incompleteness of his sentiments (their lack of a common narrative "strain") and the vague precision of their elaborate journey from Harley to "The Ghost," from the "farmer" to the curate, and finally—thanks to Rover—from the curate on to the narrator. Wadding is used to hold gunpowder in its proper place inside the barrel and, as such, its value is tied to a dialectic of substantiality: it must be heavy enough to act as a placeholder but not so bulky as to alter the bullet's course. Likewise, the narrator sustains and values Harley's letters at the threshold of their fragmentation and to the extent that they are deemed value-less within the more potent and bellicose economies of the world. At the same time that the narrator tries to obscure the sentimental commodity by emphasizing its public (non)value, he cannot help but bring forward its material thinghood—the intolerable "hand" of Harley's wadded writing and the palpable and "melancholy" air that hangs about his grave.

In the same way that the epistolary form of the sentimental romance produces the (non)valued fragments of its narrative economy, so too the erotic plot of *Julia de Roubigné* values symbolic tokens that materialize loss and fragmentation. Julia's vivid childhood fantasies, for example, eroticize the luxury of sorrow rather than any equalizing closure of desire:

> Maria! in my hours of visionary indulgence, I have sometimes painted to myself a husband—no matter whom—comforting me amidst the distress which fortune had laid upon us. I have smiled upon him thorough my tears; tears, not of anguish, but of tenderness; — our children were playing around us, unconscious of misfortune. . . . I have imagined the luxury of such a scene, and affliction became a part of my dream of happiness. (16)

Such feelings of agonizing affection are so central to the work of sentimental romance that, as Julia's "no matter whom" illustrates, they render even the sentimental object that arouses that affection superfluous. This is why Carl Schmitt argues that, in the literature of romance, "we can no longer speak of an object. This is because the object becomes the mere 'occasion,'" for sentimental reverie.[11] And so too even Savillon's physical body is strangely dispensable in the novel, his portrait providing the necessary "occasions" for Julia's sentimental distress. The text goes even further by suggesting that such erotic fetishes are *even more erotic* than the sexual body that they fetishize; hence, the raciest moment of the novel occurs when Savillon and Julia merge registration and desire into a totally aestheticized erotics of servitude. "When our master was with us," blushes Julia, "he used sometimes to guide my hand; when he was gone, at our practice of his instructions, Savillon commonly supplied his place. But Savillon's hand was not like the other's: I felt something from its touch not the less delightful from carrying a sort of fear along with that delight" (144). Julia's "fear" and Savillon's surrogate mastery only add to the erotic charge of this sentimental exchange, an exchange in which the artistic canvas and the act of painting are relegated to mere aesthetic occasions through which they channel their pained desire.

Sentimental space thus occupies queer territory outside of the heteronormative emplotments of society—a space in which tearful orphans divulge their hearts to their same-sex friends. "To speak one's distresses to the unfeeling, is terrible," argues Savillon. "[E]ven to ask the alms of pity is humiliating; but to pour our griefs into the bosom of a friend, is but committing to him a pledge above the trust of ordinary men" (128). As such, it is incorrect to assume that sentimental epistolarity uses letters between same-sex friends in order to spotlight and adumbrate the text's real, heterosexual economy of desire. On the contrary, the point of the letters is to sustain the fragments of sentiment from narrative and erotic closure—a challenge that Laurence Sterne transforms into a coquettish art in *A Sentimental Journey*.

Julia de Roubigné also takes this challenge to heart. In its determination to open up a ruined space for sentiment in the afterlife of matrimony—a space obscured from public view and utterly devoid of the "sort of happiness" that silences the sentimental narrative—the text goes so far as to insist that the erotics of victimhood and servitude penetrate even the most

Feeling 59

ideal of marriages. Madame de Roubigné's letter from beyond the grave constitutes the text's most explicit articulation of this erotics of enslavement. The contents of her letter offer marriage advice to Julia, advice that metatextually informs all sentimental interactions between masters and slaves, husbands and wives, gentlemen and their man-servants, and ladies and their *fille de chambres* in the novel:

> Let the pleasing of that one person be a thought never absent from your conduct.... This privilege a good-natured man may wave: he will feel it, however, due; and third persons will have penetration enough to see, and may have malice enough to remark, the want of it in his wife. He must be a husband unworthy of you, who could bear the degradation of suffering this in silence. The idea of power, on either side, should be totally banished from the system: it is not sufficient that the husband should never have occasion to regret the want of it; the wife must so behave, that he may never be conscious of possessing it....
>
> In this, and in every other instance, it must never be forgotten, that the only government allowed on our side, is that of gentleness and attraction; and that its power, like the fabled influence of imaginary beings, must be invisible to be complete. (79–81)

Madame de Roubigné's "system" of domestic "government" is keenly attuned to both the public and the private coordinates of modern "power." The fantasy of an absolute difference between genders—the two "sides" of marriage—is something that is to be both disguised *and* desired. The public discourse of sexual equality, often considered one of the central, liberal tendencies of the sentimental romance, is thus shown to be palpably ruined at its private core. "But *misfortune* is not always *misery*," Julia's mother insists at the close of her letter. "Then is the triumph of wedded love!—the tie that binds the happy may be dear; but that which links the unfortunate is tenderness unutterable" (81). At the same time that gender differences are publicly "banished," the discourse of sentimental equality *ruins* gender with an invisible, yet devastatingly "complete," private obligation to power.

"I know not if there is really a sex in the soul," ponders Savillon in language that Mackenzie would later borrow for his 1779 essay in the *Mirror*.[12] "[C]ustom and education," he continues, "have established one in our idea; but we wish to feel the inferiority of the other sex, as one that does not debase, but endear it" (113). Even if humans were "really" equal, winks the sentimental romantic, we still desire the luxury of mastery and the polite stigma of "inferiority" it demands. This is why the decaying husks of so many abandoned women, often called Maria, allegorically litter the landscape of sentimental romance. "It is by such private and domestic distresses," notes Mackenzie in another story published in the *Mirror*,

> that the softer emotions of the heart are most strongly excited. The fall of more important personages is commonly distant from our observation; . . . [b]ut the death of one, who, like Maria, was to shed the influence of her virtues over the age of a father, and the childhood of her sisters, presents to us a little view of family affliction, which every eye can perceive, and every heart can feel. On scenes of public sorrow and national regret, we gaze as upon those gallery pictures which strike us with wonder and admiration; domestic calamity is like the miniature of a friend, which we wear in our bosoms, and keep for secret looks and solitary enjoyment. (499)

The ruined woman and her fragmented domesticity take center stage in the erotics of "national regret." This economy of "affliction" does not so much value Maria's image as it does fetishize "domestic calamity," the thing of ruin itself. What the sentimental "gaze" desires is not Maria's subjectivity but her grief, the story of her suffering, the formal incompleteness of her self. Her name, like her subjectivity, is totally insignificant, and signals the generalized condition of sentimental ruin rather than any unique human presence. And so in Sterne's *A Sentimental Journey* we are not surprised to encounter another iteration of Maria, similarly ruined and, as is often the case with such fragmented subjectivities, hovering on the threshold of sanity as she wanders aimlessly around an idyllic country landscape:

> She was dressed in white . . . except that her hair hung loose, which before was twisted within a silk net.—She had, superadded likewise to her jacket, a pale ribband which fell across her shoulder to the waist; at the end of which hung her pipe.—Her goat had been as faithless as her lover; and she had got a little dog in lieu of him, which she had kept tied by a string to her girdle. . . .
>
> I sat down close by her; and Maria let me wipe [her tears] away as they fell with my handkerchief—I then steeped it in my own—and then

in hers—and then in mine—and then I wiped hers again—and as I did it, I felt such undescribable emotions within me, as I am sure could not be accounted for from any combinations of matter and motion.

I am positive I have a soul; nor can all the books with which materialists have pestered the world ever convince me of the contrary.[13]

Sentimental romance ruins, not revives, the aesthetics of pastoralism: it names the textual coproduction of ruin and revival. For it is only in such total fragmentation of domesticity that the voluptuous and ruined materiality of Maria's tear can appear, a materiality that congeals her unique and private suffering and enables this public spectacle of sentimental exchange to take place. Sterne's romance of the tear, like Mackenzie's sentimental shilling, brings forward the thinghood of the ruined body—the wetness of its tears and the technical process of their absorption into Yorick's handkerchief—at the same time that it presents this exchange as firm evidence for an antimaterialist, sentimental "soul" that transcends private differences. Mary Wollstonecraft, in her own fragmented and unfinished novel *Maria; or the Wrongs of Woman* (1794), will later revisit such sentimental exchanges from the viewpoint of the ruined, female body. For, as Madame de Roubigné's "system" of domestic "government" reminds us, the equality of the sexes hinted at in these public spectacles of sympathy and charity is tied to the privilege of private ruin, the endearing and utterly material stain of suffering that haunts the afterlife of sentimental equality. And so when Julia confronts the ruin of her love for Savillon, her "tears fell without control, and almost without distress" (132). This perfect sentimental tear so completely publicizes and materializes the private affective core of the sentimental subject that it treats both subjectivity and sentimentality—emotional "distress"—as entirely irrelevant factors in sentimental exchange.

THE DIALECTICS OF AMOROUS BONDAGE

The concept of a community united by universal, public sympathies and a common sentimental currency appears to level differences between human subjects.[14] We have seen how, in order to avoid the corruption of the public exchange, the economy of sentimental romance only values and circulates the always-ruined fragments of private feeling. However, as

Julia's hyperemotional tear demonstrates, these fragmented and nonvaluable affective tokens are no strangers to the logic of the commodity. If these tokens are to act as currency within the sentimental community, then they must be quantifiable: we must be able to possess them to greater or lesser degrees. Instead of democratically leveling differences between people, the sentimental romance singles out and privileges specific moments of exceptional suffering, congealing personal pain into a public token—a thing of ruined feeling. The point to be emphasized here is that these exceptional things of singular difference and unutterable private ruin help to *found* the conceptual equalities paraded by modern discourses of liberalism and sentimental democracy. The fact of servitude and the stigma of private difference are not simply excluded from the communities that are imagined by such concepts: they are not other, competing concepts that have been expelled from the sentimental community. On the contrary, and as both Giorgio Agamben and Madame de Roubigné would be quick to point out, it is the *creation* of these unutterable stains of private difference that enables the concept and the economy of public equality to emerge and sustain itself with such invisible and complete force.[15]

At stake here is the proper relationship between sentiment and servitude, romance and race.[16] In *The Politics of Sensibility*, Markman Ellis points out that the literature of sentimentality is drawn to overtly political themes such as the slave trade and racial discrimination, arguing that this attraction stems from the "asymmetrical power relation essential to slavery"—a fact that the sentimental romance uses to exploit "the scopic possibilities of violence and inequality inherent to the chattel slave economy, and the ambiguous, mute docility of the slave subject."[17] Read from such a perspective, the horror of the transatlantic slave trade thus becomes a "scopic" scene to which the sentimental novel is drawn, a rich symbolic repository that the text can plunder in order to engage its sympathetic, generic interests. But servitude names much more than a theme, a symbolic value, that economies of affection manipulate in order to assert their politically progressive agendas. As David Kazanjian has demonstrated, the tendency to separate enlightened discourses of democracy and equality from the premodern evils of racism and slavery ignores the ideological fact of their mutual *coproduction*. "[C]apacious practices of freedom," he argues, "were increasingly restricted to a formal equality fleshed out by precise—if unstable—racial, national, and gendered materialities."[18]

Feeling

Sentimental romance, driven by its "capacious" vision of a community united by shared sympathies and feelings, similarly fleshes out a precise, private space ruined by inequality and stained with unutterable suffering. This desire to produce, as well as to publicly banish, material differences between people transforms servitude from a sentimental theme into a formal aesthetic principle. And it is this aesthetics of ruin, rather than the scopic symbolism of slavery, that is responsible for the deepest structural link between romance and race, sentimentality and servitude.

When Savillon decides to save Julia and her family from financial ruin, he immediately leaves for his uncle's slave plantation in Martinique. Upon arrival, Savillon is appalled by the "treatment of the negroes," and the letters he sends to Beauvaris, his most intimate confidante, speak with sentimental vigor "of the many thousands of my fellow-creatures groaning under servitude and misery" (101). It is this humanitarian thread of the narrative that attracts the attention of Ellis, lending support to his reading of *Julia de Roubigné* as a text that draws on African slavery as a powerful thematic context. Susan Manning goes so far as to argue, in a footnote to her 1999 edition of the text, that "Savillon's (and Mackenzie's) abolitionist views are far ahead of general opinion" (97). To be sure, Savillon's letters point out the horrific evils of slavery; but it is important to remember that these comments appear only after he has relayed to Beauvaris his experiment with "a different mode of government in one plantation." Most of the slaves, Savillon observes, "neglect their work altogether; but this only served to convince me, that my plan was a good one, and that I should undoubtedly profit, if I could establish some other motive, whose impulse was more steady than those of punishment and terror" (97). Savillon's "project" is, from the outset, presented as an economic experiment designed to increase the profitability of plantation labor. The issue that drives his Martinican adventures is never the *abolition* of "punishment and terror"; on the contrary, in searching for a coercive power, an "impulse more steady" than spectacular, raw violence, his letters continue to develop the central aesthetic and thematic concerns of the sentimental romance: how can the obligation and the stain of servitude penetrate the modern subject completely and invisibly? And how can this fact of private ruin be transformed into a profitable and an erotic economy of desire?

"One slave in particular," Savillon continues, "was worth less money than almost any other in my uncle's possession. I answered him . . . that I hoped to improve his price some hundreds of livres" (97–98). What follows in these letters is an astonishing account of Savillon's conversation with this slave, Yambu, who turns out to be a "prince" and "master of all" the other slaves on this plantation (98). Notice how, in the extended dialogue that follows, the erotics and economics of sentimental power permeate the interaction between master and slave. Rather than dissipating and transcending this dialectic of power, Savillon instead transforms his lordship into a more subtle, more complete, and, he will argue, a more profitable impulse with which to control African bodies:

> I took his hand; he considered this a prologue to chastisement, and turned his back to receive the lashes he supposed me ready to inflict. "I wish to be the friend of Yambu," said I. He made me no answer: I let go his hand, and he suffered it to drop to its former posture.... "Can you speak my language, or shall I call for some of your friends, who can explain what you would say to me?" "I speak no say to you," he replied in his broken French....
>
> "Would you now go to work," said I, "if you were at liberty to avoid it?" "You make go for whip, and no man love go."—"I will go along with you, though I am not obliged; for I chuse to work sometimes rather than be idle."—"Chuse work, no work at all," said Yambu.—'Twas the very principle on which my system was founded. (98–99)

And in a moment of perverse abolitionism, Savillon decides that the best way to put his "system" into effect is to "free" Yambu:

> "[F]rom this moment, you are mine no more!."... "You would not," said I, "make your people work by the whip, as you see your overseers do?"—"Oh! no, no whip!"—"Yet they must work, else we shall have no sugars to buy them meat and clothing with."—(He put his hand to his brow, as if I had started a difficulty he was unable to overcome.)—"Then you shall have the command of them, and they shall work chuse work for Yambu."... "Your master," said I, "is now free, and may leave you when he pleases!"
>
> ... [I] told [the other slaves] that, while they continued in the plantation, Yambu was to superintend their work; that if they chose to leave him and me, they were at liberty to go; and that, if found idle or unworthy, they should not be allowed to stay.... I have had the satisfaction of

Feeling 65

observing those men, under the feeling of good treatment, and the idea of liberty, do more than almost double their number subject to the whip of an overseer. I am under no apprehension of desertion or mutiny; they work with the willingness of freedom, yet are mine with more than the obligation of slavery. (99–100)

The point is not that Savillon, and by extension Mackenzie, is either a pro-slavery apologist or an early abolitionist. On the contrary, the text parades a putative choice between distinct public values ("the willingness of freedom" and the "whip" of slavery) at the same time that it produces an invisible private "obligation" more massive than even the most spectacular system of discipline and punishment. In the afterlife of sentimental equality, Yambu retains an essential difference (as "master" to "those men" whose work he superintends) at the same time that he receives "the idea of liberty." "Speak no say" and "work chuse work": Yambu's language fully registers the paradox of a speaking subject who is at once free and enslaved, a subjectivity shaped by a living death shared by all the sentimental victims of the novel.

And so too when Matthew "Monk" Lewis visits the Jamaican plantations he has inherited in 1816, his own attempts to improve the condition of his slaves amounts to installing a better-regulated, more humane, and more complete system of obligation.[19] There is no more Gothic, more completely horrific scene in all of Lewis's scandalous fiction than the account in his *Journal of a West Indian Proprietor* of the imagined liberation of one of his slaves. "As I took no notice of him," Lewis recalls,

> he at length ventured to introduce himself by saying, "Massa not know me: *me your slave!*"—and really the sounds made me feel a pang at heart. The lad appeared all gaiety and good humour . . . but the word "slave" seemed to imply that, although he did feel pleasure then in serving me, if he had detested me he must have served me still. I really felt quite humiliated at the moment, and was tempted to tell him, "Do not say that again: say that you are my negro, but do not call yourself my slave."[20]

What Lewis can only dream of saying to his slave in Jamaica, Savillon vocalizes clearly in Martinique: "say that you are my negro"; you are "mine with more than the obligation of slavery."

While the symbolic opposition between freedom and servitude seems to hold the slave clearly and visibly in his place, separated only by the "whip of an overseer," how are we to articulate the invisible stain, the "mine" of obligation that remains after his manumission? In the same way that servitude is not simply another theme or a different concept that the sentimental romance engages, so too Lewis's "negro" is not just the white man's public Other: along with Yambu and the many sentimental Marias, he is also marked by an invisible yet complete private obligation, a living death always excluded from political community and totally obscured from public view. What is so devastating and novel about the topography of this racialized space of personal ruin is not its thematic or conceptual distance from the ideals of affective and democratic equality. On the contrary, Mackenzie's work demonstrates the secret alliance between the sentimental freedoms of the man of feeling and the unutterable obligations of servitude—the mutuality and interdependence that, like the twin images of the Rubin Vase, provides the illusion of two distinct concepts or values. The thing of racialized, private ruin forms an inseparable bond with these expansive freedoms, connected by an intimate dialectic of appearance and occlusion that does not so much exclude its stain of singular difference as it does *include* it invisibly and completely within the modern sentimental and political community.

JEFFERSON AND THE TRANSATLANTIC MAN OF FEELING

Why does it matter that Ossian was Jefferson's favorite poet? Several critics have found the relationship between ancient Scottish bard and enlightened sage of Monticello intriguing. Susan Manning, and more recently Kevin Hayes, have, for example, documented Jefferson's passion for Ossian's melancholic verse—a passion that would lead him to compose a gravestone for his close friend and brother-in-law Dabney Carr using Ossianic verse, and that would inspire him to contact James Macpherson's brother in order to obtain copies of the poems in their original Gaelic. Spare no expense, Jefferson told Macpherson—"The glow of one warm thought is to me worth more than money"—and he even asked for advice on Gaelic dictionaries and grammars, so that he could learn the language of his muse more effectively and efficiently.[21]

By the mid-1770s, Jefferson was reading Ossian on a daily basis. In 1773, he wrote that his poems "have been, and will I think during my life continue to be to me, the source of daily and exalted pleasure. The tender, and the sublime emotions of the mind were never before so finely wrought up by human hand. I am not ashamed to own that I think this rude bard of the North the greatest Poet that has ever existed."[22] The image of Jefferson riding Fingal or Ryno—horses he named after the heroes of Ossian's poetry—through the dense fog of a Virginia morning stands in stark opposition to the more traditional picture of the rational, Lockean-inspired, and deistic champion of Enlightenment epistemology and political theory. Indeed, those few scholars who have acknowledged the importance of romantic, even sentimental, aesthetics to Jefferson's work always frame the issue in terms of competing worldviews—the man of science versus the man of feeling. Such scholarship encourages us to think of two Jeffersons, and as such implies that sensibility and enlightenment, romance and reason, offer two opposing ideologies.

For Susan Manning, then, Jefferson *retreats* into a sentimental mode of perception when he is confronted with the ugly facts of U.S. imperialism. "*Ossian,*" she argues, "did not function as a register for his own domestic affections; they provided a means of distancing and harmonizing sentiments with an uncomfortably discordant and specific charge of grief and guilt."[23] Slavery and, in particular, colonial violence toward indigenous peoples is often, she argues, filtered through the lens of Ossianic romance—at which point Jefferson transfers the image of the noble, Highland savage, blessed with a potently ruined eloquence, onto the western frontier. This is why, argues Manning, Jefferson championed the speech of Logan—including it in his *Notes on the State of Virginia* (1781)—and later composing an editorial preface to accompany the numerous reprintings that this hugely popular speech would quickly demand.

I want to conclude this chapter, however, by revisiting another moment in the *Notes* in order to rethink the relationship between race, romance, and reason. Rather than view these terms as separate and distinct—and instead of offering an analysis of the ways in which the "two Jeffersons" negotiate a third, distinct problem of race—I will instead show how the *Notes* foreground the mutuality of eighteenth-century ideologies of romance, reason, and race.

PHRENOLOGIES OF FEELING

Writing less than a decade after Mackenzie completed *Julia de Roubigné*, Jefferson articulates his own system of sentimental "government" in the *Notes*:

> Whether the black of the negro resides in the reticular membrane between the skin and scarf-skin, or in the scarfskin itself; whether it proceeds from the colour of the blood, the colour of the bile, or from that of some other secretion, the difference is fixed in nature, and is as real as if its seat and cause were better known to us. And is this difference of no importance? Is it not the foundation of a greater or less share of beauty in the two races? Are not the fine mixtures of red and white, the expressions of every passion by greater or less suffusions of colour in the one, preferable to that eternal monotony, which reigns in the countenances, that immoveable veil of black which covers all the emotions of the other race?[24]

Thomas Jefferson's romance of race synthesizes the Enlightenment's thirst for taxonomic precision with the man of feeling's dream for a flawlessly unmediated blush or tear. Sharing the same grammatical structure that patterns Shaftesbury's *Sensus Communis* with such precautious certitude, Jefferson's theory of sentimental community is framed by a series of questions that promise the scientific resolution of the adverb clause ("Whether the black of the negro resides in the reticular membrane") only to deliver self-evident redundancy (even if we have no idea as to its "seat and cause," the blackness of the negro must be "fixed in nature"). The invisibility of the stain's mechanism only adds to its material force: blackness is not just a coloring of the skin; it is the "immovable veil" of ruin at the heart of sentimental registration, the "eternal" occlusion of feeling's desire to publicize itself. Jefferson's genius is to build a romance of race rooted in the aesthetics of sentimental romance and its obscured thing of ruined feeling.

The point to emphasize here is that sentimental romance and Enlightenment science are not two opposing ideologies or two different aesthetic modes: they each mutually reinforce the idea that the essence, the core of identity is to be found in some *thing* hidden deeply within the interior folds of the body. These things—blackness and feeling—are not simply private

Feeling 69

essences; they also flow out to the surface of the body, to greater or lesser degrees, and publicize themselves on the skin and skull—material echoes of our inner, most private selves. As such, both the romance of race and the romance of feeling construct their own phrenological fantasies. Consider, for example, the following passage from Hutcheson's *An Inquiry Concerning the Original of Our Ideas of Virtue or Moral Good*, one of the more important texts in the development of an eighteenth-century politics of feeling:

> it is certain, almost all *habitual Dispositions* of *Mind* form the Countenance in such a manner, as to give some Indications of them to the Spectator. Our *violent* Passions are obvious at first View in the Countenance; so that sometimes no Art can conceal them; and smaller Degrees of them give some less obvious Turns to the Face, which an accurate Eye will observe. Now, when the *natural Air* of a Face approaches to that which any Passion would form it unto, we make a Conjecture from this concerning the *leading Disposition* of a Person's *Mind*. [25]

Although ostensibly rooted in the privacy of sensation, the discourse of sensibility is always also caught up in the dilemma of publicizing the personal. It longs for, even fetishizes, material tokens of affective display—tears, blushes, and other "Turns of the Face"—and obsesses over the possibility that these echoes of privacy can be read, that the interior affective core can communicate with and make its mark on the fleshy surface of the skin. It is with little surprise, then, that we find that Harley's "skill in physiognomy," albeit limited,[26] inspired an 1886 edition of *The Man of Feeling* that was published with its own "Index to Tears," each entry chronicling a moment in the text when one of these watery things of feeling is shed.[27]

Of course, for those fortunate bodies that are open to such spectacles of feeling, the problem will become one of adjudicating the authenticity of the affective material on display. This is how we should read the sentimental fascination with melancholy, which is not a particular kind of emotion but a permanent fracture that ruins feeling from within and detaches it from the crass, inauthentic economy of everyday emotions—the kind that circulate among "men of the world." For those who fetishize the privacy of affection, all public display of emotion is thus *formally* ruined. This is why every vision of sentimental community ultimately hinges on the spectacle of the ruined body. Melancholy and unending ruin are the price that the man of feeling pays for his authentic, essential, identifying core, and it is here—with the logic of his aesthetic framework as well as with the content of his symbolic core—that we should risk reading him in conjunction with emerging, Enlightenment ideologies of racial identity—ideologies that predict the inevitable decline of the eloquent noble savage and anatomize the mute materiality of the slave.

MOURNING AND THE LASTNESS OF RACE

In 1803, the New York publishers Elliot and Hunt attempted to capitalize on the new nation's thirst for sentimental ruins by publishing an excerpt from Mackenzie's *The Man of Feeling* alongside the ever-popular "Speech of Logan." Even twenty years earlier, when Jefferson included this same speech in the "eternal monotony" section of his *Notes on the State of Virginia*, the lament of the last Mingo warrior had numerous admirers around the world and a rich publication history. As Jefferson explains in a later edition of the *Notes*:

> The speech was published in the Virginia Gazette ... (I have it myself in the volume of gazettes of that year) and though in a style by no means elegant, yet it was so admired, that it flew through all the public papers of the continent, and through the magazines and other periodical publications of Great-Britain; and those who were boys at that day will now attest, that the speech of Logan used to be given them as a school exercise for repetition. It was not till about thirteen or fourteen years after the newspaper publications, that the Notes on Virginia were published in America. Combating, in these, the contumelious theory of certain European writers, whose celebrity gave currency and weight to their opinions, that our country, from the combined efforts of soil and climate, degenerated animal nature, in the general, and particularly the moral faculties of man, I considered the speech of Logan as an apt proof of the contrary, and used it as such.[28]

For the same reason that he would send the Comte de Buffon a New Hampshire moose, Jefferson was keen to promote Logan's speech as an example of the poetical as well as the physical fecundity of the American soil.[29] Rather than refute climatological theories of racial differentiation—and profoundly aware of the implications that such theories had on European attitudes toward his new nation—Jefferson instead turns to the sublime savagery of Native American prehistory to provide evidence for a rich vein of romantic and ruined orality running deeply through the geological strata of his land.

Whereas the "black of the negro" consigns that race to mute monotony—incapable of producing any trace of affective "colour" in the geological record save its own massive veil of negativity—Logan's feelings are ruined in a different way. For if feeling is a thing that can be possessed (or utterly veiled), Logan's speech reminds us that, within the aesthetic economy of sentimental romance, even the possessor of such feelings loses their subjectivity and historicity at the precise moment that their affections are publicized:

> I appeal to any white man to say if he ever entered Logan's cabin hungry, and he gave him not meat; if he ever came cold and naked, and he clothed him not. During the last long and bloody war, Logan remained idle in his cabin, an advocate for peace. Such was my love for the whites, that my countrymen pointed as they passed by, and said, "Logan is the friend of the white men." I had even thought to have lived with you, had it not been for the injuries of one man. Colonel Cresap, the last spring, in cold blood, and unprovoked, murdered all the relations of Logan, not even sparing my women and children. There runs not a drop of my blood in the veins of any living creature. This called on me for revenge. I have sought it; I have killed many; I have fully glutted my vengeance. For my country I rejoice at the beams of peace; but do not harbour a thought that mine is the joy of fear. Logan never felt fear. He will not turn upon his heel to save his life. Who is there to mourn for Logan? Not one.[30]

As Jonathan Elmer has argued, "Logan's is a mourning without issue, isolated from both land and people, a mourning quarantined, or so Jefferson hopes, wholly within a poetic code."[31] But the point that I would stress here is the mutuality of sentimental and racial logic at play in the speech. It isn't just that Jefferson's unconscious racism seeks out the sentimental romance—and its ruined figures of solitary mourning—as a convenient aesthetic code to appropriate and then infuse with naturalized symbols of racial distinction and decay. In the same way that Sterne's longing to share in the thing of sentimental ruin produces the perfect sentimental tear—a sentimental commodity that so completely materializes affection that it renders subjective emotion irrelevant—so too the power of Logan's mourning works by creating another hypermaterial token of our essential subjectivity: racialized "blood in the veins."

At a time in which race was quickly becoming the term for a scientific species of humankind rather than just a loose collection of ancestors who bear the same name, the mournful erasure of Logan's "blood" stands at a watershed moment in U.S. ideologies of race—ideologies that will soon rely on the concept of "one drop of blood" or the illusion of racialized genetic codes in order to "quarantine" what is quintessentially human. By reading the lament of Logan's lost and last blood alongside the work of mourning in the sentimental romance, we can see how racialized blood circulates in the same kind of fragmented and ruined economy as Harley's coin or Maria's tear. As with feeling, the thing of race is visible only at the threshold of its disappearance—not simply because it is a convenient national myth that numbs us to the ugly truths of Native American genocide, but also because its materiality can never be fully present for exchange. If the spectacle of public feeling necessarily ruins the intimate privacy of our emotions, so too displays of racial affiliation must always operate invisibly beneath as well as openly on the surface of the skin. (After all, the idea of race as a simple function of skin coloration would hardly provide for the kind of ideological flexibility needed to group specific populations of people who themselves display a bewildering assortment of skin hues.) Where the "negro" is condemned to the "monotony" of a race that can only register itself negatively on the skin's surface—as the interruption of "passion" and the eternal veiling of "suffusions of color"—the race of Logan is ruined from an all too immediate connectivity between feeling and its registration in language and on the body. In the same way that Julia's perfect sentimental tear so completely materializes her affections that it occludes any subjective emotional experience, so too the uninterrupted immediacy of Logan's affective suffusions helps to produce the famous stoicism of the Indian. We should read such stoicism not as a disciplined passivity engendered by a *lack* of emotional response but, rather, as the void, the private ruin that accompanies total affective publicity.

What is Logan lamenting? What is the object of his mourning? The assumption made by scholars of this speech and its relationship to the U.S. colonization of native lands is that he is mourning the loss of his family and the demise of his race. However, Logan himself claims that his actions have "fully glutted [his] vengeance"; and given his inability to interrupt the total immediacy of his feelings, it should not come as a surprise that he is able to mobilize and materialize his mourning into effective, vengeful action. The strange lament, "Who is there to mourn for Logan?" does not mourn the loss of a valued object: it anticipates the impossibility of mourning *for* Logan and his losses. For Elmer,

> Logan's discursive isolation is melancholic, in the precise sense that it is not open to the consolations of mourning. Logan is himself melancholic, of course—Why would he mourn? For whom would his mourning have meaning, reduced as he is to the last?—but his more essential role is as the *object* of melancholic investment. . . . Logan remains unsubsumable; he is a lost object for which another could never substitute. (147)

While I agree with Elmer's assessment of Logan's melancholic function within U.S. ideologies of race and colonization, the idea that Logan himself is "melancholic" misses the mark. Within the "poetic code" of sentimentality, Logan's "race" is ruined in its total publicity of affect while the "negro" is ruined by an eternally veiled intimacy. The genius of this sentimental logic is that neither "race" actually exhibits emotion—the one because it is utterly occluded, the other because it is totally absorbed—stoicized—in the immanent materiality of its display. That leaves the delicate "suffusions of color" to whiter European bodies who manage to forge a middle ground between these two extremes.

Logan is the last of his race because the thing, the "blood" of race can appear only in fragments of loss and lastness. As such, race is always racing away from the comforting illusion of lost wholeness (the last of the race); properly speaking, there is no lost, mournable moment when Logan was at ever at home with his "race." Race functions as an uncanny gaze that, like Logan's anticipative lament, ruins itself so that mementos of its loss (blood, genes, and other *things*) can appear and circulate as exchangeable values. Within this sentimental economy of racial difference, whiteness emerges not as another kind of race but, instead, as a promise, a destiny that manifests itself between the silent latency of the "negro" and the stoic lament of the last Indian—in the shadows cast by the things of feeling and the blood of race.

3

PROPERTY/PERSONHOOD

CONJURING COMMUNITY: *ARTHUR MERVYN* AND THE AESTHETICS OF RUIN

When Arthur Mervyn, the eponymous hero of Charles Brockden Brown's 1798 romance, begins to hear reports of a yellow-fever epidemic taking root in nearby Philadelphia, he immediately filters the gruesome details through an aesthetics of the sublime. These reports, he later reflects, were

> of a nature to absorb and suspend the whole soul. A certain sublimity is connected with enormous dangers, that imparts to our consternation or our pity, a tincture of the pleasing. This, at least, may be experienced by those who are beyond the verge of peril. My own person was exposed to no hazard. I had leisure to conjure up terrific images, and to personate the witnesses and sufferers of this calamity. This employment was not enjoined upon me by necessity, but was ardently pursued, and must therefore have been recommended by some nameless charm.[1]

Literary critics often point to Edmund Burke's influential *A Philosophical Enquiry into the Origin of Our Ideas of the Sublime and the Beautiful* (1756) in order to connect the "terrific images" of the English Gothic romance with Burke's theories on the effects and the aesthetics of terror.[2] The fact that Arthur Mervyn experiences the same "tincture" of sublime peril that, for Burke, so often accompanies the threat of communal dissolution and self-annihilation raises questions that continue to haunt critics of American literature: What are the relationships between English and American romance forms? And why were so many writers in the emerging U.S. nation—from Brockden Brown to Irving, from Neal to Hawthorne, and from Poe to Melville—drawn to the "sublimity" of a literary genre whose popularity was already on the wane in London?[3] In order to answer these questions, it will be necessary to revisit and rethink the aesthetic logic of romance, race, personhood, and property.

Beginning with Leslie Fiedler's groundbreaking 1960 text *Love and Death in the American Novel*, scholars of American literature have often explored the link between the Gothic romance and the emerging U.S. nation.[4] In his preface to *Edgar Huntly* (1799), Brockden Brown observes that, although American writers cannot employ the same locales and symbols as their European counterparts—Gothic castles, for example—in order to generate the "enormous dangers" required of the genre, "[the] incidents of Indian hostility, and the perils of the western wilderness, are far more suitable; and, for a native [writer] of America to overlook these, would admit of no apology."[5] In a similar vein, John Neal also urges the nation and its national literature to look westward for its own peculiarly American images of the "terrific": "There may be no such [Gothic] ruins in America as are found in Europe, or in Asia or in Africa; but other ruins there are of a prodigious magnitude—the ruins of a mighty people . . . [and] the live wreck of a prodigious empire that has departed from before our face within the memory of man; the last of a people who have no history."[6] For Fiedler—as for many Americanists—the romantic literature of the emerging nation becomes an aesthetic medium in which Enlightenment ideologies of freedom, democracy, sovereignty, and property rights confront and negotiate the reality—the "live wreck"—of U.S. colonial violence. "A dream of innocence," Fiedler avers, "had sent Europeans across the ocean to build a new society immune to the compounded evil of the past from which no one in Europe could ever feel himself free. But the slaughter of the Indians, who would not yield their lands to the carriers of utopia, and the abominations of the slave trade . . . provided new evidence that evil did not remain with the world that had been left behind."[7]

What results from this approach to the relationship between literature and the ideology of the emerging nation is an essentially Freudian reading of the genesis of American Gothic romance. Faced with the realities of racial and colonial violence, American literature represses the ugly facts of Indian removal (where property rights have been violated) and African slavery (where personhood has itself been transformed into a kind of property) and creates its own, more palatable, myths of national triumph and the inevitable decline of the noble savage. In *The Insistence of the Indian*, for example, Susan Scheckel notes that "If Indians provided a crucial site of reflection on national identity . . . , they also represented that which had to be denied for a coherent image of the nation to be recognized."[8] A key component of this "coherent image" of the nation was, then, the ability to forget, to repress, those "Others" whose presence and resistance threatened to explode the myths of nationhood. But as Scheckel's reference to the "insistence" of the Indian points out—and as other titles, such as Renee Bergland's *The National Uncanny: Indian Ghosts and American Subjects*, suggest—the repressed, ugly facts of colonial violence return to haunt the romantic narratives of the emerging nation, paving the way for literary scholars to excavate the subversive traces of racial ghosts that threaten to disrupt nineteenth-century ideologies of expansion and political freedom. The Gothic romance thus helps the new nation to imagine the proper contours of its community;[9] or, borrowing Lauren Berlant's terminology, such texts begin to shape the "National Symbolic" by providing a space, a medium through which the new mythical stuff of a unified, coherent nation can be negotiated and imagined.[10] And like the manifest content of a dream, this symbolic, literary medium is haunted by the return of latent, repressed events that threaten to disrupt these imaginative borders of the national community.

If we were to keep pushing this Freudian methodological analogy, the problem to be emphasized here is the same one that Slavoj Žižek points to in the frequent misreadings of *The Interpretation of Dreams*, misreadings that equate the Real of the unconscious with the latent content of the dream and consciousness with its manifest content.[11] From the perspective of Fiedler's American Gothic romance, the ugly facts of Indian removal and African slavery would here function as an unconscious, repressed Reality (with a capital *R*), a latent content that forever haunts the manifest dream of American literary nationalism. But Žižek's point is that such a reading of Freud misses the truly elusive nature of the Real—that always "Unfathomable X" responsible for the traumatic force that first separates and makes possible any distinction between manifest and latent dream content.[12] What is at stake here is the very structure of haunting—the status of the specter—that inhabits the gothic romance of nation. What truly haunts the literature of the emerging U.S. nation, I will argue, is not the return of some horrific Other—some racialized

Property/Personhood 77

remainder that refuses to be removed outside the clean and proper borders of the nation. As Žižek points out, such a return of the repressed is fully provided for and anticipated by the ideology of national community, as a sort of pregiven and fully sanctioned subversion that, thanks to its absolute Otherness, dialectically reinforces the logic of self-identity at work in modern systems of community. Rather, what these systems must repress at all times is the possibility that their formal, aesthetic logic is flawed—that there is something about the singularity of experience and subjectivity that always exceeds and eludes collection into coherent communities of similar *things*.

This chapter explores how two of the most distinctive common things thought to be possessed by the modern, democratic subject—property and personhood—are coproduced with romances of contagion, immunization, mummification, mesmerism, and metempsychosis. Never simply one literary genre among many, I argue instead that the Gothic names modernity's central aesthetic regime. The Gothicity of a text like *Arthur Mervyn* is not simply to be measured by the symbolic anxiety of its content: Gothic here also idenitifies a formal aesthetic program that conjures up the generic specters—the common things—of modern community. We have already seen how an ostensibly distinct romance form, the sentimental novel, is capable of producing similarly "Gothic" special effects, rendering the ruined things of feeling—tears and blood, for example—visible for exchange within the democratic commonplace. In what follows, I show how three, more traditionally "Gothic," romance novels expose, contribute to, and resist these modern aesthetics of belonging.

PROPERTY, PERSONHOOD, PEST

Arthur Mervyn has a name for the elusive "something" at the heart of modern forms of community: the pest. The sublime "tincture" of pleasure that its hero derives from reports of Philadelphia's yellow-fever epidemic will always be fleeting. Indeed, he will soon become infected by "the pest," and the safe distance that he is able to maintain "beyond the verge of peril" is quickly exposed as an ideological fiction, the "nameless charm" of an aesthetic gaze that, not unlike recent critical approaches to the Gothic and Burke's own ideology of the sublime, safely patrols the borders of self and

Other by enjoying the possibility that these spaces are threatened with immanent contamination and destruction. Modern forms of subjectivity ("I had leisure to conjure up terrific images") are here tied to the "calamity" of community. And Brockden Brown makes us aware that such conjuring—although productive of leisure time—is itself anything but an idle, leisurely act: Mervyn's emerging sense of self-identity performs these feats of magic with all the "necessity" of a drive that "was ardently pursued." Such is the allure of ruin and infection in *Arthur Mervyn*.

The pest is not simply some pregiven, infectious thing that originates outside of the community and that then threatens to collapse the borders of its space, to open up its bodies to infection, and to expose its property to looting. This is, of course, the way that the text's characters (as well as the text's critics) tend to experience its menace.[13] Yellow fever is imagined as a potently vague Caribbean disease, transported to the early republic by refugees from the Haitian Revolution. In addition to all these important anxieties of nation, race, and property, Brockden Brown helps us to read another kind of relationship that exists between pest, personhood, and community, a relationship that focuses not so much on the subversive, sublime antagonism between these preestablished concepts but that, rather, highlights the mutuality of their coproduction.

Arthur Mervyn begins with another scene of conjuration. Dr. Stevens, who will provide a safe home both for Mervyn's infected body and for his extraordinary narrative, describes his own response to the pest and to the threat that it poses to himself and to his community:

> I was resident in this city during the year 1793. Many motives contributed to detain me, though departure was easy and commodious, and my friends were generally solicitous for me to go. It is not my purpose to enumerate these motives, or to dwell on my present concerns and transactions, but merely to compose a narrative of some incidents with which my situation made me acquainted.
>
> Returning one evening, somewhat later than usual, to my own house, my attention was attracted, just as I entered the porch, by the figure of a man, reclining against the wall at a few paces distant. My sight was imperfectly assisted by a far-off lamp; but the posture in which he sat, the hour, and the place immediately suggested the idea of one disabled by sickness. It was obvious to conclude that his disease was

pestilential. This did not deter me from approaching and examining him more closely.

He leaned his head against the wall, his eyes were shut, his hands clasped in each other, and his body seemed to be sustained in an upright position merely by the cellar door against which he rested his left shoulder. The lethargy into which he was sunk seemed scarcely interrupted by my feeling his hand and his forehead. His throbbing temples and burning skin indicated a fever, and his form, already emaciated, seemed to prove that it had not been of short duration.

There was only one circumstance that hindered me from forming an immediate determination in what manner this person should be treated. My family consisted of my wife and a young child. Our servant maid had been seized three days before by the reigning malady, and, at her own request, had been conveyed to the hospital. We ourselves enjoyed good health, and were hopeful of escaping with our lives. Our measures for this end had been cautiously taken and carefully adhered to. They did not consist in avoiding the receptacles of infection, for my office required me to go daily into the midst of them; nor in filling the house with the exhalations of gun-powder, vinegar, or tar. They consisted in cleanliness, reasonable exercise, and wholesome diet. (233–34)

What is the relationship between the pest, the body, the community, and the home for Dr. Stevens? From the outset, we understand that his decision to remain in Philadelphia during the yellow-fever outbreak is a conscious choice that runs contrary to the opinion of the community. Not only does Stevens refuse to flee the pest by making what would have been an "easy and commodious" departure from the city. He also tells us that, unlike the other remaining city dwellers, he makes no effort to avoid "the receptacles of infection"—including Mervyn's "throbbing" and "pestilential" body—that confront him during his stay. Brockden Brown foregrounds the threat that this body poses for Stevens and his *oikos*: his lethargic form merges with the walls and the "cellar door" of Stevens's home, as if burrowing its way through these boundaries by exchanging the framework of Mervyn's body—his hands "clasped in each other" and no longer reaching out into the world—for the "support" promised by the architecture of Stevens's home. While the rest of the city attempts to keep the pest at bay—and the home isolated and intact—Stevens invites it in and cares for it. This strategy of incorporation (or, better, inoculation) will be repeated throughout the text, when Stevens, for example, also takes into his home a friend who has become infected with an insane and incurable passion for one of Mrs. Villars's prostitutes (430). In contrast with the primitive conjurings of the rest of Philadelphia—who rely on talismanic "exhalations of gun-powder, vinegar, or tar" to protect them from the pest—Stevens's secret is found in the enlightened magic of hygiene: "cleanliness, reasonable exercise, and wholesome diet." Instead of threatening Stevens's body and his home, the pest paradoxically reinforces and inoculates these spaces by lending them a palatable antagonist against which to exercise their ever-strengthened powers. Even the relationship between Stevens and his wife is braced by this regimen, her "willingness and ... solicitude" to work together with her husband only amplifying domestic accord (236).

The difference between Stevens's strategy of inoculation and the quaint "exhalations" of the other city dwellers is reflected in transformations of the verb "to conjure" that were taking place in the eighteenth century. In medieval times, to conjure protection involved an appeal to a transcendent, magical, or spiritual power, such that, for example, Wyclif's Bible (1380) translates Matthew 26:63 as follows: "But Jhesus was stille. And the prince of prestis seide to hym, Y *coniure* thee bi lyuynge God, that thou seie to vs, if thou art Crist, the sone of God" (italics mine).[14] Conjuring here helps to maintain safe and proper boundaries by invoking the authority of a higher power that is cordoned off from the body. As such, conjuring constitutes a quasi-juridical action, a "constraint" that is placed on someone by putting them under oath. Chaucer's "The Prioress' Prologue and Tale" thus reads: "This yonge child to conjure he bigan,/And said, "Oh dear child, I beseech thee,/By power of the holy Trinity/Tell me what is thy cause to sind,/Since they throat is cut as it seems to me?" (644–48)[15] Where conjuring here invokes the power of a nonhuman, transcendent power to keep meaning and law in order, by the end of the eighteenth century this power has become secularized in and personified by the figure of the conjurer. The task of this conjurer is to "effect, produce, bring *out*, convey *away*" change (*OED*), and his competency hinges on his ability to directly channel the magical powers that now inhere within—rather than transcend—the modern object and its conjuring subject/body. In *Capital*, Marx famously analyzes the energy and aesthetics of this new object in his discussion of the commodity-form, a phenomenon he equates with the mid-nineteenth-century German craze in spiritualist "table turning." I invoke the spectacle of the séance here in order to suggest that the Enlightenment hygiene practiced by Dr. Stevens does not simply do away with magic: it redistributes the dynamics of its power between the inoculated confines of the body and the ever-threatening thinghood of the pest. Never satisfied with the mystical power of isolated objects—"gun-powder, vinegar, or tar"—Stevens instead invites the pest to penetrate his home and his body. And in the same way that enabling the suspicious and infected youth to tell his tale ultimately reinforces his faith in the virtue of humankind (427), so too the wholesomeness of Stevens's body and the cleanliness of his home are revivified by the proximity of immanent ruin.

At work in *Arthur Mervyn*, then, is a relationship between body, community, and pest that exceeds the traditional narratives of resistance, repression, and return so often associated with Gothic romance. Stevens's modern, hygienic body is transformed by the diet and exercise that the pest demands of it; and so too the community of his *oikos* is never simply threatened by an independent, pathogenic force from beyond its walls: the pest is also conjured up from within, incorporated into the everyday tasks of household management. In his analysis of the rise of biopolitical forms of sovereignty, Roberto Esposito locates this tactic of inoculation—what he calls the "paradigm of immunity"—at the heart of modern forms of community.[16] Immunity here describes "the essential relationship the body has with its vulnerability": "the immunitary paradigm," he argues, "does not present itself in terms of action, but rather in terms of *reaction*—rather than a force, it is a repercussion, a counterforce, which hinders another force from coming into being. This means that the immunitary mechanism presupposes the existence of the ills it is meant to counter."[17] In his reading of Hobbes, Esposito points out that the private individual is not, contrary to most readings of *Leviathan* (1651), saved from the perils of the state of nature by the sovereign command and then placed under the protection of the modern state. Rather than read these two figures—sovereign and individual—as pregiven actors in the drama of the social contract, Esposito points instead to the immunitary logic that coproduces the illusion of isolated positions, an illusion that continues to haunt our biopolitical horizon.[18] From Esposito's perspective, what Hobbesian sovereignty immunizes the individual from is precisely its exposure to the pure community of the state of nature. "[C]ommunity is not an entity," he argues, nor a collective subject, nor a group of subjects. It is the relation that makes them no longer be individual subjects, since it interrupts their identity with a bar that passes through them and thus changes them. It is the 'with,' the 'between,' the threshold on which they cross in a contact that relates them to others to the very extent that it separates them from themselves."[19] What makes Hobbes the first figure of modernity for Esposito is the way in which he cofounds sovereign power and liberal individualism through the logic of immunity:

> [I]n order to save itself unequivocally, life is made "private" in the two meanings of the expression. It is privatized and deprived of that relation that exposes it to its communal mark. Every external relation to the vertical line that binds everyone to the sovereign command is cut at the root. Individual literally means this: to make indivisible, united in oneself, by the same line that divides one from everyone else. The individual appears protected from the negative border that makes him himself and not other (more than from the positive power of the sovereign). One might come to affirm that sovereignty, in the final analysis, is nothing other than the artificial vacuum created around every individual—the negative of the relation or the negative relation that exists between unrelated entities.[20]

Both Esposito and *Arthur Mervyn* help us to rethink the same paradoxes of American democracy that Leslie Fiedler identifies at the heart of the Gothic romance: on the one hand, political freedom, liberal individualism, and secured property rights; and on the other, slavery, biopolitical colonialism, and the dispossession of indigenous lands and lifeways. For Brockden Brown and Esposito alike, it is never enough to read the modern, democratic revolution as a linear plot in which individuals contract together to form communities in which they can enjoy their freedom and protect their property. And it is equally erroneous to read the Gothic romance solely as a subversive medium through which the repressed violence and hypocrisy of this masterplot returns to haunt the modern political state. Instead, what they help to bring into view is the aesthetic regime of modernity—a truly "Gothic" aesthetics that renders the subject visible to the extent that she is already immunized by a veil of negativity, that foments community only insofar as it immediately forecloses any radical connection between actors, and that conjures magical things—property, race, feeling, personhood, rights—which animate this negativized community with all the force of the fetish.

As Dr. Stevens soon finds out, the complex plot of *Arthur Mervyn* involves the education of its naïve, bucolic hero in the ways of city life. Befriended by a confidence man named Welbeck, Mervyn is quickly introduced to the vagaries of modern forms of financial exchange and property ownership. Brockden Brown's decision to set Mervyn's fragmented narrative in the diseased, urban landscape of Philadelphia links yellow fever's "pest" with anxieties relating to these same forms of exchange and ownership in the emerging U.S. nation. If, as John Locke avers in the *Second Treatise of Government* (1689), "in the beginning, all the world was America," then the pest enables Brockden Brown to revisit the originary romance of the American liberal subject, exposing the gothic aesthetics that conjure his claim to property rights and political freedom.[21] What does it mean to have property in one's self? What is the nature of this peculiar thing that inheres within us and grants us membership in the political community? And how does this self-property reach out from our body through acts of labor, contaminating the world around us with our sovereign claims to ownership? No simple bildungsroman, *Arthur Mervyn* helps us to read the occluded subtext of Lockean liberalism and its exaltation of personhood and property, demonstrating instead how modern forms of community and individuation are infected with the table-turning magic of commodified things.

The pest brings into relief these relationships between personhood, property, and community in the city of Philadelphia:

> The usual occupations and amusements of life were at an end. Terror had exterminated all the sentiments of nature. Wives were deserted by husbands, and children by parents. Some had shut themselves in their houses, and debarred themselves from all communication with the rest of mankind. The consternation of others had destroyed their understanding, and their misguided steps hurried them into the midst of the danger which they had previously laboured to shun. Men were seized by this disease in the streets; passengers fled from them; entrance into their own dwellings was denied to them; they perished in the public ways.
>
> The chambers of disease were deserted, and the sick left to die of negligence. None could be found to remove the lifeless bodies. Their

remains, suffered to decay by piece-meal, filled the air with deadly exhalations, and added tenfold to the devastation. (346)

In this state of emergency, it is no longer possible to maintain distinctions between public and private, *polis* and *oikos*. The bonds holding together the family and the home have been destroyed, with parents leaving children and husbands deserting their wives. Experiences that were once shrouded in privacy—death, madness, pain—have been transformed into spectacles where people now "perished in . . . public ways." As a result of this insane indistinction, all claims to property have been dissolved. "Entrance" to one's home can be "denied," and those who refuse to leave soon inhabit "chambers of disease" penetrated by the decayed exhalations of devastation. The pest renders property violable, and, as a result, shakes the Lockean foundations of the early U.S. republic. But the pest destroys these foundations of community not simply by separating individuals and infecting common spaces. On the contrary, it works its deadly effect by producing an *excess* of community—an overflowing of proximity that is often experienced as claustrophobia in Mervyn's Philadelphia:[22]

> In proportion as I drew near the city, the tokens of its calamitous condition became more apparent. Every farm-house was filled with supernumerary tenants; fugitives from home, and haunting the skirts of the road, eager to detain every passenger with inquiries after news. The passengers were numerous; for the tide of emigration was by no means exhausted. . . . Few had secured to themselves an asylum . . . , every house being already overstocked with inhabitants. (355)

Community in *Arthur Mervyn*'s state of nature is, to echo Esposito, "the 'with,' the 'between,' the threshold . . . that relates [individuals] to others to the very extent that it separates them from themselves." We will revisit the topography of this community-in-excess later when we explore how Brockden Brown associates its form with ideologies of race and poverty. For now, we should note that, in returning to the chaos of the state of nature, the text forces us to revisit the problematic origins of Lockean property and its relationship to personhood and community: How can our singular, sovereign claim to property emerge from a world of indistinction?

"Of Property," the fifth chapter of Locke's *Second Treatise*, begins by acknowledging the antagonism that seems to exist between the concepts of property and community: "how [do] men come to have a property in several parts of that which God gave to mankind in common" (sec. 24)? It will be Locke's genius to devise a romance that transforms this apparent tension into a union strong enough to found the modern political order, a romance driven by a mutually reinforcing logic of personhood and property. He gives us his first secular (indeed, American) vision of the backdrop to this drama—the state of nature—immediately after introducing the ostensible antagonism between property and community:

> God, who hath given the world to men in common, hath also given them reason to make use of it to the best advantage of life, and convenience. The earth, and all that is therein, is given to men for the support and comfort of their being. And tho' all the fruits it naturally produces, and beasts it feeds, belong to mankind in common, as they are produced by the spontaneous hand of nature; and no body has originally a private dominion, exclusive of the rest of mankind, in any of them, as they are thus in their natural state: yet being given for the use of men, there must of necessity be a means to appropriate them some way or other, before they can be of any use, or at all beneficial to any particular man. The fruit, or venison, which nourishes the wild Indian, who knows no enclosure, and is still a tenant in common, must be his, and so his, i.e. a part of him, that another can no longer have any right to it, before it can do him any good for the support of his life. (sec. 25)

What is already remarkable about Locke's narrative is its joint appeal to an immaterial, unbounded, suprahuman power that provides the raw, open stuff of proto-property and a material, embodied container that is capable of enclosing and digesting this stuff. The mutual processes of spiritualization and materialization at work in Lockean property and personhood will be the focus of the next two sections of this chapter, but for now we should note the ways in which property and "life" are inextricably entwined. Earlier in the first *Treatise*, Locke links the origins of property to the "strong desire of preserving . . . life and being" that was "planted" in us by God—a desire for "self-preservation" that he equates with "*the voice of God*" in us (sec. 86). We have a right to make food our property because we have an immanent-transcendent calling to preserve our life. Again note the dual appeal that food satisfies in this Lockean logic: it works because it can function as both a spiritual principle of nourishment and, at the same time, as a material, calorific fact of consumption. Like the pest at Dr. Stevens's door, the threat to life's "support," when invited inside and "planted" as our most intimate inner voice, provides the necessary vacuum for property to fill and sustain us—a regime of ontological hygiene that conjures up the need for property's material supplement. We should, then, read the "self" of Lockean "self-preservation" not as some preexisting entity that is threatened by the devastating, pest-like threat of starvation. Instead, the "self" is an aftereffect produced by the interplay between a metaphysics of self-ruin and an economy of dietary salvation.

In his brief analysis of Locke in *Bios*, Esposito points to the immunitarian paradigm at work in "Of Property." He reads this chapter as a "qualitative intensification of... immunitary logic" because it not only produces the illusion of isolation between individuals within the common but also because, unlike Hobbes, it works to naturalize sovereignty on the side of these individuals and their powerful claim over the objects they own (63): "[W]hile sovereign immunization [in Hobbes] emerges transcendent with respect to those who also create it, that of proprietary immunization [in Locke] adheres to them—or better, remains within the confines of their bodies" (63).[23] Property thus sustains the body of the Lockean individual not only through its capacity to feed his organs but also through its incorporation into the aesthetics of his frame:

> Though the earth and all inferior creatures be common to all men, yet every man has a "property" in his own person: this no body has any right to but himself. The labour of his body, and the work of his hands, we may say, are properly his. Whatsoever then he removes out of the state that nature hath provided, and left it in, he hath mixed his labour with, and joined to it something that is his own, and thereby makes it his property. It being by him removed from the common state nature hath placed it in, it hath by this labour something annexed to it, that excludes the common right of other men: for this labour being the unquestionable property of the labourer, no man but he can have a right to what that is once joined to, at least where there is enough, and as good, left in common for others. (sec. 27)

Property is a dimension, an expression of personhood: it fragments the "common" by distributing it among singular, consumable parts, but it also hollows out an ownable enclosure within the body that infects personhood with the illusion of autonomy, interiority, and privacy.

What does it mean to have property in one's person? Although this appears a seemingly self-evident metaphysical proposition, we must—as always in Locke—remember the material subtext with which it works in tandem, coproducing the illusion of isolated, private persons who inhabit a public world of distributed property. The peculiar property to be found "in" personhood exists as both a transcendent principle and as an immanent quality. It is this abstract-material/universal-singular thinghood of the Lockean person that Marx will later develop in his notion of "congealed quantities of homogenous human labor," and its importance to the *Second Treatise* is evident in the way that it immediately begins to infect and annex the "work of [the] hands."[24] "Locke's reasoning," argues Esposito,

> unravels though concentric circles whose center does not contain a political-juridical principle, but rather an immediately biological reference.... Just as work is an extension of the body, so is property an extension of work, a sort of prosthesis that through the operation of the arm connects it to the body in the same vital segment; not only because property is necessary for the material support of life, but because its prolongation is directed to corporeal formation.... [The subject's] predominance over the object isn't established by the distance that separates it from the subject, but by the movement of its incorporation. (65)

It is tempting to read *Arthur Mervyn* as a celebration of Jeffersonian agrarianism, an homage to the good old days when value and identity were tied directly to the labor of our hands. In contrast, the mercantile speculators of the city trade in a more abstract, immaterial exchange-value, hence the fact that our hero is continually duped by what he calls these "perilous precincts of private property" (270).[25] However, like Mackenzie's man of feeling, the young Arthur Mervyn—even before he journeys to Philadelphia—cuts a frail, ghost-like figure in the fields of bucolic Chester County, the last living offspring of a dead mother with "some defect in [her] constitution"—a defect that leaves Arthur waiting "for the same premature fate" that befell his five other siblings (244). There is no idyllic agrarian option for Mervyn, where the work of his body can be "the unquestionable property of the labourer," and where the fruits of his labor reinforce his sense of, and property in, an independent self; indeed, given the ruined, temporary positions available, the city feels like more of an escape to him, and work obstructs rather than effects his "liberty" (250):

> Tilling the earth was my only profession, and to profit by my skill in it, it would be necessary to become a day-labourer in the service of strangers; but this was a destiny to which I, who had so long enjoyed the pleasures of independence and command, could not suddenly reconcile myself. It occurred to me that the city might afford me an asylum. (248)

In the world of *Arthur Mervyn*, the "labour of [the] body" and the "work of [the] hands" form complicated, prosthetic interrelationships with the "pleasures of independence" and personhood. As Sean X. Goudie has noted, Mervyn often translates "momentary loss of identity" with lost, "[p]aralyzed, or "'phantom' limbs," exposing the channels of prosthetic infection at work in his "self-identity."[26] Indeed, the pest reminds us that if the property that resides "in" Lockean personhood can extend out from the body—through the hands and limbs–and annex itself onto labor, then this contagious circuit can also operate in reverse: "Without an appropriating subject, no appropriated thing. But," continues Esposito, "without any appropriated thing, no appropriating subject" (*Bios* 67).

In *Arthur Mervyn*, property and pest work together to coproduce the illusion of the modern subject: if property is a romance of contagion enabling "the subject" to connect itself, through a labor of prosthesis, to a world of property, then the pest names the "thing" that animates its ruin. No matter which direction these circuits flow—toward accretion or decomposition, toward civilization or destitution—their contagious current produces the fantasy of isolated-but-connected things: subject, property, pest:

> I wandered over this deserted mansion, in a considerable degree, at random. Effluvia of a pestilential nature, assailed me from every corner. In the front room of the second story, I imagined that I discovered vestiges of that catastrophe which the past night had produced. The bed appeared as if some one had recently been dragged from it. The sheets were tinged with yellow, and with that substance which is said to be characteristic of this disease, the gangrenous or black vomit. The floor exhibited similar stains. (379)

For Walter Benjamin, Poe's tales work their magic by transforming bourgeoise interior space into a crime scene, a site of catastrophe and evacuation that attests, in the materiality of its ruin, to the ghostly traces of the modern subject.[27] Where the "horror of [Poe's] apartments" here involves the "arrangement of furniture [as a] site plan of deadly traps, and the suite of rooms prescribes the path of the fleeing victim," in Brockden Brown's "deserted mansion" we can already see this same aesthetic program at work.[28] Notice how the thinghood, the "[e]ffluvia," of the pest "assail[s]" the subject. In this passage, and throughout *Arthur Mervyn*, this pest is "imagined" as an "element" that "taint[s]" the air and poisons the "atmosphere" (382, 377, 376): "I seemed not so much to smell as to taste the element that now encompassed me. I felt as if I had inhaled a poisonous and subtle fluid, whose power instantly bereft my stomach of all vigour. Some fatal influence appeared to seize upon my vitals; and the work of corrosion and decomposition to be busily begun" (360). The massive and invisible materiality of the pest is thus tied to a romance of ruin that hovers over these "vestiges" of catastrophe. The pest is an aftereffect conjured by detective and crime scene: it is the thing that that must have tinged the "sheets . . . with yellow" and stained the floor with infected "vomit." And the subject of this crime is also a belated forensic reconstruction—the once-vital organism that must have expelled "black vomit" and stamped the bed with signs of a fleeting presence before being "dragged" from the scene of disaster.

In his perverse bildungsroman, Brockden Brown revisits these originary fictions of personhood and property at the Lockean heart of the U.S. nation. Instead of a hardworking and vibrant subject whose individuation animates the aesthetic framework of the novel, Arthur Mervyn's fragile, infected personhood—at least in the first volume—emerges belatedly through the good detective work of Dr. Stevens and his friends.[29] From the perspective of Lockean individualism, the form of both *Arthur Mervyn* and Arthur Mervyn are shown to be ruined at the core. Even before Mervyn contracts yellow fever, his body is already infected with the "vestiges" of impending catastrophe: "The seeds of an early and lingering death are sown in my constitution. It is vain to hope to escape the malady by which my mother and my brothers have died. We are a race, whose existence some inherent property has limited to the short space of twenty years" (351). In Brockden Brown's skillful hands, this "inherent property" of ruin immunized into the frame of the novel and its hero is exposed as modernity's pervasive aesthetic logic—a logic connecting the melancholia of the man of feeling with modern systems of identity, with the everyday operation of the modern city, and with its institutional common spaces.

In February 1798, just a few months before the *Weekly Magazine* would start publishing chapters from *Arthur Mervyn*, this same journal began serializing Brockden Brown's "The Man at Home."[30] The central drama of this text involves the narrator's decision to endorse the credit of an old friend and business partner. In so doing, he is perfectly aware that he risks his own fortune: "My existence itself is at stake," he reasons, and so when his friend defaults on the loan, the narrator is forced to hide out in the apartment of his washerwoman.[31] The story takes place during the period of his confinement, and it offers Brockden Brown the opportunity to reflect on the peculiar nature of value that property exchange requires. Like *Arthur Mervyn*, "The Man at Home" is interested in the immunitary logic that binds the risk of infection and collapse to the "good health" of modern forms of exchange and community. Debt—the infection and evacuation of value—here functions in much the same way that sleep—the "paroxysms" that erase consciousness—assists the hygenic maintenance of a healthy body. "The recurrence of these paroxysms," notes Brockden Brown, is "necessary to prevent death. We must forego our consciousness for a while that we may not lose it altogether. . . . In order to preserve our minds in a tolerably sound and active state . . . , it is requisite that these paroxysms should be regular and complete."[32] Brockden Brown observes this logic at work in economies of desire as well as in the cycles of consciouness. "The same observation may be made of love as of sleep," he insists. "They are equally diseases, that is, they are equally deviations from the truth of things and the perfection of our nature; but they are diseases whose tendency it is to exclude diseases still greater."[33] Small wonder, then, that the "pest" functions here, as in *Arthur Mervyn*, to cement rather than dissolve the erotics of plot. The narrator tells the story of a young man, Wallace, for whom "the Yellow Fever [was] the most fortunate event that could have happened."[34] Forced to leave the city, he soon makes the acquaintence of a "lady, who added three hundred pounds a year, to youth, beauty, and virtue. . . . A lovely wife, a plentiful fortune, health, and leisure are the ingredients of my present lot, and for all these am I indebted to the Yellow Fever."[35] In the same way that a "healthy" diet sustains Dr. Stevens at the threshold of disease; and just as the "pest" produces the sublime spectacle necessary for Mervyn's "leisure" time; so too the promise of infection and debt work to energize rather than enervate economies of value in "The Man at Home."

RACE, RUIN, ROMANCE

When Arthur Mervyn returns to the infected urban landscape of Philadelphia, in search of another country boy (also named Wallace) who has risked his life by venturing to city, Mervyn's fateful decision is based on the "lingering death sown in [his] constitution." This "malady" immunizes his fear of the pest; after all, he reasons, it "is better to die, in the consciousness of having offered a heroic sacrifice . . . than by the perverseness of nature" (351). After searching the "deserted mansion" for Wallace, he falls ill with a fever and is forcefully hospitalized:

> I lay upon a mattress, whose condition proved that an half-decayed corpse had recently been dragged from it. The room was large, but it was covered with beds like my own. Between each, there was scarcely the interval of three feet. Each sustained a wretch, whose groans and distortions, bespoke the desperateness of his condition.
>
> The atmosphere was loaded by mortal stenches. A vapour, suffocating and malignant, scarcely allowed me to breathe. No suitable receptacle was provided for the evacuations produced by medicine or disease. My nearest neighbour was struggling with death, and my bed, casually extended, was moist with the detestable matter which had flowed from his stomach.
>
> You will scarcely believe that, in this scene of horrors, the sound of laughter should be overheard. While the upper rooms of this building, are filled with the sick and the dying, the lower apartments are the scene of carrousals and mirth. The wretches who are hired, at enormous wages, to tend the sick and convey away the dead, neglect their duty and consume the cordials, which are provided for the patients, in debauchery and riot. (386)

Mervyn's description of the hospital further develops the thinghood, the "detestable matter," of the pest's passing. Again, it is as if we have stumbled upon a crime scene where some *thing* has happened. It is these "evacuations" of the body that belatedly attest, through the material negativity of their ruin, to the fact that once-existing persons were joined in battle against a deadly, pestulant foe. In addition to the massive materiality that "casually" creeps and flows in the room, we are also reminded that this breakdown of social order is associated not with the destruction of community but, rather, with its excess. There is a palpable sense of proximity, of bodies opened and exposed to each other, that produces bacchanalian signs of revelry: "laughter," "debauchery," and "riot." While this chaotic state of emergency might seem like a reasonable representation of the yellow-fever epidemic in Philadelphia, what is especially important and notable in *Arthur Mervyn* is the way in which this scene of belated personhood and ruin will repeat itself throughout the text, infecting a variety of different social systems—race, gender, and poverty, for example—with its aesthetic structure.

In the previous chapter, we saw how visions of sentimental community coproduce material spectacles of the ruined female body, and in Brockden Brown's novel there is no shortage of these Marias. The second volume of *Arthur Mervyn* finds its protagonist venturing beyond the city walls of Philadelphia, desperately trying to make amends for the ethical and financial wrongdoings of his former associate, the forger, embezzler, and murderer Welbeck. For example, Arthur is eager to rescue Clemenza Lodi, Welbeck's mistress, from the ruined life into which she has been forced. Even before we encounter her figure, however, we enter the "parlour" of the prostitutes with whom she lives, fully prepared to recognize the architectural and aesthetic principles governing its space:

> The parlour was spacious and expensively furnished, but an air of negligence and disorder was every where visible. The carpet was wrinkled and unswept; a clock on the table, in a glass frame, so streaked and spotted with dust as scarcely to be transparent, and the index motionless, and pointing at four instead of nine; embers scattered on the marble hearth, and tongs lying on the fender with the handle in the ashes; an harpsichord, uncovered, one end loaded with *scores*, tumbled together in a heap, and the other with volumes of novels and plays, some on their edges, some on their backs, gaping open by the scorching of their covers; rent; blurred; stained; blotted; dog-eared; tables awry; chairs crouding each other; in short, no object but indicated the neglect or ignorance of domestic neatness and economy. (515)

The familiarly "open," crowded, and "stained" nudity of these household objects testifies to their scorched ruin. In the vestiges of the parlour's catastrophe, it is "negligence" rather than the pest that is palpable in the "air." This room has personality: its property channels the ruin of the women who occupy the hiatus of its space. If the pest threatens to open up the *oikos* to looting from the outside, thereby interrupting the crucial Lockean connection between persons and their property, we can see that there are other pests at work in Brockden Brown's Philadelphia, other spaces in which similarly disconnected and vulnerable objects are on display. There is, indeed, an obscenity to the way in which Mervyn moves about this emptied house—"Did I act illegally," he asks himself, "in passing from one story to another" (521)?—but it is the violation of the voyeur rather than the thief, since property this open, this unowned, and this promiscuous is incapable of being stolen. Here is Mervyn's encounter with Clemenza:

> Presently I reached a front chamber in the third story. The door was ajar. I entered it on tiptoe. Sitting on a low chair by the fire, I beheld a female figure, dressed in a negligent, but not indecent manner. Her face in the posture in which she sat was only half seen. Its hues were sickly and pale, and in mournful unison with a feeble and emaciated form. Her eyes were fixed upon a babe, that lay stretched upon a pillow at her feet. The child, like its mother, for such she was readily imagined to be, was meagre and cadaverous. Either it was dead, or could not be very distant from death.
>
> The features of Clemenza were easily recognized, though no contrast could be greater, in habit and shape, and complexion, than that which her present bore to her former appearance. All her roses had faded, and her brilliances vanished. Still, however, there was somewhat fitted to awaken the tenderest emotions. There were tokens of inconsolable distress. (523)

The negligence of the parlour's "air" now firmly impressed upon her "manner," Clemenza and her offspring embody the "mournful" catastrophe of seduction and abandonment. However, while the sentimental romance fixes its attention on such tokens of love's ruin, obsessively repeating scenes of amorous catastrophe in order to register, in its belated passing, the veiled presence of affection, *Arthur Mervyn* instead exposes how pervasive this aesthetic logic is under modernity. Indeed, in its conclusion the text offers its own reworking of sentimentality's erotic and melancholic plot: Mervyn will choose the blemished cosmopolitanism of Ascha over the pastoral Eliza, sounding a hopeful rather than plaintive note at the novel's end.

When Mervyn visits Baltimore in order to return money connected with the Caribbean plantation economy, he stumbles across another iteration of Clemenza's "feeble" figure in the slave quarters of the Watson "mansion":

> Beside the house was a painted fence, through which was a gate leading to the back of the building. Guided by the impulse of the moment, I crossed the street to the gate, and, lifting the latch, entered the paved alley, on one side of which was a paled fence, and on the other the house, looking through two windows into the alley.
>
> The first window was dark like those in front; but at the second a light was discernible.... [I]n a rocking-chair, with a sleeping babe in her lap, sat a female figure in plain but neat and becoming attire. Her posture permitted half her face to be seen, and saved me from any danger of being observed.
>
> This countenance was full of sweetness and benignity, but the sadness that veiled its lustre was profound. Her eyes were now fixed upon the fire and were moist with the tears of remembrance, while she sung, in low and scarcely audible strains, an artless lullaby. (568)

In what way is this "artless lullaby" of the slave connected to Clemenza's "inconsolable distress"? What is the relationship between slavery, property, and ruin in *Arthur Mervyn*? These are, of course, extremely complex questions, and recent scholarship has explored how "intimate relations in Philadelphia are built on the infrastructure of slavery and the Caribbean economy."[36] Given the intricacies of this circumatlantic network within which Mervyn and the emerging U.S. nation are inscribed, it is not hard to imagine the reverberations that the "increasingly democratic, creolized, and fractious West Indian societies [would have had on] U.S. ambitions for commercial empire and 'pure' notions of national character and culture."[37] While I acknowledge the importance of these insights into the anxieties of the "national imaginary," I want to conclude by exploring another relationship between slavery and property in the text, a relationship that does not so much treat slavery as a repressed fact or event that returns to haunt the new, fragile nation but that, rather, outlines its formal, aesthetic link with property and modern personhood. At stake here, as in chapter 2, is the function of sentimental romance and its relationship to themes of race and slavery. Critics often account for the persistence of this aesthetic form—and for the presence of such lullabies—in *Arthur Mervyn* by pointing out the ways in which Brockden Brown's sentimentalism supports or critiques emerging discourses of race. For Sean X. Goudie, Mervyn adopts the gaze of the man of feeling in order to "'naturalize'" his "evolving [racialist] patterns of thought by overlaying them with discourses of travel writing and sentimentalism;"[38] whereas for Stephen Shapiro, this same sentimentalism is mobilized by the text in order to channel its liberal and abolitionist appeal. Of particular interest to both critics, then, is the famous "stagecoach" scene, where Mervyn is forced to confront and cohabit with colonial and racial Otherness during his journey to Baltimore:

> I mounted the stage-coach at day-break the next day, in company with a sallow Frenchman from Saint Domingo, his fiddle-case, an ape, and two female blacks. The Frenchman, after passing the suburbs, took out his violin and amused himself with humming to his own *tweedle-tweedle*. The monkey now and then mounched an apple, which was given to him from a basket by the blacks, who gazed with stupid wonder, and an exclamatory *La! La!* upon the passing scenery; or chattered to each other in a sort of open-mouthed, half-articulate, monotonous, and singsong jargon.
>
> The man looked seldom either on this side or that; and spoke only to rebuke the frolicks of the monkey, with a Tenez! Dominique! Prenez garde! Diable noir!
>
> As to me my thought was busy in a thousand ways. I sometimes gazed at the faces of my *four* companions, and endeavored to discern the differences and samenesses between them. I took an exact account of the features, proportions, looks, and gestures of the monkey, the Congolese, and the Creole-Gaul. I compared them together, and examined them apart. I looked at them in a thousand different points of view, and pursued, untired and unsatiated, those trains of reflections which began at each change of tone, feature, and attitude.
>
> I marked the country as it successively arose before me, and found endless employment in examining the shape and substance of the fence, the barn and the cottage, the aspect of earth and of heaven. How great are the pleasures of health and of mental activity. (566)

While Goudie points to the conventions of sentimental travel writing that work to naturalize Mervyn's emerging taxonomic thought, Shapiro reminds us that the scene echoes a famous moment in Laurence Sterne's *A Sentimental Journey through France and Italy* (1768) where Yorick "begins a polemic against Atlantic slavery after hearing a starling trapped in a cage singing, 'I can't get out,—I can't get out.'" "The refugee Creole," continues Shapiro, "insinuates the same undertones of racial tension as he attempts to hold back the 'black devil,' Dominique (Domingo/Haiti) trying now to get out."[39] However, there is much more than the insinuation of "racial tension" at stake in these Sternean echoes. As we will see, for Brockden Brown and Sterne what is also at issue is the way in which their protagonist's emerging sense of personhood—both the confident, classifying "I" in the above passage and Yorick's famously aloof, sentimental gaze—conjures the racial Other in order to secure the illusion of its own isolation and power.

It is important to remember that Sterne's caged starling appears only after Yorick has already begun to fear his own imprisonment in "the Bastile." Our sentimental hero, so lost in the exercise of his own voyeurism, has ignored the ways in which politics and the nation inscribe his body and its travels: he forgets to bring along his passport. "I had left London with so much precipitation," he confides, "that it never entered my mind that we were at war with France; and had reached Dover, and looked through my glass at the hills beyond Boulogne, before the idea presented itself."[40] Faced with the prospect of immanent confinement, he conjures a creative journey of the imagination in order to dispel this threat to his personhood:

> —And as for the Bastile! the terror is in the word—Make the most of it you can, said I to myself, the Bastile is but a word for a house you can't get out of....
>
> [T]he Bastile is not an evil to be despised—but strip it of its towers—fill up the fossé—unbarricade the doors—call it simply a confinement, and suppose 'tis some tyrant of a distemper—and not a man which holds you in it—the evil vanishes, and you bear the other half without complaint. (96)

As if by magic, Yorick finds his writerly exercise quickly complemented by the voice of a starling:

> I was interrupted in the hey-day of this soliloquy, with a voice which I took to be of a child, which complained "it could not get out." ... I saw

it was a starling hung in a little cage.—"I can't get out—I can't get out," said the starling....

I vow, I never had my affections more tenderly awakened; or do I remember an incident in my life, where the dissipated spirits, to which my reason had been a bubble, were so suddenly called home. Mechanical as the notes were, yet so true in tune to nature were they chanted, that in one moment they overthrew all my systematic reasonings upon the Bastile. (96)

It will take another conjuring act of the sentimental imagination to defuse this new threat to Yorick's "dissipated" freedom:

 The bird in his cage pursued me into my room; I sat down close to my table, and leaning my head upon my hand, I begun to figure myself the miseries of confinement. I was in a right frame for it, and so I gave full scope to my imagination.

I was going to begin with the millions of my fellow-creatures born to no inheritance but slavery; but finding, however affecting the picture was, that I could not bring it near me, and that the multitude of sad groups in it did but distract me—

—I took a single captive, and having first shut him up in his dungeon, I then looked through the twilight of his grated door to take his picture.

I beheld his body half wasted away with long expectation and confinement, and felt what kind of sickness of the heart it was which arises from the hope deferred. Upon looking nearer I saw him pale and feverish: in thirty years the western breeze had not once fanned his blood—he had seen no sun, no moon in all that time—nor had the voice of friend or kinsman breathed through his lattice—his children .... I heard his chains upon his legs.... [H]e gave a deep sigh—I saw the iron enter into his soul—I burst into tears—I could not sustain the picture of confinement which my fancy had drawn—I started up from my chair, and calling [my servant], I bid him bespeak me a *remise*, and have it ready at the door of the hotel by nine in the morning. (97–98)

What is the relationship between slavery, personhood, and the sentimental gaze in Yorick's "soliloquy"? And how can it help us to read the taxonomic exaltations of Arthur Mervyn on his travels to the American South? To begin with, we should note that slavery is not simply an ugly fact of history to which Sterne's hero gives his full sympathetic "scope." Indeed, the institution of slavery—with its abstract "multitude of sad groups"—proves a useless "distract[ion]" for Yorick. What he needs—or, rather, what his "I" needs in order to restore its sense of traveling detachment—is to bring the tantalizing prospect of ruin into manageably catastrophic proportions. What is truly horrific to this sentimental self is the undifferentiated backdrop of "millions of my fellow-creatures" or the possibility that his singular travels can be stamped out and incarcerated according to the edicts of any abstract, passported multitude. In order to immunize himself from this threat of indistinction and community, Yorick installs into his "frame" a ruined fragment of personhood—the slave or the "captive" who has become mere property. Sterne emphasizes the way in which the voyeuristic freedom of the sentimental hero—the aesthetic distance required to "Take [a] picture"—is a belated fiction wrought by such sacrifices: before Yorick can call for his carriage, his tears act as ontological tokens that, not unlike Dr. Stevens's home economics, bolster the illusion of personhood by opening it up to the threat of dissolution and infection, to pain and to the pest. Travel is not something that preexisting sentimental subjects go on in order to write about affecting themes such as slavery: travel names the exercise required to "sustain" the interplay between exalted personhood and ruined property. *A Sentimental Journey* is wonderfully attuned to both these dimensions of transcendent sensibility and bawdy materiality, and in its opening pages offers one of the most powerful and succinct allegories of sentimental travel writing.[41] Yorick is sitting alone in his chaise composing the preface to the text, but attracts the attention of passersby due to the strange movement of his carriage—a small "*Desobligeant*" designed for a single traveler. "We were wondering," notes one of the onlookers, "what could occasion its motion.—'Twas the agitation, said I coolly, of writing a preface." "I never heard . . . of a preface wrote in a *Desobligeant*," responds the onlooker. "It would have been better," rejoins Yorick, "in a *Vis a Vis*" (37). With dual attention to both the material conditions of its composition and to the lofty detachment of its solitary voyeur, Sterne makes us aware that, within the sentimental romance, writing *travels* the self.

Slavery and confinement agitate rather than arrest the momentum of the sentimental traveler, and it is this immunitary intimacy between personhood and its fragmented captivity that is registered by Sterne's starling.

After Yorick's servant purchases the bird for him, the starling begins his own journey:

> In my return from Italy I brought him with me to the country in whose language he had learned his notes—and telling the story of him to Lord A—Lord A begged the bird of me—in a week Lord A gave him to Lord B—Lord B made a present of him to Lord C—and Lord C's gentleman sold him to Lord D's for a shilling—Lord D have him to Lord E—and so on—half round the alphabet—From that rank he passed into the lower house, and passed the hands of as many commoners....
>
> It is impossible but many of my readers must have heard of him; and if any by mere chance have ever seen him—I beg leave to inform them, that that bird was my bird—or some vile copy set up to represent him.
>
> I have nothing further to add upon him, but that from that time to this, I have borne this poor starling as the crest to my arms. (99)

The Latin name for the starling is *sternus*, and in the same way that Sterne welcomes this captive muse into his prose, so too Yorick installs him at the symbolic core of his crest. Indeed, the momentum provided by his exchange energizes language itself and animates the alphabet as it passes between noble and commoner alike. The ornithological subtext that thus links Sterne's starling back to the chirping tunes of "*tweedle-tweedle*" and "*La!La!*" echoed by the different species inside Arthur Mervyn's carriage is, again, Lockean. In *An Essay Concerning Human Understanding* (1690), Locke enlists the help of another bird—this time a parrot—in order to conjure personhood and to establish the ground for a taxonomic hierarchy of matter.[42] While Descartes sought out the secret to personal identity in the split between immaterial mind and material body, Locke's genius is to immunize (*not* to resolve) this dialectic into the stuff of matter itself. If, in the *Second Treatise*, the Lockean individual emerges as a belated effect of the infectious interplay between personhood and property, in the *Essay* Locke's "rational parrot" helps to create another distinction within the individual—between the "*Man*" and the "*Person*"—that works to coproduce the illusion of "*personal Identity*."[43] Citing William Temple's account of this strange bird from his *Memoires of What Past in Christendom from the War Begun in 1672 to the Peace Concluded 1679*, Locke relates the story of "an old *Parrot*... that spoke, and asked, and answered common questions like a reasonable Creature" (333, sec. 8). When "*Prince Maurice*" went to visit this bird, the parrot came first into the Room where the Prince was, with a great many *Dutchmen* about him [and] said presently, *What a company of white men are here?* They asked it, what it thought that Man was, pointing to the Prince. It answered, *Some General or other;* when they brought it close to him, he asked it, *D'ou venes-vous?* It answered, *De Marinnan.* The Prince, *A qui estes-vous?* The Parrot, *A un Portugais.* The Prince, *Que fais-tu la?* Parrot, *Je garde les poulles.* The Prince laughed, and said, *Vous gardez les poulles?* The Parrot answered, *Oui, moi; et je scai bien faire;* and made the Chuck four or five times that People use to make to Chickens when they call them. I set down the Words of this worthy Dialogue in *French,* just as Prince *Maurice* said them to me. I asked him in what Language the *Parrot* spoke, and he said, in *Brasilian;* I asked whether he understood *Brasilian;* he said No, but he had taken care to have two Interpreters by him, the one a *Dutch-man,* that spoke *Brasilian,* and the other a *Brasilian,* that spoke *Dutch;* that he asked them separately and privately, and both of them agreed in telling him just the same thing that the *Parrot* said. . . .

[T]he Prince, 'tis plain, who vouches for this Story, and our Author who relates it from him, both of them call this Talker a *Parrot;* and I ask any one else who thinks such a Story fit to be told, whether if this *Parrot,* and all of its kind, had always talked as we have a Princes word for it, this one did, whether, I say, they would not have passed for a race of *rational Animals,* but yet whether for all that, they would have been allowed to be Men and not *Parrots?* For I presume 'tis not the *Idea* of a thinking or rational Being alone, that makes the *Idea* of a *Man* in most Peoples Sense; but of a Body so and so shaped joined to it; and if that be the *Idea* of a *Man,* the same successive Body not shifted all at once, must as well the same immaterial Spirit go to the making of the same *Man.* (333–35, sec. 8)

Where Yorick transforms slavery into a spectacle of personal sympathy—establishing his sentimental community with the captive starling and, at the same time, emphasizing the detached, voyeuristic isolation of his gaze—Locke's parrot works its magic through a similar play of identity and difference. On the one hand, Locke elevates the bird to the height of reason: as a member of the "race of *rational Animals,*" the parrot is, perhaps surprisingly, included into our community of reason. At the same time, however, Locke uses this inclusion to effect still further divisions within this "race," divisions that establish the material difference of the "Body" and shape of "*Man.*" In both Sterne and Locke, the vigor of Yorick's "I" and the conceptual solidity of Lockean identity are belated by-products of this immunitary aesthetics. Later in this same chapter, Locke defines a "*Person*" as a "thinking, intelligent Being, that has reason and reflection, and can consider it self as it self, the same thinking thing in different times and places; which it does only by that consciousness, which is inseparable from thinking" (335, sec. 9). For Locke, identity is always thus a "Forensick Term"—a retroactive gaze that can only grasp its concept in passing (346, sec. 26). Not only is identity split within the confines of the body—between an "immaterial Spirit" of personhood (open even to parrots) and the materiality of the "Body" of "*Man*"—but it is then also tied to another concept, "consciousness," that is folded back into this already-split "*Person*" along with its immunitary companion, the "soul." Designed to counter contemporary theological and philosophical arguments concerning identity, resurrection, reincarnation, and the inadequacies of Cartesian dualism, these moves will produce some of the more famous claims in the *Essay*, claims that establish the truly gothic coordinates of Enlightenment personhood. In the next section, we will see how this logic continues to inform the special effects of metempsychosis and mesmerism in Montgomery Bird and Cooper, but for now, with the menagerie of *Arthur Mervyn*'s "stage-coach" in mind, we should again note how both starling and parrot produce lively, if uncanny, spectacles of language: simultaneously familiar and distant, sentimental and "mechanical," their notes open up a space in which language can resonate. If Sterne's starling animates the alphabet through tokens of its exchange, Locke's parrot reinforces the difference between nations and national languages by securing the possibility that these differences can also be overcome, infected, translated. Combining the transcendent power of "*rational*" thought with the ruined, nonhuman material of the flesh, it is as if this bird comes to allegorize both communication and community, generating "worthy Dialogue[s]" in "*French*," "*Brasilian*," and "*Dutch*" and infecting the "*company of white men*."

We can now return to *Arthur Mervyn* and explore the relationship between infection, language, race, and community in the "stage-coach." In the *Histoire naturelle des oiseaux* (*Natural History of Birds*, 1770–83), the eminent natural historian and racial theorist the Comte de Buffon borrows Locke's parrot in order to further delineate the contours of the human "Body":

> What would have happened if, through a combination in nature just as possible as any other, the monkey had received the parrot's voice and

like the parrot the faculty of speech? The speaking monkey would have stunned into silence the entire human species and would have charmed it [*l'auroit séduite*] to the point that the philosopher would have had great trouble demonstrating that with all these beautiful human attributes the monkey was not, for all that, any less an animal. It is thus fortunate for our intelligence that nature separated and placed into two very distinct species the imitation of speech and the imitation of our gestures.[44]

Here, as in Locke, the "human" is the belated by-product of an immunitary operation that opposes the "faculty of speech" to the physical "gestures" of the body. Split so decisively, the "human species" can then be conjured in the synthesis of these two now-distinct "attributes." What Goudie calls the Enlightenment's "regulatory mechanisms of classification" do not, then, work their magic by establishing axes of distinction against which isolated and discrete "species" can be plotted; and the exalted individual subject does not simply preexist and discover these patterns of order.[45] As we see in *Arthur Mervyn*'s "stage-coach" scene, this taxonomic distribution of the sensible is made possible by the aesthetic interplay between the "*tweedle-tweedle*" of rational parrots, the "half-articulate . . . singsong jargon" of the slave, and the mute "gestures of the monkey." Like Yorick's "*Desobligeant*," Mervyn's carriage is propelled, rather than arrested, by the threat of entombment and overproximity, and Brockden Brown similarly connects its comforting cacophony with the emerging sensibility—"those trains of reflections which began at each change of tone, feature, and attitude"—of his sentimental traveler. In so doing, *Arthur Mervyn* shows how the "mental activity" of Enlightenment personhood is propelled by its romance of "differences and samenesses." The "Frenchman from Saint Domingo," the "open-mouthed" monotony of the slave, and the "frolics of the monkey" are not preexisting racial and colonial ghosts that return to haunt the journey of U.S. democracy and freedom: they are conjured from within this American dream, fellow travelers wrought into its aesthetic framework.

"MY EXTRAORDINARY DUALITY": THE METEMPSYCHOSIS OF MODERN PERSONHOOD IN *SHEPPARD LEE*

In *Sheppard Lee*, Robert Montgomery Bird's 1836 romance of spirit-hopping metempsychosis, we encounter another man of Enlightenment science, similarly obsessed with preserving the integrity of the body from overproximity and infection. Here is Doctor Feuerteufel's plan to cure the emerging U.S. nation of such pests:

> "Now, zhentlemens, I have devise my plan for de benefit of America, vich is de most unwholesome land in de earth, full of de exhalation and de miasm, de effluvium from de decay animal and vegetable. You shall adopt my plan for embalm your friends, and you no have no more pad air for de fevers, de bilious, de agues, and de plack vomit.... Here you see de ox-heart, de catfish, de bullfrog, de six hands and feet, and done into flesh and plood mummee. Here is de woman's head. It has been done dis tree year. But you shall see de grand specimen, de complete figure, de grown man turn into de mummee."[46]

Feuerteufel's genius stems from his unusual method of embalming the "flesh": "the man is a chymist such as was never heard of before. Davy, Lavoisier, Berzelius.... They stopped short at the elements—our doctor here converts one element into another!" (400). Earlier in the novel, when our eponymous narrator first encounters this "man of de science," we are alerted to rumors that "he was a counterfeiter in disguise" or perhaps even "a conjurer" (401, 37). His Enlightenment magic hinges on the possibility of separating the spirit of the *"Person"* from the material flesh of the *"Man,"* and thus extends Brockden Brown's investigation into the Gothic coordinates of Lockean personhood. If, in *Arthur Mervyn*, property and the pest name mutual processes of infection that work to immunize personhood, to solidify the illusion of self-coherence, and to spatialize a community of distinct, ownable things, in *Sheppard Lee* these same processes are converted into a regime of aesthetic effects that include metempsychosis, galvanic reanimation, and Feuerteufel's conversions of the flesh. Instead of ridiculing these practices as nonsciences, Montgomery Bird, who had been trained as a physician at the University of Pennsylvania before becoming a novelist and dramatist, shows how they work together to conjure the "fleshly matrix" that ultimately synthesizes spirit and matter, person and man, in the figure of the white, Anglo Saxon "human" (141). In Locke, Montgomery Bird, and Brockden Brown, the contours of this figure are established by immunitary processes that inject the threat of dissolution and indistinction "inside" its borders. We have seen how it is through this project of risk management that the "human" can emerge retroactively as the *thing* that has been compromised, put into danger. *Sheppard Lee* exposes the ways in which Enlightenment science, ideologies of race, and the commodity culture of the emerging U.S. nation rely upon a similar logic, and its text links these discourses with other technologies that, like Dr. Feuerteufel, conjure thingified spirits and spiritualized matter.

Of course, Feuerteufel's claim to convert spirit into matter is immediately undermined when his "grand specimen" is reanimated: the reader learns that this "mummee" is in fact the body of our protagonist, and the text closes with Sheppard Lee reclaiming the flesh from which his spirit had been separated earlier in the novel. Completing the circuit of exchange that had seen his spirit move between a succession of different bodies, Sheppard Lee's deflation of Feuerteufel's hygienic "plan for de benefit of America" seems to satirize Enlightenment projects such as Locke's that hinge on the distinction between the matter of "*Man*" and the spirit of the "*Person*." Indeed, Feuerteufel is not alone in his fantasies of the flesh: when Lee earlier inhabits the body of Abram Skinner, a scheming miser, we are introduced to another plan for "converting the human body into different mineral substances" (229):

> According to the economical Chinese method, each [dead body] could be converted into five tons of excellent manure; and the whole number would therefore produce just one hundred and fifty millions of tons; of which one hundred and fifty thousand, being their due proportion, would fall to the share of the United States of America, enabling our farmers, in the course of ten or twelve years, to double the value of their lands. This, therefore, would be a highly profitable way of disposing the mass of mankind. (228)

If Skinner seeks to harvest the value of the body by reinvesting its latent energy in the crops of the nation, Arthur Megrim—the scientist who experiments with "that extraordinary fluid, galvanism, on [one of Lee's earlier] lifeless bodies" (372)—is connected to a similar economy of "method" when he reanimates this slave's flesh:

> The first thing I did upon feeling the magical fluid penetrate my nerves, was to open my eyes and snap them twice or thrice; the second to utter a horrible groan, which greatly disconcerted the spectators; and the

third to start bolt upright on my feet, and ask them "what the devil they were after?" In a word, I was suddenly resuscitated ... to the great horror of all present, doctors and lookers-on, who ... fled from the room, exclaiming that I "was the devil, and no niggur!" (372–73)

Instead of a world of stable identity, hygienically cordoned off from the infectious, decaying flesh of the body, *Sheppard Lee* offers us an "America" in which personhood, property, and slavery are driven by Gothic economies of exchange and conversion.

As Steve Fraser points out, "[r]ather than symbolizing that rock-solid independent, self-affirming individual so central to the ethos of democratic capitalism, Sheppard's experience suggests that the self melts away into a series of performances staged in the theater of the marketplace."[47] But what is most troubling about Bird's novel is its refusal to step outside this "theater" in order to effect its critique. Even before Lee's digging accident provokes the "extraordinary duality," the split between spirit and body, that sets his metempsychotic journey in motion (at the end of each of the eight "books" in the novel, Lee finds different bodies for his spirit to inhabit), Bird makes us aware that this is just the latest of his recent tumultuous conversions. Swindled out of his inheritance by Aikin Jones, overseer of his family's "property," Lee's world has already been turned upside down at the beginning of the novel: "In a word, Mr. Jones became a rich man, and I a poor one; and I had the satisfaction, every day when I took a walk over my forty-acre farm ... to find myself stopped ... by the possessions of Mr. Aikin Jones ... while I was trudging along through the mud" (17). Lee is born into a world in which the stability of even agrarian ideals has already been sacrificed to the whims of the urban market. His father, for example,

> was a farmer in very good circumstances, respectable in his degree, but perhaps more famous for the excellent sausages he used to manufacture for the Philadelphia market, than for any quality of mind or body that can distinguish one man from his fellows. Taking the hint from his success in this article of produce, he gradually converted his whole estate into a market-farm, raising fine fruits and vegetables, and such other articles as are most in demand in a city; in which enterprise he succeeded beyond his highest expectations, and bade fair to be ... a rich man. The only obstacle to a speedy accumulation of riches was a disproportionate increase in the agents of consumption,—his children

multiplying on his hands almost as fast as his acres, until he could count eleven in all; a number that filled him at one time with consternation. He used to declare that no apple could be expected to ripen on a farm where there were eleven children. (8–9)

As with the rural infection of *Arthur Mervyn*'s landscape, the demands of the "Philadelphia market" have already transformed the Lockean/Jeffersonian ideal of the small family farm. Indeed, the fecundity of the family has become a "consternation," an obstacle that hurts the enterprise's bottom line through its excessive "consumption." Unlike Mervyn, however, Lee will ultimately return to the land, his peregrinations of the spirit spotlighting the ungrounded life of chaos produced by modern forms of "accumulation"—systems of exchange that alienate and thingify human subjectivity: "My estate is small, and it may be that it will never increase. I am, however, content with it; and content is the secret of all enjoyment. I am not ashamed to labor in my fields" (424). We have seen this same contentment in the novel's most controversial figure, "nigga Tom"—a happy slave whose body Lee occupies and who is incited to rebel against his master by the "fatal . . . sentimental notions about liberty" contained in an abolitionist pamphlet (357). Before he is corrupted by this pamphlet, Tom shares the same "secret of all enjoyment" with Lee: "There was scarce a slave on the estate who . . . did not labour more for himself than his master; for all had their little lots or gardens, the produce of which was entirely their own, and which they were free to sell to whomsoever they listed. . . . The truth is, my master was, in some respects, a greater slave than his bondmen" (345). Echoing the argument of Hegel's famous section entitled "Lordship and Bondage," and anticipating the direction that Marx will soon take its argument, Tom's happiness promotes the same agrarian myth of property and unalienated labor that Lee claims to have found at the novel's close.[48]

Critics have understandably been troubled by the way in which this abolitionist pamphlet interrupts Tom's contentment. If, as Edgar Allan Poe notes in his *Southern Literary Messenger* review of Bird's novel, *Sheppard Lee* enforces "the very doubtful moral that every person should remain contented with his own," then it would seem that the pamphlet—as well as the text's conclusion—supports a return to an agrarian, perhaps even to a plantation, economy.[49] Bird's attitudes toward slavery are further tested by his refusal to let Lee's spirit speak through the body of the slave. Here, as Christopher Looby notes, "Bird risks a compromise with his own theory of metempsychosis, for while he held that in every one of his successive existences Sheppard Lee retained a shadow of a memory of his previous incarnations . . . now he 'ceased to remember all my previous states of existence.'"[50] This was either, Looby continues, "because as an African he naturally dwells in the present and has no sense of the past . . . or because in his new condition his 'mind was stupified.' That is, he is mentally limited either because of an innate racial characteristic or because circumstances–his enslavement–had degraded him."[51] What is particularly noteworthy about *Sheppard Lee*—and what makes "the politics of this novel resist paraphrase . . . [so] insistently and frustratingly"[52]—is the way in which both the ideology of racial difference and the romance of agrarian property and labor so totally frame the aesthetic world of the text. From its opening page, the novel is perfectly aware of its place inside the economy of print, and Bird's decision to publish it in New York, rather than in his native Philadelphia, as the work of Sheppard Lee quickly became a futile hoax that emphasized—rather than challenged—the impossibility of anonymity in the emerging print culture of the nation. As readers, then, we are taught to be suspicious of the kind of "isolated" freedom that Lee boasts of in the novel's first paragraph—a liberal power that is already couched firmly in and secured by the language of commerce:

> The importance of any single individual in society, especially one so isolated as myself, is so little, that it can scarcely be supposed that the community at large can be affected by his *fortunes*, either good or evil, or *interested* in any way in his fate. Yet it sometimes happens that . . . man may safely consider himself of some *value* in his generation. . . . Such a man I consider myself to be; and the more I reflect upon my past life, the more I am convinced it contains a lesson which may be studied with *profit*. . . . [W]hile I leave these learned gentlemen to discuss what may appear most wonderful in my revealments, I am most anxious that the common reader may weigh the *value* of what is, at least in appearance, more natural, simple, and comprehensible. (7, emphasis mine)

And in the same way that Bird alerts us to the ways in which commodity culture controls the parameters of our freedom, so too Tom's chapters quickly disabuse any sentimental notions of liberty that may circulate within U.S. democracy:

"I intend to run away," said I....

"Whaw! what a fool!" cried the [old slave], regarding me with surprise and contempt; "what you do when you run away, ha? Who'll hab you? who'll feed you? who'll take care of you? who'll own a good-fo'-nothing runaway nigga, I say ha? Kick him 'bout h'yah, kick him 'bout dah, poor despise nigga wid no massa, jist as despise as any free nigga! You run away, ha? what den? ... take up constable, clap him in jail, salt him down cowskin. Dat all? No! sell him low price, send Mississippi—what den?" (333)

As the previous chapters demonstrate, even an abolitionist, "philanthropic" Quaker has to "pay the piper" within this world (77). Bird's spiritual economy of metempsychotic exchange foregrounds such realities when Lee's soul jumps from Zachariah Longstraw, about to be lynched by a southern mob, into Tom's enslaved body. Notice how Bird insists on reading the violence of such a scene of "Lynchdom" as fully compatible with the rhetoric of U.S. political freedom and juridical order:

"The virtues that once distinguished ... the immortal Colossus, have fled from the old, to find their home in the New World. I look for them only in the bosoms of Americans!"

Here the orator, who had pronounced this sublime exordium with prodigious earnestness and effect, paused, while the welkin rung with the shouts of rapture.... As for me, I felt a doleful skepticism ..., having the very best reason to distrust that love of liberty, law, order, and justice, which was about to consign me to ropes and flames....

"Abolition, my fellow-citizens!" said the orator, "it is my intention to address you on the subject of abolition.... I have said, and I repeat, that the love of liberty, of law, of order, of justice, belongs peculiarly to the free sons of America.... Beware lest, in what you now intend to do, you give occasion to the enemies of freedom to doubt your virtue...."

These words filled me with joyful astonishment. I began to believe the [orator] was about to interfere in my favor....

"By no means," said the [orator]...; "what I have to advise is, that if we are to do execution upon the wretch, we shall proceed about it in an orderly and dignified way, resolve ourselves into a great and solemn tribunal, and so adjudge him to death with a regularity and decorum which shall excite the admiration and win the approbation of the whole world." (323–24)

Property/Personhood 109

Yet another commodity up for exchange, the rhetoric of "liberty, law, order, and justice" does not simply oppose the violence and "regularity" of racism. Instead, the novel illustrates how personhood must always be negotiated within the parameters of this commodity culture, as if identity were a token that could be circulated and be exchanged—like Lee's spirit—for different values at different times. In this sense, "abolition" is not so much a threat to the order of the plantation as it is another form of ideological enslavement, a "fatal . . . sentimental" notion, that helps to coproduce and give voice to the rhetorical platitudes of American freedom.

In the same way that "liberty" is not simply slavery's Other, so too *Sheppard Lee* helps us to read the Lockean/Jeffersonian ideal of agrarian property and labor as a mythical complement—rather than a viable alternative—to the commodity culture of the emerging U.S. nation. Indeed, Bird mocks our "sentimental notions" about this form of resistance with the novel's unlikely ending, as if we could imagine a retreat from the systematic transformations of personhood and property that so vividly beset Lee's America. Lee's father had no such faith in the isolated stability of rural agriculture, and his success was achieved by integrating, not separating, the demands of the city from the bliss of the countryside. And it is his son's commitment to locating a stable value in the ground, in the soil, that leads to Lee's downfall as well as to his problematic restoration: after all, it is while he is digging for Captain Kid's buried treasure that he succeeds "in lodging [his] mattock, which was aimed furiously at a root, among the toes of [his] right foot . . . [and] fell straightaway into a trance" (47); and it is this "trance" that first splits Lee's identity into the "extraordinary duality" that patterns the remainder of the novel. Bird refuses to locate the "value" of property or personhood in either the comfort of the soil or the whims of the market: he shows, instead, how these use- and exchange-values are engaged in a romance of dialectical mutuality rather than a logic of identity and difference.

If *Arthur Mervyn*'s pest, in threatening the borders of the "self," ultimately reinforces rather than collapses the distinction between the liberal subject and the world "outside," we might say that *Sheppard Lee*, in exposing the ontological fragility and economic convertibility of this same "self," helps to reestablish the fiction of a stable-value-under-threat. Like Brockden Brown, Bird helps us to read the Gothic aesthetics of Enlightenment science and economic value. Instead of a rational parrot, the blueprint for Lee's metempsychotic method could have been Locke's discussion of the "Prince and the Cobler" in the same *Essay*:

> For should the Soul of a Prince, carrying with it the consciousness of the Prince's past Life, enter and inform the Body of a Cobler as soon as deserted by his own Soul, every one sees, he would be the same Person with the Prince, accountable only for the Prince's Actions: But who would say it was the same Man? The Body too goes to the making the Man. . . . I know that in the ordinary way of speaking, the same Person, and the same Man, stand for one and the same thing. And indeed every one will always have a liberty to speak, as he pleases, and to apply what articulate Sounds to what *Ideas* he thinks fit, and change them as often as he pleases. But yet when we will enquire, what makes the same *Spirit*, *Man*, or *Person*, in our Minds; and having resolved with our selves what we mean by them, it will not be hard to determine, in either of them, or the like, when it is the *same*, and when not. (340, sec.15)

Where Locke's earlier distinction between the "*Person*" and the "*Man*" hinges on the special effects induced by his rational parrot, here this same distinction is achieved through the magic of metempsychosis. If there is something of the Gothic in these aesthetics of Lockean identity, *Sheppard Lee* reminds us that such ostensibly supernatural "*Ideas*" are never simply *post festum*, Counter-Enlightenment responses to the empire of reason. Bird's attention to the thinghood of the spirit—its ability to exchange and circulate—highlights the strangeness of the "immaterial Substance" at the heart of the Lockean "*Person*" (340, sec. 16). His romance foregrounds its own participation in—rather than its transcendent isolation from–the aesthetic regime of Enlightenment reason and the culture of commodity capitalism. As a result, the "liberty to speak" that concludes Locke's reasoning and the "contentment" that frames Lee's idyllic retreat to the agrarian origins of U.S. democracy are exposed as wholesome fictions rooted in a violent economy of alienation and enslavement, an economy that metempsychotically circulates the fragmented stuff of personhood.

COOPER, MESMERISM, AND THE "IMMATERIAL SUBSTANCE" OF TASTE IN *THE AUTOBIOGRAPHY OF A POCKET-HANDKERCHIEF*

In *Arthur Mervyn*, we explored the mutual codependence that sustains property, personhood, and the pest—corelationships that both publicly lament and secretly value the ruined fragments of person-things. If the pest names the mysterious agent that opens up the borders of personhood and property for such exchanges, then we can see how metempsychosis in *Sheppard Lee* functions as a similar, subversively necessary pathway. In addition to the ways in which it destabilizes the notion of an essential, unchanging personal identity, metempsychosis is also allied with the mutability of matter that magically transforms objects into commodities. In the world of the novel, the essential value of things as well as persons is opened up for exchange, a lesson that Lee learns well when he is prepared to be sold as a Quaker abolitionist in the South: "I was taught [that] merchants designed giving a value to their merchandise not inherent and instrinsic to it" (318). Because his spirit inhabits a relatively unknown abolitionist, his captors decide that "To make [him] valuable, it was necessary [he] should be made famous" (318). Within the economy of the novel, both persons and property participate in a Gothic regime of convertibility, their once-stable values now opened up to the whims of modern exchange. Bird shows how such transformations of "instrinsic" value function as the norm for, rather than the exception to, the markets of the emerging U.S. nation. And, again, we see how the rhetoric of abolitionism is located firmly within—rather than hovering above and resisting outside—the metempsychotic logic of exchange-value. In this sense, both personhood and property are out of joint with themselves, a fact that even the man of Enlightenment science, Arthur Megrim, cannot escape, thanks to his "digestive apparatus [which] is out of order" (391). It is this ruined value, this "inherent and intrinsic" crime at the core of personhood and property that provides the potential for commodification, and so we are fully prepared when Megrim's tale describes a metempsychosis of the spirit that inhabits objects as well as bodies:

> I experienced divers other transformations, being now a chicken, now a loaded cannon, now a clock, now a hamper of crockery-ware, and a thousand things besides; all which conceits the doctor cured without

much difficulty, and with as little consideration for the roughness of his remedies. Being a chicken, he attempted to wring my neck...; he dischanged the cannon from my fancies by clapping a red-hot poker to my nose; and the crate of crockery he broke to pieces by casting it on the floor, to the infinite injury of my bones. The clock at first gave him some trouble, until, pronouncing it to have a screw out of order, he seized upon one of my front teeth with a pair of pincers, and by a single wrench dissipated the illusion for ever. (394)

Here the curative power of Megrim's doctor is linked to a practice that violently sustains rather than transcends the metempsychotic ramblings of his spirit. If, as some critics have astutely observed, *Sheppard Lee* turns into an "it-narrative" here, we should be careful to note that such animations merely extend the logic of exchange developed throughout the novel:[53] In refusing to distinguish the metempsychotic pathways of the spirit from the "table turning" "transformations" of the commodity-form, Bird reminds us that "it" functions here as an effective placeholder for both property *and* personhood.

In the *Autobiography of a Pocket-Handkerchief* (1843), James Fenimore Cooper crafts his own critique of U.S. commodity culture through the genre of the "it-narrative." Like Brockden Brown and Bird, Cooper describes an America beset by a crisis of value: as we follow his handkerchief around the world through a series of different owners, we are introduced to the vulgar democratic ways of American "free trade,"[54] a form of economy that services the whims of fashion and the artifices of exchange-value. And like *Arthur Mervyn* and *Sheppard Lee*, the *Autobiography* also performs its critique of this gauche community of "the *nouveaux riches*" by rooting its own values in the firmly agrarian soil of a stable, preindustrial, past. Cooper traces the origins of his handkerchief back to the "fields of Normandy," where its "threads of unusual fineness" first grew in the "Innocence" of their "virtues" (14, 24,_26). After harvesting, these threads assume their proper position in a "rare fabric, among which I remember that I occupied the seventh place in the order of arrangement, and, of course, in the order of seniority also" (25). The fabric is crafted by a young girl, Adrienne, amid the noble ruins of the French Revolution:

> the Chateâu de la Rocheiamard . . . had been the property of the Vicomte de la Rocheaimard previously to the revolution that overturned the

> throne of Louis XVI. The Vicomte . . . joined the royalists at Coblentz [and perished] in battle, but the son escaped and passed his youth in exile; marrying . . . a cousin, whose fortunes were at as low an ebb as his own. One child, Adrienne, was the sole issue of this marriage. . . . Both the parents died before the Restoration, leaving the little girl to the care of her pious grandmother, la Vicomtesse, who survived, in a feeble old age, to descant on the former grandeur of her house, and to sigh, in common with so many others for *le bon vieux temps*. (34–35)

Throughout the *Autobiography*, the French Revolution constitutes the watershed moment separating "*le bon vieux temps*" from the "republican reign" of "bankers" who thrive on its "great principle of liberty and equality" (50). As if Cooper's veiled, Federalist critique of U.S. democracy were not obvious enough, after the revolution the chateâu is "converted into a workshop and filled with machinery" (36), and the text foregrounds Adrienne's devotion to the Vicomtesse in language that echoes Burke's *Reflections on the Revolution in France* (1790):

> The strength of the family tie in France, and its comparative weakness in America, have been the subject of frequent comment among travelers. . . . Respect for years, deference to the authors of their being, and submission to parental authority, are inculcated equally by the morals and the laws of France. . . . [These laws assist] in maintaining that system of patriarchal rule, which lies at the foundation of the whole social structure. Alas! . . . The wars, the guillotine, and exile had [destroyed] it. (36–37)

Not surprisingly, the handkerchief hates to leave the comforts of this family, but it is soon subjected to the vagaries and vulgarities of the market. Before the July Revolution of 1830, however, it enjoys a tasteful seclusion in the drawer of an exclusive Paris retailer, but the reverberations of this new wave of republicanism soon set the handkerchief in motion. Adrienne is swindled by her landlady and, in order to support her grandmother, she is encouraged to sell her possessions according to the "new fashion[s] that had sprung out of the Revolution of July" (78). After it is bought by "Colonel Silky," the handkerchief is transported to the U.S. marketplace, where it quickly learns that "money makes both beauty and distinction . . . in this part of the world" (109). Celebrated as "the highest-priced handkerchief, by twenty dollars, that ever crossed the Atlantic," it enters into a world of financial speculation and "tasteless... luxury" built on artificial wealth, a world in which its identity hinges on its extravagant price rather than the noble pedigree of its fabric (132). After spotlighting the prosaic vacuity of characters such as Tom Thurston and Henry Halfacre, the handkerchief will again be united with its creator, Adrienne, who has since travelled to the United States in order to become a governess. Cooper's ending thus attempts to inject American soil with some of Adrienne's *ancienne noblesse* by marrying her off to Betts Shoreham, a "third cousin... whose great-grandmother had been a *bonâ fide* de la Rocheaimard" (229).

Although Cooper shares Bird's and Brockden Brown's critique of U.S. commodity culture—each author exposing the ways in which it unhinges the values of personhood and property from their ostensible stability in "*le bon vieux temps*"—his elitism evinces a different response to this dilemma of valuation. Where Bird indicts the powerfully interconnected ideologies of freedom and the free market by demonstrating how intimately our identity is underwritten by them; and where Brockden Brown espouses his own Woldwinite values as progressive alternatives to this spectacularization of U.S. society; in the *Autobiography*, Cooper's "it-narrative" will utilize this unfixed exhangeability of value in order to conjure a new kind of immanent, *un*changing aesthetic value: taste.[55] What is so fascinating about Cooper's handkerchief is that it embraces and, literally, grows out of a world in which the singularity of identity is to be sacrificed to universalizing economic, spiritual, and scientific forces *at the same time* that it secures a unique, tasteful space—a different kind of difference—for itself. As such, the *Autobiography* helps us to revisit the shared aesthetic program that links romance, race, and class in the emerging U.S. nation.

In what might, at first, appear a strange way to open a treatise on the singularity of refined taste, Cooper's novel draws on the scientific language of natural history, Enlightenment taxonomy, and emerging theories of racial difference in order to situate his handkerchief within the hierarchy of "civilization" (13):

> Certain moral philosophers... have shown that every man is equally descended from a million of ancestors, within a given number of generations; thereby demonstrating that no prince exists who does not share in the blood of some beggar, or any beggar who does not share in the blood of princes. Although favored by a strictly vegetable descent myself, the laws of nature have not permitted us to escape from the influence of

this common rule. The earliest account I possess of my progenitors represent them as a goodly growth of the *Linnum Usitatissimum*, divided into a thousand contemporaneous plants . . . remarkable for an equality that renders the production valuable. . . .

While our family has followed the general human law in the matter just mentioned, it forms a marked exception to the rule that so absolutely controls white blood, on this continent, in what relates to immigration and territorial origin. When the American enters on the history of his ancestors, he is driven, after some ten or twelve generations at most, to seek refuge in a county in Europe; whereas exactly the reverse is the case with us, our most remote extraction being American, while our more recent construction and education have taken place in Europe. When I speak of the "earliest accounts I possess of my progenitors," authentic information is meant only; for, like other races, we have certain dark legends that might possibly carry us back again to the old world in quest of our estates and privileges. . . . Under these limitations, I have ever considered my family as American by origin, European by emigration, and restored to its paternal soil by the mutations and calculations of trade. (10–11)

Although this remarkable passage begins with the threat of a monogenetic "equality" at the ancestral root of "man"—a threat that would spawn numerous polygenetic responses so vital to proslavery theories of racial difference—Cooper soon manages to color his account with the kind of "white blood" that was being created at the time by Saxonist antiquarians.[56] Notice how these singularities of blood—and the "territorial" "extraction[s]" of nation that accompany them—are immunized within the universalizing "moral" flow of a different kind of blood in the first paragraph. As readers of Locke, Brockden Brown, and Bird, we should already be prepared for the way in which this spiritualized aesthetics of "blood" shared between "prince" and "beggar" requires, in turn, a massively material deposit. And in the same way that Locke's metempsychotic exchange between the "Prince and the Cobler" ultimately works to singularize rather than universalize the "immaterial Substance" of personhood, so too Cooper's "common rule" of a blood transcending all differences and uniting all species is coproduced along with a taxonomic "exception to the rule that so absolutely controls white blood"—a rule that essentializes singular "races" and naturalizes "authentic" national "origin[s]."

What the *Autobiography* brings into focus, then, is the fact that all "it-narratives"—insofar as they invoke the spiritualization of matter so central to the aesthetics of commodification—are always also "thou narratives," propelled by a dematerialized, divine force that hovers, metempsychotically, above and between the stuff of "it." This is why the language (the "articles of *genus*" [31]) of Enlightenment classification and empiricism can coexist with the "Providence" of a nonmaterial, spiritual power in the text: "Each [linen plant] is an incident in the progress of civilization; the man and the vegetable alike taking the direction pointed out by Providence for the fulfillment of his or its destiny" (13).[57] "I was but a speck among a myriad of other things produced by the hand of the Creator," opines the youthful "*Linum Usitatissimum*" plant:

> It was my duty to live my time, to be content, and to proclaim the praise of God within the sphere assigned to me. Could men and plants but once elevate their thoughts to the scale of creation, it would teach them their own insignificance so plainly, would manifest the futility of complaints and the immense disparity between time and eternity, as to render the useful lesson of contentment as inevitable as it is important. (18)

It is this kind of "contentment" with the "scale of creation" that Poe reads as "the very doubtful moral" of *Sheppard Lee*; but where Bird exposes the ways in which this myth of "destiny" ultimately complements commodity culture and its related ideologies of mastery, Cooper instead fuses its spiritual "Providence" with racialist theories of natural hierarchy in order to support his idea of an endangered "*ancienne noblesse*":

> I will here digress a moment, to make a single remark on a subject of which popular feeling, in America, under the influence of popular habits, is apt to take an *ex parte* view. Accomplishments are derided as useless in comparison with what is considered household virtues. The accomplishment of a cook is to make good dishes; of a seamstress to sew well; and of a lady to possess refined tastes, a cultivated mind, and agreeable and intellectual habits. The real *virtues* of all are the same, though subject to laws peculiar to their station; but it is a very different thing when we come to the mere accomplishments. To deride all the refined attainments of

human skill denotes ignorance of the means of human happiness, nor is it any evidence of acquaintance with the intricate machinery of social greatness and a lofty civilization. These gradations in attainments are inseparable from civilized society, and, if the skill of the ingenious and laborious is indispensable to a solid foundation, without the tastes and habits of the refined and cultivated, it never can be graceful or pleasing. (139–40)

The point to be emphasized here is that the singular, "very different *thing*" evidenced by these tasteful "gradations in attainments" emerges through— not outside of or strictly against—the equalizing logic of "household virtues." Cooper's romance of "it" works to establish a significant "insignificance" within this naturalized, providential order, a "thing" of taste visible only to a "refined" few who remain both included within the "destiny" of social order and, at the same time, excused from its mundane "household" duties and values. If Locke utilizes a metempsychotic pathway to help create the "immaterial Substance" of personhood, Cooper instead draws on another important U.S. "pseudo" science, mesmerism, as a Gothic medium capable of conjuring the invisible stuff of taste:[58]

> I have already hinted that pocket-handkerchiefs do not receive and communicate ideas by means of the organs in use among human beings. They possess a *clairvoyance* that is always available under favorable circumstances. In their case, the mesmeritic trance may be said to be ever in existence, while in the performance of their proper functions. It is only while crowded into bales, or thrust into drawers, for the vulgar purposes of trade, that this instinct is dormant.... By virtue of this power, I had not long been held in the soft hand of Adrienne, or pressed against her beating heart, without becoming the master of all her thoughts.... This knowledge did not burst upon me at once, it is true, as is pretended to be the case with certain somnambules, for with me there is no empiricism—everything proceeds from cause to effect, and a little time, with some progressive steps, was necessary to make me fully acquainted with the whole. The simplest things became the first apparent, and others followed by a species of magnetic induction, which I cannot stop now to explain. (57–58)

Like the late-night "table turning" of Marx's commodity-form, the secret magic of Cooper's "it" comes fully to life only after its "vulgar" and mundane adventures in "trade" have ceased. There is a certain luxury to this timeless "trance" that eschews the logic of the "burst," as if the calm grandeur of Burkean patriarchal transfer were itself reflected in its gently "progressive" moments of mesmeritic acquaintance. In chapter 2, we witnessed the similarly immanent transfer of feeling's "thing" between Yorick and Maria, an exchange made possible by an equally talented handkerchief. In his *Autobiography*, Cooper's romance extends this "magnetic" logic beyond mere "vegetable *clairvoyance*" (14) and demonstrates how it functions as the tasteful glue cementing all members of refined society. And so when Betts Shoreham takes the "soft hand" of Adrienne, we find that they "understood each other perfectly" (205)—a species of "induction" that, like the pest's immanent pathway, undergirds the aesthetic framework of personhood and property in the emerging U.S. nation.

4

EVENT/HIATUS

THE AESTHETICS OF AMERICAN IDLING

In the previous chapter, we saw how modern forms of property and personhood invoke Gothic conjurations of the flesh, metempsychotic wanderings of the spirit, and mesmeric pathways of pestilence and infection. Although frequently employed by discourses of democracy and abolition, I argued that these peculiar common things are already deeply implicated in Atlantic modernity's romance of racial difference. We need only turn again to the figure of John Locke in order to see how *claiming* property—as well as outlining its formal qualities—involves animating an equally impressive array of special aesthetic effects.

For Locke, the question of property's form is always linked to colonial expansion and the *dis*possession of indigenous peoples. For example, the "work of [the] hands" that, in the *Second Treatise*, adds some thing to "the state that nature hath provided" comes into relief only to the extent that it eclipses a different kind of relationship to the land (sec. 25). If "in the beginning, all the world was America," then what Locke's romance of history offers is a particular form of temporality, a destiny that favors European modes of labor and a futurity that naturalizes colonial ideologies of possession (sec. 49). James Tully argues that "Locke defines property in such a way that Amerindian customary land use is not a legitimate type of property. Rather, it is ... assimilated to an earlier stage of European development in the state of nature."[1] As secretary to Lord Shaftesbury, the most important "Lord Proprietor" of Carolina, Locke was intimately involved in the colonization of North America; in addition to drafting *The Fundamental Constitutions of Carolina* (1669), he also invested in various slave-trading and mercantile enterprises in the Americas and frequently acted as an advisor on matters of colonial governance and commerce.[2] However, his most important contribution to the colonization of the Americas remains his distinction between a precolonial "state of nature" and the work of colonial "hands" that transforms this "nature" into property. At stake in Locke's distinction is both a particular form of temporality (progression from the precolonial to the colonial) and a specific mapping of space (the transition from a radically open "state of nature" to the world of enclosure that property demands). "[I]n the first ages of the world," Locke claims, "men were more in danger to be lost, by wandering from their company, in the then vast wilderness of the earth than to be straitened for want of room to plant in" (sec. 35). An aesthetics of idling thus operates at the heart of Locke's romance of property and colonial progress, where to be idle implies a certain figuration of space and a specific form of time: the emptiness of a "vast wilderness" and the aimless, nonprogressive "wandering" that such a "vast" space makes possible.

In *The Law of Nations* (1758), Emeric de Vattel further adumbrates this "idle mode of life" when he describes Europe's duty to "cultivate" property in the new world:

> The cultivation of the soil ... is ... an obligation imposed upon man by nature. ... Every Nation is therefore bound by the law of nature to cultivate the land which has fallen to its share. There are others who, in order to avoid labour, seek to live upon their flocks and the fruits of the chase. ... Now that the human race has multiplied so greatly, it could not subsist if every people wished to live after that fashion. Those who still pursue this idle mode of life occupy more land than they would have need of under a system of honest labour. ... [W]hen the Nations of Europe, which are too confined at home, come upon lands which the savages have no special need of and are making no present and continuous use of, they may lawfully take possession of them and establish colonies in them.[3]

Idling here implies a discontinuity in both space and time: the savage avoids the space of structured "labour" by wandering randomly across the land with the "flocks and the fruits of the chase," and he gives himself up to the desultory temporal rhythms of this lifestyle. "Although the vast country ... was inhabited by countless native tribes," notes Alexis de Tocqueville in *Democracy in America* (1835), it is justifiable to assert that, at the time of its discovery, it formed only a desert. The Indians took up residence there but did not possess it.... The ruin of these races began the day the Europeans landed on their shores; it has continued since then; it is reaching its completion at the present time. Providence, in placing them in the midst of the races of the New World, seemed to have granted them only a short period of enjoyment; they had, in some sense, a waiting brief. [*La Providence, en les plaçant au milieu des richesses du nouveau monde, semblait ne leur en avoir donné qu'un court usufruit; ils n'étaient là, en quelque sorte, qu'en attendant.*][4] These shores so ready for commerce and industry, these deep rivers, this inexhaustible Mississippi Valley, this entire continent thus appeared like the still empty cradle of a great nation.[5]

For Tocqueville as for Locke, the idle savage provides the engine for the progressive flow of national history. The co-event of "European" landing and Indian "ruin" is not to be read simply as happening in an isolated moment in the history of this "great nation." Rather, we see that it is the "ruin" of the "Indian" that *inaugurates* the play of a national past, present, and future (it "began," "it has continued," and "it is reaching its completion")—a play of differences that makes thinkable a temporal axis against which the thinghood of isolated, national events can be imagined and plotted. As such, the relationship between idle "Indians" and industrious colonials is far more complex than one of simple opposition. They do not occupy two different forms of space and two separate moments of time: idling is the name for the atemporal and aspatial occlusion that enables the nation to manifest itself so squarely *in* "the present time." In a remarkable turn of phrase, Gerald Bevan translates Tocqueville's description of this idling exception ("*qu'en attendant*") as having a "waiting brief," and like the dead letters and passive retorts that Melville's Bartleby will locate at the heart of his Wall Street law office, at stake in this "brief" is the relationship of a peculiar hiatus to the norm—a hiatus that both interrupts and originates modern forms of national and juridical space-time.[6] Borrowing the legalistically inflected term "*usufruit*" to describe the kind of "enjoyment" enjoyed in this "short period" of idling, Tocqueville again reminds us of the link between the aesthetics of American idling and the origins of property and possession in Atlantic modernity.[7]

HIATUS AND HISTORY

In his 1801 review of George Richards Minot's *Continuation of the History of the Province of Massachusetts Bay*, Charles Brockden Brown establishes another kind of aesthetic relationship between the time of the nation and its idling hiatus. His review begins by noting, "with unspeakable regret, that [Minot's] plan, which comprehended the northern as well as southern colonies of America, was left unfinished." However, Brockden Brown is quick to transform the regretful hiatus in Minot's "plan" into an exciting future opportunity: "This regret is, in some degree, diminished by the hope, that the honour of completing so great and arduous an undertaking is reserved for some native citizen." After all, he reasons,

> [i]n the number, variety and authenticity of his materials, the historian of the United States possesses many advantages unknown to the narrator of the events of a remote age, or of a distant nation. There is little necessity of seeking truth by the process of conjecture, or by painful collation of doubtful and discordant authorities; since there are few facts worthy of relation, concerning which written or printed documents may not be found, without extraordinary exertion or laborious research.[8]

Where the hiatus of the idle Indian brings into relief Tocqueville's "still empty cradle of a great nation," here Brockden Brown offers the promise of a temporal vacuum crying out to be filled by the palpably accessible events of American history.[9] In the years that followed, Washington Irving would indeed take on the "great and arduous" duty of national historian. But he would accomplish this task not simply by providing the missing "facts" necessary to fill in this historical hole: on the contrary, Irving's work obsessively maintains, rather than resolves, the originary tension between hiatus and national history. Like Locke, Vattel, and Tocqueville, he establishes an aesthetics of American idling that reinforces the new nation's claims to property and futurity. Irving thus renders the common wholeness of national space and time thinkable by ceaselessly mourning the fragmented ruin of the dispossessed idler.

Irving's *A History of New-York* (1809) could hardly appear more antithetical to Brockden Brown's vision of an authentic collation of unproblematic national facts. Indeed, as Jeffrey Insko points out, "[o]ne of the functions of *A History of New-York* was to deflate the high moral import of nationalist historiography."[10] For Robert Ferguson, Irving achieves this goal by "demolish[ing] the intellectual foundations for a progressive interpretation of American culture [and by challenging c]onventional beliefs in natural law, the virgin land, manifest destiny, and republican order and virtue."[11] And in a similar vein, Christopher Looby celebrates "Irving's deconstruction of the epistemological assumptions and causational structures of historical writing"—a methodology that aims "to diminish the power of accumulated historical understanding, to destroy precedent, and reopen historical time to creative possibilities."[12] "Far from being outmoded," insists Insko, this "Irving has never been more timely than right now":[13] and it is the counter-Enlightenment force of his project—coupled with the ironic "posture of obsolescence" employed by its pseudonymous author, Diedrich Knickerbocker[14]—that helps to make Irving's quixotic account of the nation's Dutch colonial past so familiar to modern readers and critics. But if these early works seem so "timely," then Irving's later histories and fictions—in particular the massively popular biographies of Columbus (1828), Astor (1836), and Washington (1855–59)—prove all the more distant for the uncritical Romanticism with which they celebrate the forefathers of the emerging U.S. nation. In order to resolve this apparent tension between the irony of youth and the assuredness of old age, the structure of the hiatus is often fruitfully deployed by literary critics. William Hedges, for example, makes sense of the trajectory of Irving's career by locating *A History of New-York* in a temporal no-man's-land: "*Knickerbocker's* confusion comes from belonging to an age which fell directly between Bolingbroke and Emerson. Without any underlying assumptions of its own, that age seemed determined to exhaust itself, if need be, by exposing its own impotence and unreality."[15] The confusing paradoxes of Irving's texts are here transferred over to the historical record, so that what "we discover is that [Irving] is a personification of contradictions implicit in the eighteenth century itself."[16] Enabling the play of differences between ostensibly distinct "age[s]," the exception of the hiatus again restores the normal flow and proper progression of history. "It was only in the middle stage of his career," concludes Hedges, "that Irving began the long climb out of the grave of neo-classicism, which he had been helping to dig ever deeper, toward a positive romanticism."[17]

For other critics, the hiatus of this "middle stage"—epitomized by one of the most important idlers in American literary history, Rip Van

Winkle—reinforces various interpretations of Irving's own personal history. It is the figure of Rip as storyteller that, for Jeffrey Rubin-Dorsky, helps Irving to find comfort amid the chaos of the modern world. While Irving himself travels through old Europe like a dispossessed and homeless American[18]—his financial ground as fluid and uncertain as his geographic—Rip Van Winkle helps to "satisfy [Irving's] hunger for cultural continuity" after "[h]aving been excluded from participation in the continuous flow of an ordered society."[19] In narrating and collecting the fragments of the old, Irving "discovered that storytelling . . . was an uncircumscribed, timeless activity."[20] Michael Warner also situates Irving's work at the threshold between the old and new, specifically at the point of "transition between patriarchy and modern heterosexuality."[21] At stake in the "antihistorical rhetoric of anachronism" practiced by the author, Rip, and the other bachelors who populate his work is an "apprehension of history through which Irving attempts to remediate modernity" by "idealiz[ing] patriarchy just at the moment when it was clearly being displaced."[22] "Irving writes history," concludes Warner, "as though his aim were to have historical consciousness without inhabiting time"[23]—a conclusion that is "odd" for such a "nationalist . . . writer, who capped his career with a five-volume biography of Washington" and who was "caught up in political history" like "no other writer after Franklin and Jefferson."[24]

What all these critics of Irving's work share is their sense of its detachment from time and space, its "uncircumscribed" and idling hiatus from the norms of neoclassicism, the Enlightenment, U.S. "political history," and modernity itself. How "odd," then, that this same work should both inaugurate U.S. literary history and introduce the new nation to its first professional author. In what follows, I argue that Irving's work—in particular *The Sketch-Book* and *A Tour on the Prairies* (1835)—offers an alternative approach to the oddness of this paradox, an approach that refuses to reduce the hiatus and its aesthetics of idling to a time and a place strictly *outside* the modern U.S nation and its history. Irving, like *The Sketch-Book*'s Rip Van Winkle, is never simply modernity's Other: in the same way that he will both critique and reinforce progressive myths of nationalist history over the course of his career, so too Rip will both eschew and, ultimately, embrace the "rising generation, with whom he soon grew into great favor."[25] Instead of resolving the oddness of these important tensions in Irving's work, I argue that that their dialectical mutuality works to *establish* rather than resist the peculiarly modern space and time of the U.S. nation. Following Jean-Luc Nancy, Giorgio Agamben has called the strange relationship between an established juridical norm and the originary hiatus of its exception "a relation of ban": no simple opposition between inclusion and exclusion, the "ban" is "the originary structure in which law refers to life and includes it in itself by suspending it."[26] Moreover, Agamben approaches the structure of this "ban" as an aesthetic form tied to modernity, a form of relation that blurs distinctions between politics and "life" and that soon begins to permeate and pattern our biopolitical horizons. Deploying this same structure of the "ban," Irving's dialectics of hiatus and wholeness, of idle homelessness and destined homeland, are always intimately political forms of relation before they can become symbolically potent themes.[27] Throughout Irving's work, this idling hiatus is transformed into much more than a missing hole in the nation's historical register; and throughout his career, Irving reminds us that there are many other functions that a national historian can fill.

IRVING AND THE FERTILE FRAGMENTS OF THE NATIONAL PAST

Even before we are introduced to one of the most out-of-joint protagonists in American literature, *The Sketch-Book of Geoffrey Crayon, Gent.* (1820–21) establishes fragmentation as its formal, aesthetic framework: "The following papers, with two exceptions, were written in England, and formed but part of an intended series for which I had made notes and memorandums" (4). "Before I could mature a plan," Irving continues, "circumstances compelled me to send them piecemeal to the United States, where they were published from time to time in portions or numbers" (4). *The Sketch-Book* is brought to life by the promise of ruined completion: not only is its subject matter incompletely whole (with the two U.S. "exceptions" of "Rip Van Winkle" and "The Legend of Sleepy Hollow" interrupting the English origins of the text); prior serialization has also punctured its integrity with the fragmented flow of "piecemeal . . . portions." Here and throughout this text, wholeness emerges as a belated aftereffect of the play of ruined "portions," ruins that owe their hiatus to some silent and nameless trauma.[28] Irving continues to develop this framework in his narration of the text's publication history. Although initially expecting a smooth, uneventful transition into print ("It was said . . . that a London bookseller intended to publish" the text [5]), the process is soon interrupted by an uncomfortable "silence" in communication between publisher and author, a traumatic and "disheartening" interlude that could only be "construed [as] tacit rejection" (5–6). When Irving's fears materialize, he turns to Walter Scott for help, sending "him the printed numbers of the Sketch Book in a parcel by coach, and at the same time . . . hinting that since I had had the pleasure of partaking of his hospitality, a reverse had taken place in my affairs which made the successful exercise of my pen all-important" (6). With fears of financial ruin and the trauma of this first rejection fresh in his mind, Irving hoped that his friend would use his influence to secure publication elsewhere in England. Scott did, eventually, help to publish his manuscript, but only after it had "failed" with another "bookseller unknown to fame" that Irving is forced to deal with (9). "The sale was interrupted," notes Irving, adding yet another traumatic hiatus into the text's publication history—a prefatorial gesture that works to reinforce the generosity of Scott and to emphasize the belated wholeness of the fragments that follow (9).

Scott's initial reaction to Irving's inquiry was to offer him a job as editor of a new "weekly periodical . . . about to be set up in Edinburgh" in competition with its *Review* (7). Irving's response to this job offer is worth quoting at length:

> [I] went on to explain that I found myself peculiarly unfitted for the situation offered to me, not merely by my political opinions, but by the very constitution and habits of my mind. "My whole course of life," I observed, "has been desultory, and I am unfitted for any periodically recurring task. . . . I have no command of my talents, such as they are, and have to watch the varyings of my mind as I would those of a weather-cock. Practice and training may bring me more into rule; but at present I am as useless for regular service as one of my own country Indians, or a Don Cossack.
>
> "I must, therefore, keep on pretty much as I have begun; writing when I can, not when I would. I shall occasionally shift my residence, and write whatever is suggested by objects before me, or whatever rises in my imagination; and hope to write better and more copiously by and by." (8)

Not only is *The Sketch-Book*'s publication history fragmented by ruin and traumatic detour; so too Irving's persona is riven by idling and the "desultory... varyings [of] mind" that interrupt its periodicity. Again, we should be wary of reading such interruptions as strictly anathema to the periodical progression of personal and publication history: the preface is composed in 1848 and included in the text's revised edition. As Irving composes this preface—his hugely successful career marked by anything but the wild ramblings of "useless" talent—such ruined fragmentation bequeaths a retroactive wholeness to his legacy and to *The Sketch-Book* that follows.

In the same way that these traumatic interruptions of periodicity work to reinforce the palpable flow of time, so too the tales of Irving's traveler will, in their fragmented dispersal, reinvigorate the homeland as a now-distant, ruined memory. Borrowing imagery and language from Oliver Goldsmith's "The Traveller,"[29] one of the first stories in *The Sketch-Book* demonstrates how the interruption of a "sea voyage" can sever and, thus, bring into mournful relief a "'lengthening chain'" connecting us to the temporal and spatial origin of the home. "In traveling by land," Irving avers,

> there is a continuity of scene, and a connected succession of persons and incidents, that carry on the story of life, and lessen the effect of absence and separation. We drag, it is true "a lengthening chain" at each remove of our pilgrimage; but the chain is unbroken: we can trace it back link by link; and we feel that the last still grapples us to home. But a wide sea voyage severs us at once. It makes us conscious of being cut loose from the secure anchorage of a settled life, and sent adrift upon a doubtful world. It interposes a gulf, not merely imaginary, but real, between us and our homes—a gulf... rendering distance palpable and return precarious. (14)

This same "precarious" comfort makes "conscious" the palpability of both temporal and spatial "remove." To voyage, then, is to create a "fragment of a world" (15), a fragmentation that—like the "wrecked... remains" of the vessel Irving encounters during his Atlantic crossing—works to punctuate "the story of life" by hollowing out interruptions and periods that, in their ruin, testify to the passing of space and time (16). This is why *The Sketch-Book* opens with this epigraph from Lyly's *Euphues*:

> I am of this mind with Homer, that as the snaile that crept out of her shel was turned eftsoons into a toad, and thereby was forced to make a stoole to sit on; so the traveller that strageleth from his owne country is

in a short time transformed into so monstrous a shape, that he is faine to alter his mansion with his manners, and to live where he can, not where he would. (10)

Although this might seem like a strange way to begin a travel romance, we should by now recognize in it the mournful imprimatur of the sentimental voyeur. Here and throughout *The Sketch-Book*, Irving employs his "sauntering gaze" to register the "monstrous" form of a spatio-temporal progression that simultaneously inaugurates and fragments its origin (13)—a Homeric "pilgrimage" that "grapples us to home" only insofar as it "stragleth from" its ruined "shel."

These opening passages thus help to establish the key formal, aesthetic patterns of fragmented hiatus that will feature so famously in "Rip Van Winkle." Indeed, from the story's first lines, we see how the "desultory" interruptions of trauma and sea voyage now hollow out the sleepy contours of the "Kaatskill mountains." "They are a dismembered branch of the great Appalachian family," the "late Diedrich Knickerbocker" informs us from beyond the grave,

> and are seen away to the west of the river, swelling up to a noble height, and lording it over the surrounding country. Every change of season, every change of weather, indeed every hour of the day, produces some change in the magical hues and shapes of these mountains, and they are regarded by all the good wives, far and near, as perfect barometers. (34)

Here again we witness a dismembered nobility that, in its ruined exception, enframes the Hudson valley with its "swelling" contours and establishes the normal barometric conditions for the passing of time ("Every change of season [and] every hour of the day"). This "noble" aesthetics of fragmented hiatus will soon be transferred to an Indian "abode of spirits" that patrols the spatial borders and manifests the temporal destiny of the new nation; but it is Rip's out-of-jointedness that, in this story at least, most fully embodies the spirit of originary dismemberment offered up by the "Kaatskill mountains." Notice how, in the following introductory passage, our protagonist is associated with a desultory, interrupted form of temporality even before his more famous twenty-year slumber in the mountains:

> At the foot of these fairy mountains, the voyager may have descried the light smoke curling up from a village.... It is a little village, of great

antiquity, having been founded by some of the Dutch colonists, in the early times of the province, just about the beginning of the government of the good Peter Stuyvesant, (may he rest in peace!) and there were some of the houses of the original settlers standing within a few years, built of small yellow bricks brought from Holland. . . .

In that same village, and in one of these very houses (which, to tell the precise truth, was sadly time-worn and weather-beaten), there lived many years since, while the country was yet a province of Great Britain, a simple good-natured fellow, of the name of Rip Van Winkle. He was a descendent of the Van Winkles who figured so gallantly in the chivalrous days of Peter Stuyvesant, and accompanied him to the siege of Fort Christina. He inherited, however, but little of the martial character of his ancestors. . . . [H]e was, moreover, a kind neighbor, and an obedient hen-pecked husband. Indeed, to that latter circumstance might be owing that meekness of spirit which gained him such universal popularity; for those men are most apt to be obsequious and conciliating abroad, who are under the discipline of shrews at home. (34–35)

In the same way that Rip's "meekness of spirit" punctuates the end of the Dutch era of martial "gallantry," so too the "time-worn" materiality of his house testifies to the temporal distance that now separates him from the "original" days of "antiquity." Caught between the pastness of the past ("there lived many years since") and the promise of the national future ("while the country was yet a province of Great Britain"), Rip rips the temporal into the play of "since" and "yet," a play of colonial differences that will enable the history of the new U.S. nation to awaken fully in time.

"The great error in Rip's composition," Knickerbocker continues, "was an insuperable aversion to all kinds of profitable labor. . . . In a word Rip was ready to attend to any body's business but his own; but as to doing family duty, and keeping his farm in order, he found it impossible" (35). In addition to the fecundity of Rip's temporal hiatus, he and his "companions in idleness" form "a kind of perpetual club of the sages, philosophers, and other idle personages of the village" (36, 37), fragmenting and thus bringing into relief the Lockean spatial coordinates of the new nation. Drawing on Locke's and Vattel's aesthetics of Indian idleness, Rip's neglect of "his farm" functions as a originary exception to the modern agrarian norm, and his nonlabor ("telling endless sleepy stories about nothing" [37]) infects existing forms of property with ruin (his "fences were continually falling to pieces" [36]) and even dispossesses the idler of any reproductive fruit: "His children, too, were as ragged and wild as if they belonged to nobody" (36). Rip's impotence functions in both this physical, spatial sense—as a hiatus in property and possession—and also as a profound out-of-jointedness in the temporal: "how sagely [he] would deliberate upon public events some months after they had taken place" (37). "I'm not myself," Rip will declare after his slumber (45), and it is as if he has simply been passed over by time and history, his son now become the perfect "ditto of himself" (47). Michael Warner has already provided nuanced commentary on the function of bachelorhood and the perils of "family duty" in Irving's work, but I would argue here that Rip's interruption of the erotic plot—his meek inheritance from the past and his "hen-pecked" impotence in the present—provides the engine for, as well as the exception to, the inexorable unfolding of the modern present. Where Mackenzie's men of feeling maintain the tension of the erotic plot by endlessly deferring its closure ("romances always end with a marriage," declares Julia de Roubigné, "because, after that, there is nothing to be said"),[30] Irving emphasizes the surprising fecundity of impotence and ruin. In "The Art of Book-Making," for example, Irving juxtaposes the virility of a modern press "teem[ing] with voluminous productions" with the activity of "some strange-favored being, generally clothed in black," who would "steal forth, and glide through" the rooms of the British Museum (69). We soon find out that "these mysterious personages, whom I had mistaken for magi, were principally authors . . . in the very act of manufacturing books [by] sequester[ing] pools of obsolete literature . . . and draw[ing] buckets full of classic lore . . . wherewith to swell their own scanty rills of thought" (70). As such, this "pilfering disposition" through which "the beauties and fine thoughts of ancient and obsolete authors . . . bear fruit in a remote and distant tract of time" offers an alternative economy of reproduction to modern forms of progress and publication (71). Nowadays, Irving continues, "we burn down a forest of stately pines [to find] a progeny of dwarf oaks start up in their place: and we never see the prostrate trunk of a tree mouldering into soil, but it gives birth to a whole tribe of fungi" (72).[31] The ostensibly nonproductive labor of the "magi" does not so much interrupt modernity and its technologies of publication and reproduction; rather, it offers its own "mouldering" form of inheritance propelled by the fertile fragments of a ruined past, fragments that "undergo a kind of metempsychosis, and spring up under new forms. What was formerly a ponderous history revives in the shape of romance—an old legend changes into a modern play" (71). As we saw in the previous chapter, the magic of metempsychotic exchange is included in, rather than simply opposed to, modern, Enlightenment logics of property and personhood. So too in *The Sketch-Book* we continue to witness the infectious magic of those discontinuous moments that, like the rough "particularities of ancient rural life," have been "almost polished away" by the onset of modernity (173). Establishing the threshold between the rough and the smooth—between the ruin of a disconnected past and the promise of an endlessly virile future—such "obsolete" moments do indeed continue to "bear fruit."

Irving revisits the dialectical mutuality of modernity and antiquity in "London Antiques," where he encounters the "relics of a 'foregone' world locked up in the heart of the city" of London. In place of the obsolete "magi" who wander around the reading room of the British Museum, Irving finds at the Charter House "a number of gray-headed old men, clad in long black cloaks [who proceed] without uttering a word" (209). These men appear to be "ghosts of the departed years" who guard the fragments of antiqued things: "implements of savage warfare; strange idols and stuffed alligators; bottled serpents and monsters decorated the mantelpiece; while on the high tester of an old-fashioned bedstead grinned a human skull, flanked on each side by a dried cat" (209). Such ruined things, stamped with the mouldering authority of times past, help bring into relief the "modern changes and innovations of London" (211); or, as Irving puts it, they are "swallowed up and almost lost in a wilderness of brick and mortar; but deriving poetical and romantic interest from the commonplace prosaic world around them" (207). The relics of the Charter House, like the obsolete wanderings of the magi, are not simply excluded from the spatio-temporal experience of a prosaically modern London; they are, instead, occluded and banned into its very heart—a "realm of shadows, existing in the very centre of substantial realities" (209).

Rip Van Winkle meets with another ghost "of the departed years" when he discovers in the mountains "a strange figure slowly toiling up the rocks" dressed in "the antique Dutch fashion" (39). In many ways, stories like "London Antiques" and "Little Britain" help to reinforce the formal, aesthetic relationship between Rip's Dutch colonial hiatus and the business of the emerging U.S. nation. Where the privileged spaces of Irving's "Kaaterskill mountains" are protected by "The Sleepy Hollow Boys" and Rip's "perpetual club of the sages, philosophers, and other idle personages of the village" (292), in London this same task is left to "the Roaring Lads of Little Britain" (217). Like the magi of the Charter House, the "sheltered" and "decayed gentry" of "Little Britain" may truly be called the heart's core of the city; the strong-hold of true John Bullism" (213). This "is a fragment of London," continues Irving,

> as it was in its better days, with its antiquated folks and fashions. Here flourish in great preservation many of the holiday games and customs of yore.... [Its inhabitants] still believe in dreams and fortune-telling, and an old woman that lives in Bull-and-Mouth Street makes a tolerable subsistence by detecting stolen goods, and promising the girls good husbands.... There are even many ghost stories current [and] Lords and ladies, the former in full-bottomed wigs, hanging sleeves, and swords, the latter in lappets, stays, hoops, and brocade, have been seen walking up and down the great waste chambers, on moonlit nights; and are supposed to be the shades of the ancient proprietors in their court-dresses. Little Britain has likewise its sages and great men. (213–14)

While the "old Dutch inhabitants" of Sleepy Hollow "say Hendrick Hudson and his crew are at their game of nine-pins" when it thunders (48), the "Lords and ladies" of Little Britain preserve their own "holiday games and customs" and are equally drawn to supernatural explanations of the mundane.

IRVING AND THE RUINED CHANNELS OF FUTURITY

What, then, is the relationship between these sleepy, timeless places "of yore" and the waking busy-ness of modernity? How do Little Britain and Sleepy Hollow function in terms of the awakened fullness of their respective Big nations? In the same way that the ruined fecundity of the British Museum brings modernity's "whole tribe of fungi" into relief, we learn that Little Britain, "[t]hus wrapped up in its own concerns, its own habits, and its own opinions, ... has long flourished as a sound heart to this great fungous metropolis" (219). Rather than situate the idle fragments of the nation's past strictly outside of the modern metropole, Irving instead insists on their continued productive centrality within its borders. Never simply antimodern, they offer up a ruined spatio-temporal hiatus against which the flow of national time and space can be measured. Rip does not sleep *through* the American Revolution: in testifying to the antiqued pastness of the past, he hollows out a discontinuous space and time that brings into relief the full flow of the modern, that makes "the revolution" thinkable as an isolated, national event along time's axis. Such little spaces are included into the big nation, banned as originary exceptions that, like the "dismembered" fragments of the "Kaatskill mountains," bequeath their contours to channel the current of the modern, "moving on its silent but majestic course" like the Hudson River through Sleepy Hollow (38). They provide the promise of a pristine benchmark against which the fated events of history can appear and be chronicled: "All empires," Irving informs us, "are doomed to changes and revolutions. Luxury and innovation creep in; factions arise; and families now and then spring up, whose ambition and intrigues throw the whole system into confusion" (219). We see this same comforting confusion inevitably beset Little Britain itself, with its "tranquillity . . . greviously disturbed, and its golden simplicity of manners threatened with total subversion, by the aspiring family of a retired butcher" (220). Needless to say, the French have a hand in all this: after becoming "smitten with a passion for high life," "reading novels, [and] talking bad French" (220), "the infection had taken hold" such that this family "even went so far as to attempt patronage, and actually induced a French dancing-master to set up in the neighborhood" (222). Before too long, however, "the worthy folks of Little Britain took fire at it, and did so persecute the poor Gaul, that he was fain to pack up fiddle and dancing-pumps, and decamp with such precipitation, that he absolutely forgot to pay for his lodgings" (222). Notice here how it is the always-imperiled sanctity of Little Britain ("I apprehend," cautions Irving, "that it will terminate in the downfall of genuine John Bullism" [223]) that makes possible the play of national differences and the inevitable march of modern time.

What is so remarkable about *The Sketch-Book* is its aesthetic coproduction of antiquarian nostalgia and modern nationalism. Rather than structure these concepts antagonistically, Irving instead reveals their dialectical mutuality. As Milton's epigraph to "English Writers on America"—the proudly nationalistic defense of the emerging U.S. nation that follows "Rip Van Winkle—reminds us, a sleepy hiatus has the potential to energize as well as to arrest the spirit of the modern: "Methinks I see in my mind a noble and puissant nation, rousing herself like a strong man after sleep" (50). By focusing exclusively on the ostensibly antimodern out-of-jointedness of Rip Van Winkle, critics often ignore the manifest timeliness he bequeaths to figures such as "John Bull." Where Rip hollows out the time of nation with the gift of his discontinuous slumber—dittoed and passed over by the temporal—"there is scarcely a being in actual existence more absolutely present to the public mind than that eccentric personage, John Bull" (265): "Crouched in his little domain, with these filaments stretching forth in every direction, he is like some choleric, bottle-bellied old spider, who has woven his web over a whole chamber, so that a fly cannot buzz, nor a breeze blow, without startling his repose, and causing him to sally forth wrathfully from his den" (267). Reaching "in every direction" out into time and space, John Bull's absolute presence is never startled with the surprises of slumber and "repose." Fully conscious and incapable of idleness, he "is one of those fertile humorists, that are continually throwing out new portraits, and presenting different aspects from different points of view" (266). There is something about the expansiveness of his form—even before it takes on particular "aspects" of national content—that seems to embody the "English." As such, he is not so much a static symbol of the nation imagined by its citizenry: on the contrary, *he* gives birth to *them*: "Men are apt to acquire particularities that are continually ascribed to them. The common orders of English . . . endeavor to act up to the broad caricature that is perpetually before their eyes" (265). Where Rip is impotent and scrawny, every "thing that lives on [John Bull] seems to thrive and grow fat" (268):

> His manor is infested by gangs of gipsies; yet he will not suffer them to be driven off, because they have . . . been regular poachers upon every generation of the family. He will scarcely permit a dry branch to be lopped from the great trees that surround the house, lest it should molest the rooks, that have bred there for centuries. Owls have taken possession of the dovecote; but they are hereditary owls, and must not be disturbed. . . . In short, John has [a] reverence for every thing that has been long in the family. (271)

While Rip stands dispossessed—his empty home "sadly time-worn and weather-beaten"—John Bull allegorizes the ever-expanding space of the colonial homeland and its temporal gifts of generational inheritance.

Irving thus writes to the fecundity of the future as well as to the ruined antiquity of the past. The mutuality of these aesthetic perspectives is brought into full view in Irving's most explicit meditation on progress and obsolescence, "The Mutability of Literature." "Beguiled by the solemn monastic air" of the "vaulted passages and mouldering tombs" of Westminster Abbey, Geoffrey Crayon enters into conversation with one of the books contained in its "literary catacomb" (113, 112, 113). It is this book, a "testy" quarto unhappy with its isolation from the world (115), that eulogizes the "fixed" exceptionalism of English literature and language, not Irving's pseudonymous author (116). "[A]lmost all the writers of your time have . . . passed into forgetfulness," retorts Crayon (116):

> The purity and stability of language, too, on which you found your claims to perpetuity, have been the fallacious dependence of authors of every age. . . . Even now many talk of Spenser's "well of pure English undefiled," as if the language ever sprang from a well or a fountain-head, and was not rather a mere confluence of various tongues, perpetually subject to change and intermixtures. It is this which has made English literature so extremely mutable, and the reputation built upon it so fleeting. Unless thought can be committed to something more permanent and unchangeable than such a medium, even thought must share the fate of every thing else, and fall into decay. This should serve as a check upon the vanity and exultation of the most popular writer. (116)

In coproducing the antiquarian elitism of the "little quarto" along with Crayon's sense of mutability and fated progress, Irving taps into a rich aesthetic vein of modernity. We fail to give a full account of this formal, dialectical process if we focus exclusively on one side of its generative pair. Indeed, scholars have often ignored aspects of *The Sketch-Book* that voice an almost Malthusian delight in serving "check[s] upon the vanity" of a stagnating elite. Such is the role of the critic for Crayon: "Criticism may do much," he insists. "It increases with the increase in literature, and resembles one of those salutary checks on population spoken of by economists" (118). In his 1798 *An Essay on the Principle of Population*, Malthus uses the same language to discuss "The Checks to Population in the Less Civilized World" (the title of book 1) and "The Checks To Population In The Different States of Modern Europe" (the title of book 2).[32] Drawing on the work of the Swiss mathematician Jean-Louis Muret, Malthus attempts to account for Muret's observation that "the most healthy countries, having less fecundity, will not overpeople themselves, and the unhealthy countries, by their extraordinary fecundity, will be able to sustain their population."[33] While Malthus does not directly extend his theory of population change to questions concerning the mutability of language and literature, Irving makes precisely this connection in the extraordinary passage that follows:

> [W]e daily behold the varied and beautiful tribes of vegetables springing up, flourishing, adorning the fields for a short time, and then fading into dust, to make way for their successors. Were not this the case, the fecundity of nature would be a grievance instead of a blessing. . . . Language gradually varies, and with it fade away the writings of authors who have flourished their allotted time; otherwise, the creative powers of genius would overstock the world. (117)

As we will see in "Traits of Indian Character" and "Philip of Pokanoket"—stories that deal more explicitly with the Native American "tribes" who have used up "their allotted time" and now "fade away" in order "to make way for their successors"—the formal, aesthetic structure of Irving's dialectics of progress and nostalgia is, like Locke's *Second Treatise*, always also involved in the politics of colonial expansion and the ideology of racial difference.

For Irving, the American frontier provides a spatial image for this dialectical tension, materializing the threshold between a noble and antiqued prehistory and the ruthless and fated march of progress. In "Traits of Indian Character," the frontier is not a particular location in space; rather, it is a principle, an engine of spatio-temporality—a promise of hybridity and infection that belatedly reinforces the distinction between a fated modernity and a ruined nobility. It is populated by "the miserable hordes which infest the frontiers, and hang on the skirts of the settlements" (241). These no-people, Irving continues, are

> commonly composed of degenerate beings, corrupted and enfeebled by the vices of society, without being benefitted by its civilization. That proud independence, which formed the main pillar of savage virtue, has been shaken down, and the whole moral fabric lies in ruins. . . . Society has advanced upon them like one of those withering airs that will sometimes breed desolation over a whole region of fertility. It has enervated

their strength, multiplied their diseases, and superinduced upon their original barbarity the low vices of artificial life. (241)

Their bodies marking the passage of advancing time, this "miserable horde" offer themselves up to "civilization" so that progress can attain material form—the "withering airs" that, like Crayon's critic, perform the necessary checks on the nation's population. Ever in ruinous flux, they have no particular shape other than that imposed upon them by the progress of "Society," and they do not function in time so much as bequeath to it an "enervated" sense of its passing.

In contrast to these "degenerate beings" of the frontier stands the noble figure of "Philip of Pokanoket." If the infected "fabric" of the frontier "horde" will, in the movement of its decay, remain indistinguishable from the temporal flow of modernity, the "savage virtue" of Philip will offer an occluded, atemporal perspective from which to gaze at this fateful and tragic spectacle: "He saw the whole race of his countrymen melting before them from the face of the earth; their territories slipping from their hands, and their tribes becoming feeble" (253). "[H]is friends . . . swept away from before his eyes," Philip is utterly outside of time's movement, an immaterial witness to the comfort of its disaster (261).[34] Although Irving wants us to think that this "race" has "long since disappeared . . . and scarce any traces remain of them in the thickly-settled states of New England," *The Sketch-Book* was composed during a period of renewed resistance to U.S. Indian policy, and such a notorious enemy as King Philip might, in any other historian's hands, offer somewhat discomforting material (248).[35] But by situating the Indian on the originary thresholds of space and time—as frontier "beings" who register the infectious imprint of history's movement and as noble savages who stoically observe history's passing—Irving includes him in the historical record only as an exceptional absence: "They will vanish like a vapor from the face of the earth," he assures his readers. "Their very history will be lost in forgetfulness; and the places that now know them will know them no more for ever" (248–49). What Irving contributes to the aesthetics of national memory is not, then, a particular content that fills in a gaping hole in its chronicle. On the contrary, if Irving adds anything to the memory of the nation it is, precisely, the "forgetfulness" of a formal hiatus that both inaugurates national space and time and, at the same moment, "vanish[es]" in its originary gesture. Such forgetfulness is not simply excluded from history as a repressed blind spot: it is included as its enabling ruin.[36]

Throughout *The Sketch-Book*, Irving promotes these comfortably haunting ghosts of the emerging nation, Indians who "have left scarcely any authentic traces on the page of history, but [who] stalk, like gigantic shadows, in the dim twilight of tradition" (251). In the previous chapter, we saw how these same "shadows" animate a reading of the Gothic romance as a privileged site of resistance to U.S. colonial expansion—as the ugly facts that continue to "stalk" the literature and the politics of the nation. "There may be no such [Gothic] ruins in America as are found in Europe, or in Asia or in Africa," notes John Neal, "but other ruins there are of a prodigious magnitude—the ruins of a mighty people. . . . [and] the live wreck of a prodigious empire that has departed from before our face within the memory of man; the last of a people who have no history."[37] Similarly for Irving, "Indians [are] the mere wrecks and remnants of once powerful tribes," and like the ruined fragments of shipwreck that work to spatialize and punctuate the transatlantic duration of "The Voyage," so too the "remnants" of these once "mighty people" provide the material occasions of history that testify, in their decay, to the tearfully reassuring fatedness of national progress (241). In this play of immediate affective response and fated, wrecked oblivion, Irving is working in a distinctly sentimental vein. Notice how, for example, the aesthetics of Irving's "Voyage" already prepares us for the littered wreckage of Indian history on display in the later, more explicitly racialized stories:

> We one day descried some shapeless object drifting at a distance. At sea, every expanse attracts attention. It proved to be the mast of a ship that must have been completely wrecked; for there were the remains of handkerchiefs, by which some of the crew had fastened themselves to this spar, to prevent their being washed off by the waves. There was no trace by which the name of the ship could be ascertained. The wreck had obviously drifted about for many months; clusters of shell-fish had fastened about it, and long sea-weeds flaunted at its side. But where, thought I, is the crew? Their struggle has long been over—they have gone down amidst the roar of the tempest—their bones lie whitening among the caverns of the deep. Silence, oblivion, like the waves, have closed over them, and no one can tell the story of their end. What sighs have been wafted after that ship! (16)

What Irving finds punctuating the flowing "expanse" of the "sea" is not simply a haunting object, *a* shipwreck. It is an occasion, a petrified event—"a ship that must have been completely wrecked." Even the unusual syntax of his discovery—the epistemic modality of the "must have been"—fills out the dimensions of a prejacent event, engaging the reader in what theorists of modal logic would call an "evidential meaning component."[38] This wreck is a crime scene, and what such scenes give evidence of, even before they can register the forensic "struggle" of victims and villains, is the happening, the eventness of time. Necessarily traumatic, such events hollow out a silent "oblivion" *in* the temporal, a hiatus that, in its withdrawal, establishes the mournful currency of the now.[39] This aesthetics of haunting does not simply resist a pregiven consciousness by offering up tempestuous elements repressed from its record. It also establishes the recordable parameters of the present, providing a belated and melancholic backdrop against which the lengthening chain of consciousness can be clustered and "fastened."

There are other sentimental wrecks in *The Sketch-Book*, other chasms that bring into mournful relief the smooth, inexorable "expanse" of modern progress. The physiognomy of Irving's noble savage, for example, is itself wrecked by a silent, affective abyss: "The solitary savage feels silently, but acutely. His sensibilities are not diffused over so wide a surface as those of the white man; but they run in steadier and deeper channels" (243). Indian feeling thus occupies the nonplace channeled out of the surface of the "white" homeland, its very form tied to its removal from the space of the face. Indian sensibility is not a particular display or content of feeling: it is an aesthetics of affective dispossession, a subterranean depression coproduced along with the topographic illusion of a "wide," contoured "surface." Irving finds other such channels "among the hearty old holiday customs" of the rural English (164). What these "strong local peculiarities" offer, of course, is their capacity to be smoothed out by the progressive character of the modern, urban nation. "One of the least pleasing effects of modern refinement," Irving informs us, "is the havoc it has made" among such "customs. It has completely taken off the sharp touchings and spirited reliefs of these embellishments of life, and has worn down society into a more smooth and polished, but certainly a less characteristic surface" (164–65). And in "The Broken Heart," the affective "recesses" of a rural woman's "bosom" will supply the "silent and devouring melancholy" to fuel modernity's antimodern nostalgia. Irving's version of the sentimental Maria will become the muse for the "distinguished Irish poet" Thomas Moore (68),[40] and the poem he composes could pass for one of the popular "Indian Maid" laments that will soon appear on the other side of the Atlantic:

> She sings the wild songs of her dear native plains,
>   Every note which he loved awaking—
> Ah! little they think, who delight in her strains,
>   How the heart of the minstrel is breaking!
>
> He had lived for his love—for his country he died,
>   They were all that to life had entwined him—
> Nor soon shall the tears of his country be dried,
>   Nor long will his love stay behind him!
>
> Oh! make her a grave where the sunbeams rest,
>   When they promise a glorious morrow;
> They'll shine o'er her sleep, like a smile from the west,
>   From her own loved island of sorrow! (68)

Here, as with the other sentimental wreckage of *The Sketch-Book*, the smooth "promise" of the nation and the westward expansion of "country" is fueled by the sharp, mournful abyss of these lovers' graves.

In the tumultuous years following its initial publication, "Rip Van Winkle" would prove to be one of the most versatile fictions of the emerging U.S. nation. "With dozens of *Sketch Book* rip-offs appearing in the decades that followed," notes Sarah Wood, "Irving's cataleptic Dutchman would be repeatedly revived by authors, translators, poets, and especially playrights, looking to bring Rip Van Winkle up to date and into dialogue with their own political, social, and cultural contexts."[41] For example, in the early 1830s, just after the election of Andrew Jackson, a play by John Kerr entitled *Rip Van Winkle; or Demons of the Catskill Mountains!!! A National Drama* was performed in Albany and Philadelphia.[42] Where Irving's Rip initially resists the vigor of the new postrevolutionary nation, Kerr's "Van Winkle admires the changes that have taken place during his absence, marveling how the place that was once a 'long straggling village' has been 'converted into a populous and extensive town.'"[43] Kerr's play even "introduces its own Indian vignette, a song called 'The Indian Maid,' which tells... a cautionary tale of unrequited love, singing of the 'white man' who has come exploring in 'the Indian grove.'"[44] Instead of reading Kerr's revisions of "Rip Van Winkle" as strictly antithetical to the original text's ostensibly antimodern nostalgia, I would argue that such adaptations are *propelled*—rather than resisted—by Irving's aesthetics, an aesthetics rooted in the dialectical mutuality of antiqued past and fateful future. That Rip ultimately helps us to inherit this future is, perhaps, his most surprising legacy.

INDIAN REMOVAL AND THE GRIMACE OF RUINED HISTORY

Buoyed by the success of his *Sketch-Book*, Irving would spend the next decade and a half traveling around Europe and serving as a cultural ambassador to Spain and England. While Irving was receiving honorary degrees in civil law from Oxford University and gold medals from the Royal Society of Literature for his services to history, the emerging U.S. nation continued to be confronted by the "live wreck" of an indigenous people who had "no history." Speaking very generally, during the period immediately following the American Revolution to the end of the War of 1812, the most prevalent solution to the so-called "Indian problem" had been thought to be assimilation. Driven by its faith in the improvability of humankind—a faith now bolstered by the age of Enlightenment's rapid scientific advances—the United States sought to peaceably include Native Americans in their new republic. Of course, financially crippled by the revolution, and lacking a strong central government to control its frontier peripheries, it was in the new nation's best interests to maintain close ties, especially military alliances, with Native American nations. And so when the new republic desired land occupied by indigenous peoples, it generally sought first to purchase these lands for a "fair price."[45]

However, as the nation became more and more powerful, many of the states, especially those slave states seeking to expand their plantation economies, began to insist that Native American nations existing within state limits should either immediately assimilate into U.S. culture and abide by state laws or be forced to relocate outside the borders of the United States. President Andrew Jackson was an outspoken advocate of states' rights: to him it was unthinkable that distinct Native American nations, with their own laws and their own political constitutions, were considered outside of a state's jurisdiction. So when Jackson assumed office in 1829, the first order of business for him was to pass the Indian Removal Act—a bitterly disputed act that only just made it through the House of Representatives by a vote of 102 to 97.

Although the Indian Removal Act did not explicitly condone the use of force or the violation of treaties to effect the relocation of Native Americans, critics of Jackson and the proremoval faction of his government feared that the president would inevitably resort to these measures should Native American nations refuse to relocate voluntarily. In his first message to Congress in 1829, Jackson describes the strange relationship between Native Americans and the civilizing forces of American progress as follows:

> Our conduct toward these people is deeply interesting to our national character. . . . Our ancestors found them the uncontrolled possessors of these vast regions. By persuasion and force they have been made to retire from river to river and from mountain to mountain, until some of the tribes have become extinct and others have left but remnants to preserve for awhile their once terrible names. Surrounded by the whites with their arts of civilization, which by destroying the resources of the savage doom him to weakness and decay, [a sad] fate surely awaits them if they remain within the limits of the states. . . . Humanity and national honor demand that every effort should be made to avert so great a calamity.[46]

Here, as elsewhere in his speeches on Indian affairs, Jackson makes use of the aesthetics of tragedy in order to naturalize the "doom" and the "fate" of the Indian and to deemphasize the active role that U.S. colonization is playing in the dispossession of native lands. It is as if the president's narrative voice takes a step outside of the flow of time and history and, in observing the inevitable pattern of decline that dooms the Indian, appeals to our "humanity" and "national honor" in order to avert the impending temporal "calamity." To borrow John Neal's phrase, Jackson reads the "remnants" of Indian nations as living wrecks with "no history." What ruins them is not so much a specific event but, rather, the flow of time itself, which has become a palpable, external force bringing about their inevitable decline. To borrow language from Irving's *Sketch-Book*, they are simply "casual relics of antiquity ... left like wrecks upon this distant shore of time, telling no tale but that such beings had been and had perished" (149). Indians have "no history," then, not because they have no tradition or culture but, rather, because they stand *outside* of time, watching on as the fateful flow of colonial destiny manifests itself. They have no history because they have no time, because their bodies are never in time, because time is an agent that acts casually upon them rather than a property that they can possess or a dimension that they can access.

In his numerous sketches and paintings of Native American subjects, again and again George Catlin registers this strange gaze of the live wreck.[47] As Indians were being forced to relocate during the 1830s, Catlin toured the West and produced numerous canvasses that he would later exhibit in American and European cities—often accompanied by tribal members of the Indian nations that he perceived to be vanishing from the earth. Indian resistance to Jackson's removal policies was at its height during Catlin's tour. In 1831, for example, Black Hawk and his followers were driven from their homelands in order to make land available for white settlers; but in 1832 Black Hawk led one thousand people back across the Mississippi to land in Illinois that had been secured for them in an 1804 treaty with the U.S. government. After an early, stinging victory over the Illinois militia—a militia that included a number of future U.S. dignitaries such as Abraham Lincoln and Jefferson Davis—Black Hawk's followers soon ran out of supplies and were massacred at the Bad Axe River just before Catlin's visit with the leader of the rebellion. After their capture, the captives were immediately transferred by steamboat to the barracks at Fort Jefferson, where they were imprisoned and placed in chains (figure 2). Their celebrity was such that even the famous Irving would make time to meet them, rearranging the itinerary of his tour of the American West that we will be discussing shortly.[48]

In the image of the captives at Fort Jefferson, Black Hawk and his followers look out of the canvas at us, figuratively and literally arrested. Catlin sketches their faces in an almost identical fashion, as if all that matters is the repetition of their common gaze. They each carry the heavy fate of time in their own hands, frozen within the canvas like daguerrotyped subjects—static victims of the immense exposure time required by the photographic plate. Consider, however, the following, third-person account of the sketch. In response to Catlin's request to paint his portrait, it seems that one of these figures, Neapope, "seized the ball and chain that were fastened to his leg, and

FIGURE 2. George Catlin, Saukie. 87. *Muk-a-tah-mish-o-ka-kaik (the Black Hawk) War Chief of the Saukie tribe*. Pencil drawing. In *Souvenir of the N. American Indians, as They Were in the Nineteenth Century*, by George Catlin (1850). Pl.29. Courtesy of Rare Books Division, The New York Public Library, Astor, Lenox, and Tilden Foundations.

raising them on high, exclaimed with a look of scorn, 'make me so, and show me to the great father.' Upon the artist's refusing to paint him as he wished, he kept varying his countenance with *grimaces*, to prevent him from catching a likeness."[49] What is most uncanny and subversive about the Indian is not so much a specific quality of his or her savagery—some ugly, repressed fact or event that visibly haunts the symbolic surface of the colonial canvas and exposes the empty fiction of American civility. Indeed, as this brief anecdote suggests, the subaltern here really cannot speak, his acts of resistance notably, if predictably, absent from Catlin's finished product. What haunts this image is not some latent thing or event that is secretly hidden within the symbolic texture of the canvas but, rather, what is always erased by the painting's *form*: the sheer fact of Indian survival, of animation, of extension in time. For if the wreck of the Indian is ruined by time and yet somehow still lives, moves, grimaces, what kind of time does it live and move in? How could we register or paint the force, the torsion of Neapope's grimace?

Event/Hiatus 145

What shapes the aesthetic confrontation between Catlin and Black Hawk—as we have already seen with Jackson's political address to Congress—is the idea that time and experience is a property, a manifest thing, that can be owned in different ways. Precisely because of its thinghood, time can now be separated from the subject—a fact that produces both the possibility of Jackson's detached, tragic voice and the frozen Indian gaze that Catlin captures on his canvas. The Noble Savage is the name for a body whose time is up, a body that does not possess time or history and that is, therefore, destined to gaze motionless at its fateful progress. What I am suggesting here is that the politics of Indian removal and the aesthetics of American art are intimately linked to what we might call the changing experience of experience—to a transformation in our approach to time and temporality that makes the formal structure of the great eighteenth- and nineteenth-century national histories possible. From texts such as Hume's *History of England* and William Robertson's *History of Scotland* in the 1750s to Washington Irving's histories of the frontier, *Astoria* (1836) and *The Adventures of Captain Bonneville* (1837), we listen to the newly detached voice of the national historian who presides, like the narrator of Jackson's address to Congress, over a manifest series of events that ineluctably give themselves, and their trajectories, up to the historian's knowing gaze.

We might also say that the experience of time has been commodified and that, like the commodity, it begins a paradoxical life as a common thing that both possesses and is possessed by the subject, so that history becomes an economy that circulates discrete, quantifiable events. If the experience of time and history is to be transformed into a manifest destiny that is possessed by the colonial subject, what must be repressed is the grimace of *a* life, of a temporality, that somehow exceeds this time and fate, a body that continues to die even after it is dead. This grimace is not simply a subversive thing, a sign, that somehow symbolizes the Indian's nonplace within the public sphere: it is a force without object—the pure activity of an excessive drive that Freud will locate beyond the pleasure principle but still very much within the uncanny perimeters of human experience.[50]

Both on the canvas of its national art and in the topography of its natural spaces, the new nation tries to arrest this force and to distinguish its own experience of fated temporality from the live wreck of ruined Indian history. It is no accident, then, that Catlin provides what scholars consider to be the first expression of the national park idea:

> [W]hat a splendid contemplation ... when one ... imagines [Indians] as they might in future be seen, ... preserved in their pristine beauty and wildness, in a magnificent park, where the world could see for ages to come, the native Indian in his classic attire, galloping his wild horse ... amid the fleeting herds of elks and buffaloes. What a beautiful and thrilling specimen for America to preserve and hold up to the view of her refined citizens and the world, in future ages! A nation's Park, containing man and beast, in all the wild and freshness of their nature's beauty![51]

The point to be emphasized here is that Catlin's national park is not just a space of Otherness, of subversive savagery, that has been removed beyond the borders of the new nation; on the contrary, the live wreck of the Indian, forever stuck in the repetition of the same scenic moment, provides the *complementary myth of timelessness* that is necessary for the colonial subject to manifest himself so squarely and fatefully *in* and *of* time. "Indian ghosts" and "American subjects" are not pregiven, discrete entities engaged in a struggle for repression and spectral return; they are mutually *co*produced myths, each needing the screen of the other in order to secure the illusion of their own coherent self-identity. To describe their relationship visually, we might think again about the famous image of the Rubin Vase, where the contours of one image help to establish the outline of the other image, but only at the cost of the other's total occlusion. We get the sense of two discrete images—of a vase and two faces—but we can never hold both of these images in focus at the same time.

As mutual participants in the ideological myth of an Enlightened, American subject, Indians are not removed to a subversive region beyond the proper borders of the emerging U.S. nation. They are ruined and occluded into the very heart of its political and natural topography, as inclusive exceptions that help to generate the myth, the possibility of "national" space and common time. Our own national parks have inherited this same temporal topography, as evidenced by the rhetoric of the 1964 Wilderness Act:

> A wilderness, in contrast with those areas where man and his own works dominate the landscape, is hereby recognized as an area where the earth and its community of life are untrammeled by man, where man himself is a visitor *who does not remain.* An area of wilderness is further defined to mean in this Act an area of undeveloped Federal land retaining its *primeval* character and influence, without permanent improvements or

human habitation, which is protected and managed so as to preserve its natural conditions and which (1) generally appears to have been affected primarily by the forces of nature, with the imprint of man's work substantially unnoticeable; (2) has outstanding opportunities for solitude or a *primitive* and unconfined type of recreation.[52]

In order for the idea of a "primitive" and wild spatiality to emerge, what must be occluded and ruined is the presence of the civilized human. As a space in which "man himself is a visitor who does not remain," we can see that this process of occlusion helps to articulate the idea of two different, yet intimately related, concepts of presence and temporal experience: the timeless "primeval" state of wilderness and the always timely "imprint" of "man's" worldly "work."

THE EVENTNESS OF EXPERIENCE IN *A TOUR ON THE PRAIRIES*

In the literature of the early republic, the mutuality of these myths of timely, national progress and time*less*, primeval stasis is, as we have already seen, most famously expressed in Washington Irving's "Rip Van Winkle." After all, what transforms Rip from a peripheral figure of his prerevolutionary Dutch community into an indispensable member of the modern American nation is precisely the timeless hiatus that he installs at the heart of its memory. In order for the nation to emerge—and for Rip to become the archetypal modern historian—he does not so much sleep *through* history as he does provide it with the necessary myth of an occluded, ruined temporality, a timeless space, that makes possible the idea of history and time as a flowing thing, as a fateful property of experience. I will proceed by exploring how these themes of hiatus and removal continue to shape Irving's later frontier fiction by helping him to negotiate his encounters with the live wreck of the Indian.

In 1832, after spending seventeen years in Europe, Washington Irving returned to his native soil. While Irving had been traveling in Europe and writing about Germany, England, and Spain, his American audience had begun to wonder whether they had lost their favorite literary son. Faced with these doubts, Irving was eager to reinvigorate the Americanness of his authorial persona and his literary production. "Thus," as Richard Batman observes, "when [Irving] returned to America. . ., he seemed determined to see as much of his native country as possible and to sink roots once again into its soil."[53] In his two-volume biography of the author, *The Life of Washington Irving*, Stanley T. Williams contextualizes Irving's return to the United States as follows:

> Frontier posts, now within easy reach, Indian tribes, new laws, new cities, new harbors—everywhere was the turmoil of a self-confident, eager nation, with an optimism based upon a consciousness of almost illimitable resources.... The first years of his return marked the real beginning of the growth of the railway systems. All this [Irving's friends] and his brothers had attempted to describe by letter; his visitors at London and Madrid had pictured faintly this millennium of Mammon; but only now could he credit the gigantic nature of the American enterprise.[54]

"[T]he power of these nationalistic... forces," continues Williams, "was in [Irving's] mind in the spring of 1832."[55] With notebook in hand, Irving immediately made several excursions—to the Catskills and to Niagara Falls—and, after a chance meeting with Henry Leavitt Ellsworth aboard a steamer bound for Detroit, quickly made plans to visit the western frontier, Indian Territory, with him. What better place to witness the self-confidence of this "eager nation"? Anticipating the language of Catlin's "nation's Park," Irving admits that Ellsworth's "offer was too tempting to be resisted. I should have an opportunity of seeing the remnants of those great Indian Tribes, which are now about to disappear as independent nations.... I should see those fine countries of the 'far west,' while still in a state of pristine wildness, and behold herds of buffaloes scouring their native prairies, before they are driven beyond the reach of a civilized tourist."[56] Ellsworth had recently been appointed a commissioner of the newly formed Board of Indian Affairs. With the passage of the Indian Removal Act, Jackson's government was now committed to removing those Native American nations who lived on valuable eastern lands to "Indian Territory," west of the Mississippi. In particular, the so-called "Five Civilized Tribes"—the Cherokee, Choctaw, Chickasaw, Creek, and Seminole—were urged to leave their homelands and to make new lives on the western prairies. Needless to say, these relocations made for extremely strained relations between Indian nations in Indian Territory and also between Indian nations and the numerous white squatters who had settled on the lands now set aside for these removals. As Native Americans were removed to Indian Territory, the struggle for rights to hunting grounds,

Event/Hiatus 149

not to mention the struggle for land itself, fueled rivalries between nations. In order to help keep the peace, President Jackson arranged for the commissioners of the Board of Indian Affairs to travel to Indian Territory. And so Ellsworth, with Irving in tow, headed to the western frontier "to study the country, to mark the boundaries, to pacify the warring Indians, and, in general, to establish order and justice."[57]

In his own account of the 1832 tour, *Washington Irving on the Prairie*, Ellsworth praises Irving's "microscopic eye [that watches] the hidden wheels that move men along, on the common walks of life."[58] According to Ellsworth, Irving's "microscopic eye" is avowedly apolitical: the political mechanisms that might move the "hidden wheels" of common life are, apparently, off-limits for Irving: "He dislikes political or polemic discussions," Ellsworth insists (71). But separating aesthetics from politics is never that easy in *A Tour on the Prairies*. Indeed, as Ellsworth himself reminds us, after Colonel Samuel E. Stambaugh—commander of the Menominee in the Black Hawk War—failed to show up in time to Ellsworth's party, the secretary of war, Lewis Cass, appointed Irving as secretary and enlisted his "microscopic eye" to help record the details of their military tour. "Although . . . he will refuse the compe[n]sation of a regular Secreetary [sic] ($5 a day)," Ellsworth notes, "still, he will permit me to remunerate him for some losses which he has sustained, and may sustain in the excursion" (9). The "hidden wheels" of Irving's aesthetic tour are, then, nudged along by the secretary of war's coffers.

When Irving was working on the materials that were later published in *The Sketch-Book*, Indian removal was just beginning to emerge as a viable solution to the "Indian Problem." Resigned to what they perceived as the inevitable reality of colonial dispossession, Native American nations that remained in the East, and certain factions within those nations, often opted to sell portions of their territory in return for land west of the Mississippi. This relatively peaceful Native American exodus posed no direct threat to the "discourse of noble savagery"; on the contrary, voluntary relocations helped fuel the image of a tragic race destined to extinction. However, when Irving returned to the United States from Europe in 1832, Native American nations were actively resisting removal. For example, in 1832 the Cherokee sought, and won, a Supreme Court injunction (*Worcester v. Georgia*) against the State of Georgia, which was insisting that the Cherokee leave their gold-rich homelands. President Jackson ignored the Supreme Court decision and insisted that the removals were now to be enforced whether the Native American nations were willing to be dispossessed of their land or not. The heated political and juridical debates surrounding such policies captured the attention of the nation. Indeed, as Michael Paul Rogin observes:

> Andrew Jackson wrote after he left the Presidency [that Indian removal] was the "most arduous part of my duty, and I watched over it with great vigilance." The Indian-removal bill, Alabama Congressman Dixon Lewis maintained, was "known as the leading measure" of the Jackson administration. Massachusetts Congressman Edward Everett called it "the greatest question that ever came before Congress, short of the question of peace and war."[59]

We have already seen how *The Sketch-Book* opens by formalizing an aesthetics of hiatus and by celebrating voyages of removal and dispossession. These severed "fragment[s] of a world" help bring into mournful relief a "lengthening chain" connecting the artist, both in space and time, to his homeland. *A Tour on the Prairies* begins by revisiting this same transatlantic voyage. "As I saw the last blue line of my native land fade away, like a cloud in the horizon," Irving writes, "it seemed as if I had closed one volume of the world and its concerns, and had time for meditation, before I opened another. That land, too, now vanishing from my view, which contained all that was most dear to me in life; what vicissitudes might occur in it—what changes might take place in me before I should visit it again!"[60]

Dispossessed of "all that was most dear to" him, the narrative that follows constitutes Irving's rebirth as an American and as an American artist.[61] Indeed, the author encourages us to read his return to the new nation as a repetition of Rip Van Winkle's rude awakening in the Catskills. "I passed through places that ought to be familiar to me, but all were changed," observes Irving.[62]

> Huge edifices and lofty piles had sprung up in the place of lowly tenements; the old landmarks of the city were gone; the very streets were altered.
>
> As I passed on, I looked wistfully in every face: not one was known to me—not one! Yet I was in haunts where every visage was once familiar to me. I read the names over the doors: all were new. They were

Event/Hiatus 151

unassociated with any early recollection. The saddening conviction stole over my heart that I was a stranger in my own home! (7)

If history is nothing more than a space to be filled or a record of events to be chronicled, then Irving's task in *A Tour on the Prairies* appears quite straightforward: he must atone for his European hiatus by bringing himself (and his readership) up to speed with developments on the frontier. But again and again, the relationship between narrator and event—between experience and its registration—proves extremely vexed. As several critics of the text have noted, Irving's *Tour* is perhaps most notable for the near-misses and notable absences that pattern its pages. As Mark K. Burns notes:

> Irving's party will encounter none of [the traditional] components of the frontier in quite the way the text foreshadows: the promised Native tribes will be nearly impossible to meet in spite of the many clear signs of their presence throughout this territory; the prairie will prove to be far more monotonous and difficult a terrain than it at first appears; and the animals spread throughout the frontier will be more elusive, and hunting them will prove less stimulating than the men first suppose.[63]

A Tour on the Prairies, then, is neither an explicit epic of noble savagery nor a drama of frontier warfare: the only danger of Indian attack, for example, comes when Irving's party mistakes its own scouts for fierce Pawnee raiders. Indeed, as critics of the time noted, very little happens in the narrative: it is as if the hiatus has come to dominate even the economy of plot in Irving's romance. In its July 1835 review of Irving's text, the *North American Quarterly* admitted that the *Tour* "can scarcely be called a book of travels, for there is too much painting of manners and scenery, and too little statistics;—it is not a novel, because there is no story; and it is not a romance, for it is all true."[64] Burns concludes that such "absences, near-misses, delays, and disappointments [force] the text's characters as well as the reader to reconsider, perhaps, the easy transparent manner in which the American frontier was often thought to reveal itself and its significance."[65] But as our reading of *The Sketch-Book* discovered, absence, hiatus, and removal are all names for a formal aesthetic program in Irving's work, not just symbolic tropes that are deployed to various ends with varying "significance." To be sure, Irving's aesthetics of hiatus is concerned with modernity and the author's relationship to its spatial and temporal "frontier[s]." However, this aesthetic program does not simply or symbolically reflect back on a pregiven subject fatefully adrift in the age of the new: it also *coproduces* the illusion of these separate spheres and different temporalities. Rip misses the American Revolution not because he sleeps through it but, rather, because his timeless hiatus establishes the natural flow of the nation and its historical events; so too, Irving will fail to capture events on the frontier not because his party just misses them but, paradoxically, because he is looking too hard for them—because he is looking for the "it," the eventness of experience that his out-of-jointedness and ruined occlusion from the temporal have made visible, tangible.

What Irving does find on the prairies illustrates the way in which the symbolic content of his fiction supplements its formal aesthetic patterns of hiatus and dispossession. After his month-long tour of Indian Territory with Ellsworth had been completed, Irving decided to head for New Orleans. On board the Mississippi river steamboat *Little Rock*, he happened to meet John James Audubon, the naturalist and ornithologist who would later become famous for his artistic catalogues of North American bird life.[66] This chance meeting turned into a friendship that would last for years; indeed, Irving would later use his political connections to help further Audubon's career, writing, for example, an 1836 letter that introduced Audubon to the future president, Martin Van Buren.[67] But the influence ran both ways. Over the next two years, Irving reworked the journal entries from his tour of Indian Territory, paying special attention to his own representations of the natural world. By the time he finished *A Tour on the Prairies*, he had developed an intricate network of symbols that further deflected the violence attending the nation's Indian removal policies. Like Irving's frontier hybrids—whose bodies and blood bare the tension "between civilized and savage life, . . . light and darkness"—the prairie landscape was also redrawn in order to justify westward expansion and to help recode the violence of Indian removal. Richard Slotkin argues in *Gunfighter Nation* that "what is distinctively 'American' is not necessarily the amount or kind of violence that characterizes our history but the mythic significance we have assigned to the kinds of violence we have actually experienced, the forms of symbolic violence we imagine or invent, and the political uses to which we put that symbolism."[68] Irving's aesthetic approach to the natural world recodes the material and political violence associated with Indian removal and, by extension, with Ellsworth's tour; *A Tour on the Prairies* writes its own richly symbolic natural history.

When Irving writes about his first encounter with a wild horse—the "first time I had ever seen a horse scouring his native wilderness in all the pride and freedom of his nature"—he also observes how different these horses are "from the poor, mutilated, harnessed, checked, reined-up victim of luxury, caprice and avarice, in our cities!" (114). However, like the decaying spectacle of the noble savage, the inexorable encroachment of civilization signals the end for these wild horses, too. In his description of how the company's scout, Beatte, tames a wild horse, Irving uses this symbolism to encode the violence of the civilizing movement:

> The native pride and independence of the animal took fire at this indignity. He reared, and plunged, and kicked, and tried in every way to get rid of the degrading burden. The Indian was too potent for him. At every paroxysm he renewed the discipline of the halter, until the poor animal, driven to despair, threw himself prostrate on the ground, and lay motionless, as if acknowledging himself vanquished. A stage hero, representing the despair of a captive prince, could not have played his part more dramatically. There was absolutely a moral grandeur in it. . . .
>
> I could not but look with compassion upon this fine young animal, whose whole course of existence had been so suddenly reversed. From being a denizen of these vast pastures, ranging at will from plain to plain and mead to mead, . . . he was suddenly reduced to perpetual and painful servitude, to pass his life under the harness and the curb, amid, perhaps, the din and dust and drudgery of the cities. The transition in his lot was such as sometimes takes place in human affairs, and in the fortunes of towering individuals:—one day, a prince of the prairies— the next day, a pack horse! (121–22)

In this scene of symbolic dispossession, the violence of colonization is naturalized and encoded so that the "transition . . . in human affairs" forced upon the Native American nations can now be read as a theatrical drama possessing "absolutely a moral grandeur." Irving casts Beatte in the leading role of his drama—a "stage hero" who, despite his mixed Native American and European heritage, is fashioned in this text as the ultimate "Indian"—so that the violence of Indian removal is deflected even further: we watch as

Irving's putative "Indian" reduces the noble horse to "perpetual and painful servitude." Irving's clever manipulation of the discourse of noble savagery reverses the colonial dynamic so that it is the Native American who actively enslaves and tames what has, until recently, roamed free on the prairies. But at the same time as Irving recodes the violence of colonial contact, he also reinscribes this violence within the inexorable civilizing movement westward: the "drudgery of the cities" awaits the "native pride and independence" of the noble wild horse, much as the reservation awaits the noble savage. While Irving's sketch certainly elicits sympathy for the wild horse and his ignoble fate, the spectacle, the "moral grandeur," of the drama—the advancing of the frontier—more than compensates for the unfortunate corollaries of colonial expansion. And we watch as even the noble savage participates in this ineluctable and natural drama of captivity and dispossession.

This symbolic system is later utilized and reinforced by Irving when he describes a potentially awkward conversation he has with Beatte about the realities of Indian removal:

> When [Beatte] talked to me of the wrongs and insults that the poor Indians suffered in their intercourse with the rough settlers on the frontiers: when he described the precarious and degraded state of the Osage tribe, diminished in numbers, broken in spirit, and almost living on sufferance in the land where they once figured so heroically, I could see his veins swell, and his nostrils distend with indignation; but he would check the feeling with a strong exertion of Indian self-command, and, in a manner, drive it back into his bosom. (162)

Here Irving inverts the drama of the previous horse taming scene and casts Beatte as the once-wild horse with "veins swell[ing]" and "nostrils distend[ing]." "Dying Indians," as Michael Rogin comments, "betrayed whites. They threatened to force them to encounter the consequences of their own policies and desires" (243). But in this scene with Beatte, *A Tour on the Prairies* plays on the nobility of the savage in order to sidestep the "consequences" of the "encounter." Although Irving's representation of noble savagery is, like his description of the "rabble rout" at the Osage Agency, mediated somewhat by the "precarious and degraded state of the Osage tribe," the author nevertheless paints a picture of a proud animal swallowing his pride and accepting his inexorable fate as a dying Indian.

The carefully wrought description of the "Republic of Prairie Dogs" in chapter 32 of *A Tour on the Prairies* similarly demonstrates how removal and dispossession operate as aesthetic principles of the text. As Irving began his tour in 1832, the Cherokee were engaged in a series of Supreme Court cases—*Cherokee Nation v. Georgia* (1830) and *Worcester v. Georgia* (1832)—that caught the nation's attention. In *Worcester v. Georgia*, Chief Justice John Marshall ruled that Georgia had no jurisdiction over the Cherokee Nation—a decision that allayed Cherokee fears of a forced removal to Indian Territory. Marshall's decision turned on his belief that the "Cherokee nation... is a distinct community, occupying its own territory, with boundaries accurately described, in which the laws of Georgia can have no force."[69] In the 1820s, the Cherokee had worked hard to establish the forms of "civilization" held up to them as necessary for an independent nation. In addition to publishing the first Native American newspaper, the *Cherokee Phoenix* (1828–32), the Cherokee also created their own written language and adopted their own constitution. However, President Andrew Jackson, a firm advocate of states' rights, chose to ignore the Supreme Court's ruling. "The decision of the Supreme Court has fell still born," Jackson claimed. "The arm of the government is not sufficiently strong to preserve [the Indians] from destruction" (qtd. in Rogin 218).

Irving's "Republic of Prairie Dogs" allegorizes the Cherokee cases and the politics of Indian removal. Like the noble savage and the new Cherokee system of government, the "prairie dog is one of the curiosities of the Far West, about which travellers delight to tell marvellous tales, endowing him at times with something of the politic and social habits of a rational being, and giving him systems of government and domestic economy" (189). And in an echo of his earlier description of the gossiping Indians, Irving "could not help picturing to [himself] the inhabitants gathered together in noisy assemblage and windy debate, to devise plans for the public safety, and to vindicate the invaded rights and insulted dignity of the republic" (192). In the same way that Irving naturalizes the violence of colonial expansion in the "moral grandeur" of the horse-taming scene, here the removal of Native Americans and their pseudo-rational political and social organizations is effected symbolically through the author's representation of the perpetually invaded "Republic of Prairie Dogs." Indeed, Irving insists that these "politic animals" possess "moral attributes," further developing his own symbolic system of discursive dispossessions (192). Rather than acknowledge the role that Ellsworth and his company of Rangers were playing in the removal of Native Americans, Irving's gaze instead converts the violence of the removal program into a drama rooted in the natural world. From this narrative perspective, Ellsworth's company is portrayed as an invading and dispossessing force; but the arena of conflict is so far removed from the politics of U.S. colonial expansion as to be rendered benign: as the author approaches this "village," he notes that "it had been invaded in the course of the day by some of the rangers, who had shot two or three of its inhabitants, and thrown the whole sensitive community in confusion" (191).[70]

Wild bees, as well as prairie dogs, are victims of similarly inscrutable forces of dispossession and removal.[71] In another scene of "moral grandeur," Irving recodes the politics of colonial expansion into yet another romantic scene that naturalizes the violence of forced relocation. The first step in this aesthetic process involves associating the wild bees with westward expansion:

> The Indians consider [the bees] the harbinger of the white man, as the buffalo is of the red man; and say that, in proportion as the bee advances, the Indian and buffalo retire. . . . I am told that the wild bee is seldom to be met with at any great distance from the frontier. They have been the heralds of civilization, steadfastly preceding it as it advanced from the Atlantic borders. . . .
>
> At present the honey-bee swarms in myriads, in the noble groves and forests which skirt and intersect the prairies. . . . It seems to me as if these beautiful regions answer literally to the description of the land of promise, "a land flowing with milk and honey." (51)

Like the invasion of the prairie-dog village, Irving's depiction of the "Bee Hunt" displaces the violence associated with dispossession onto the natural world: "Nor was it the bee-hunters alone that profited by the downfall of this industrious community," Irving observes.

> I beheld numbers from rival hives, arriving on eager wing, to enrich themselves with the ruins of their neighbors. These busied themselves as eagerly and cheerfully as so many wreckers on an Indiaman that has been driven on shore. . . . It is difficult to describe the bewilderment and confusion of the bees of the bankrupt hive who had been absent at the

Event/Hiatus 157

time of the catastrophe.... At first they wheeled about in the air, in the place where the fallen tree had once reared its head, astonished at finding it all a vacuum. At length, as if comprehending their disaster, they settled down in clusters on a dry branch of a neighboring tree, whence they seemed to contemplate the prostrate ruin, and to buzz forth doleful lamentations over the downfall of their republic. (53)

It is tempting to read such moments in the text as thinly veiled symbolic allusions to the fate of Native Americans under Jackson's removal programs. But what links Irving's "Republic of Prairie Dogs" with the "downfall" of the republic of wild bees is *not* some knowable, factual event—the violence of Indian removal, for example—that has to be repressed and disguised by the text. On the contrary, what is repeatedly revisited is the traumatic hiatus, the absence "at the time of catastrophe" that destins these republics to ruin.

"The experience of trauma," argues Cathy Caruth, consists "not in the forgetting of a reality that can hence never be fully known, but in an inherent latency within the experience itself. The historical power of the trauma is not just that the experience is repeated after its forgetting, but that it is only in and through its inherent forgetting that it is first experienced at all" (17). What returns to haunt Irving's text, then, is not some repressed memory or displaced symbol of a specific, given event but, rather, the traumatic fact that, within the fateful flow of colonial time, subject and event are always *non*coincident, forever separated by the same vacuum, the same ruined hiatus responsible for producing the strange idea of a temporal property, a manifest destiny, that can be *owned by* the subject.

POE AND THE "AIR DISTINGUÉ" OF IMPERIAL MODERNITY

In his putative travel narrative set in the American West, "The Journal of Julius Rodman" (1840), Edgar Allan Poe draws on the numerous romantic histories of his age that glorified westward expansion. In particular, he looks to Washington Irving's recent work on the West—*A Tour on the Prairies* (1835), *The Adventures of Captain Bonneville* (1837), and *Astoria* (1836), Irving's history of John Jacob Astor's fur enterprise in the Pacific Northwest. In his 1837 *Southern Literary Messenger* review of *Astoria*, Poe praises the "masterly manner ... with which a long and entangled series of detail ... has been wrought into completeness and unity."[72] "No details more intensely exciting," Poe insists, "are to be found in any work of travels within our knowledge."[73] In "Julius Rodman," Poe lifts many of these details straight from the pages of Irving's western works—a practice that he also employs in his enigmatic 1838 novel *The Narrative of Arthur Gordon Pym*. Like *Pym*, however, "Julius Rodman" lays bare the aesthetic mechanisms shared in common by Irving's historical romances and the political discourses of colonial expansion and Indian removal.

As we have seen, by transforming dispossession and removal into aesthetic principles, Irving's works often mask the violence attending westward expansion. Poe challenges the symbolic logic underpinning Irving's strategy by bringing attention to these aesthetic devices. In place of Irving's discriminating eye for distinction and taxonomy, Poe's narrators instead bring forward the artificiality of such classificatory enterprises. "The line which demarcates the instinct of the brute creation from the boasted reason of man," argues Poe in another story he composed in the late 1830s, "is, beyond doubt, of the most shadowy and unsatisfactory character—a boundary line far more difficult to settle than even the North-Eastern or the Oregon."[74] Here Poe draws our attention, albeit tacitly, to another racial fiction—the superiority of European civility and reason—that undergirds U.S. colonial expansion.[75] And in "Julius Rodman," Poe emphasizes, rather than masks, the connection between the aesthetics of the symbol and the violence of colonial expansion. Consider, for example, his description of a potentially dangerous confrontation between U.S. explorers and Sioux Indians—a confrontation that revolves around the explorers' "medicine," their howitzer cannon:

> I determined to assume a bold stand, and rather provoke hostilities than avoid them. *This was our true policy.* The savages has no fire arms which we could discover.... Their position was one which would expose them to the full sweep of our cannon.
>
> [T]he [Indian's] interpreter spoke again [asked] whether our great medicine was not a very large and strong green grasshopper.... Jules replied ... that it was a good thing for them (the Sioux) that our great medicine had not overheard their last query, respecting the "large green grasshopper;" for, in that case, it might have gone very hard with them (the Sioux). Our great medicine was anything but a large green grasshopper, and *that* they should soon see, to their cost, if they did

Event/Hiatus 159

> not immediately go, the whole of them, about their business.... As soon as a good opportunity presented itself, the word was given to fire, and instantly obeyed. The effect of the discharge was very severe, and answered all our purposes to the full. Six of the Indians were killed, and perhaps three times as many badly wounded.[76]

While Irving's frontier romance recodes the politics of colonial expansion by occluding it—as removal, hiatus, and dispossession—into the very heart of its symbolic systems, Poe instead lays bare the violence of this aesthetic process by unveiling the hidden signifier that provides it with such compelling authority: the howitzer cannon.

Published in the August 1839 edition of *Burton's Magazine*, "The Man That Was Used Up: A Tale of the Late Bugaboo and Kickapoo Campaign" similarly unmasks the aesthetic mechanisms that undergird westward expansion. The story begins by introducing us to a narrator obsessed with uncovering what is so "*remarkable*" about "Brevet Brigadier General John A. B. C. Smith." Smith, we are told, is

> six feet in height, and of a presence singularly commanding. There was an *air distingué* pervading the whole man, which spoke of high breeding, and hinted at high birth.... The bust of the General was unquestionably the finest bust I ever saw. For your life you could not have found a fault with its wonderful proportion.... I wish to God, my young and talented friend Chiponchipino, the sculptor, had but seen the legs of Brevet Brigadier General John A. B. C. Smith.... There was a primness, not to say stiffness, in his manner—a degree of measured, and if I may so express it, of rectangular precision, attending his every movement.... He was a *remarkable* man—a *very* remarkable man—indeed one of the *most* remarkable men of the age. He was an especial favorite, too, with the ladies—chiefly on account of his high reputation for courage.[77]

Despite the narrator's keen eye for physical detail and social prestige, he is still incapable of remembering how the general earned his "high reputation for courage." Indeed, the story is marked by both the narrator's and his "age's" incapacity to remember and articulate history. The story begins with the narrator's admission that he "cannot just now remember when or where I first made the acquaintance of" the general, and his quest to uncover this history is endlessly frustrated and deferred by the various socialites he encounters on his travels. Several critics have noted that Poe's attention to the intricacies of fashion and taste should be read as a satirical critique of the emerging "polite" society of the 1830s. Joan Tyler Mead, for example, argues that Poe "heavy-handedly excoriates the American polite society of his day,"[78] and for Ronald Curran, the general "reflects the imitative vision of this time and place: a perfectly fashionable copy, yet worn out, beaten, defeated, and dead—a 'used up' man."[79] What I am interested in here, however, is how the society that Poe depicts fosters a strategic forgetting of General Smith's disastrous "swamp-fight away down south, with the Bugaboo and Kickapoo Indians" (67).

As we follow the narrator on his quest to uncover the history behind the general's *"remarkable"* reputation, we are inducted into the key rituals of "polite society." As Curran notes, the narrator's quest involves his passing "through a rite of initiation made up of visits to the major social rites of early nineteenth-century eastern American society—Church, Theater, Card Party, and Ball." Unfortunately for the irascible narrator—who is put into a "pitiable state of agitation" whenever there is "the slightest appearance of mystery" (66)—just as his informants are about to divulge the specifics of the general's *"prodigies* of valor" they are immediately interrupted by another eager participant in the social gathering. The pattern of these encounters is similar throughout the story: the informants make it a point to vent their surprise that the narrator knows nothing about the general's past, and then they proceed to wax lyrical about Smith's valor and the "wonderfully inventive age" that produces "parachutes and rail-roads—man-traps and spring guns!" (67). We also become gradually aware of a "horrid affair" that is somehow connected to "savage" Indian "wretches" and a "tremendous swamp-fight away down south." However, it is at this moment that the informants are always interrupted: "'Smith?—O yes! great man!—perfect desperado—immortal renown—prodigies of valor! *Never heard!!* (This was given in a scream.) Bless my soul!—why he's the man'—" (68). Not surprisingly, these frustrating encounters force the narrator to visit the "fountain head": "I would call forthwith upon the General himself, and demand, in explicit terms, a solution of this abominable piece of mystery" (69). But the narrator's fascinating final encounter with the general reveals more to him than he is ready to know: instead of finding the general and his celebrated panoply of physical attributes and distinctive voice, the narrator stumbles across a bundle of clothes that, much to his surprise, speaks to him in "one of the smallest, the weakest, and altogether the funniest little voices, between a squeak and a whistle" (69). This squeaking mass of clothes, we find out, is nothing less than the general himself—a fact that his slave, Pompey, is only too eager to point out:[80]

> "He! he! he! he-aw! he-aw! he-aw!" cachinnated that delectable specimen of the human family, with his mouth fairly extended from ear to ear, and with his forefinger held up close to his face, and levelled at the object of my apprehension, as if he were taking aim at it with a pistol.
> "He! he! he! he-aw! he-aw! he-aw!—what, you want Mass Smif? Why dar's him!" (69)

Pompey proceeds to reconstruct the general, marvelous limb by marvelous limb, until his palate and eyes have been installed. Finally, the narrator—much-disturbed by the proceedings—finds out that Smith was "used up" like this in an Indian campaign and abruptly leaves the general "with a perfect understanding of the state of affairs—with a full comprehension of the mystery which had troubled [him] so long" (70).

As Curran and Mead have noted, the conclusion to the story reveals that "The hero is a fitting image of the smug and pretentious society which espouses hollow values" (Mead 281): "In Poe's humorous tale the General as automaton not only amounts to a fitting 'hero' to lionize but also a perfect vehicle through which to satirize an imitative people in the wonderful age of invention" (Curran 19). However, it is also possible to read the story as an allegory of the emerging nation—as fiction that uncovers and remembers what is erased and left unspoken as Jacksonian democracy marches onward. As Colin Dayan points out, read through the eyes of Pompey the story deconstructs the myths of white masculinity on which the nation is founded:

> [E]ven though Poe used racist stereotypes in stories like "The Man That was Used Up". . . he exercised these images in order to tell another story. . . . Not only does Poe describe the dismemberment and redemption of Brigadier General John A. B. C. Smith, but he writes the "other" into the white hero's tale, putting those called "savages" or "things" into the myth of Anglo-Saxon America. Reduced to "an odd looking bundle of something" by the Bugaboo and Kickapoo Indians in a "tremendous swamp-fight away down South" (doubtless, an illusion to the Dismal Swamp), the General is put together every morning by Pompey, his black

valet. With each successive body part replaced, the General regains the voice of the consummate Southern gentleman while remaining utterly dependent on the "old negro" he debases.[81]

However, by reading General Smith and his Bugaboo and Kickapoo campaigns in the context of the forced relocation of Native Americans during the 1830s, Poe's tale can also be read as a complex reflection on the place of dispossession, hiatus, and removal in the emerging U.S. nation.

With the exception of Curran's and Mead's discussions of Poe's satirical attack on the "Fashionable Thirties," critics have paid little attention to "The Man That Was Used Up." The story most often surfaces in debates concerning the "true" identity of Brevet Brigadier General A. B. C. Smith. Ortwin de Graef notes that critics often "read the story as a kind of *histoire à clef*, and then exert themselves to convince us that their particular key is the right one."[82] I agree with de Graef and Curran that "[s]pecific identification of General Smith becomes a fruitless task" (Curran 19), but in order to situate the text historically it is important to discuss how the text fashions the general. The text itself encourages us to read Smith as a representation of the "age of invention" or, perhaps, as a metaphor for "the class of brevet generals lionized by title-happy American society" (Curran 19). Nevertheless, it is interesting that Poe chose a "used up" Indian fighter to represent and satirize his "age" and his "society." Indeed, it is hard to disagree with the arguments made by Richard Alekna and Daniel Hoffman that Poe's General Smith would have reminded his readers of Brevet Brigadier General Winfield Scott.[83] Aside from their similarities in military rank, Scott, like Smith, possessed a tall and imposing figure,[84] was "popular with the ladies," and was "as vain and egotistic as Poe's character."[85] Scott was also, according to his aide Erasmus Darwin Keyes, dependent on his black servant: "He [Scott] required to be waited upon, to be observed, and to be attended without intermission, and his body servant was to be always within call. He occasionally excused himself for this last necessity from the fact that his left arm was partially disabled by a terrible wound he received at Lundy's Lane."[86] Alekna also notes that Poe's reference to the "Bugaboo and Kickapoo Campaign" brings to mind the Black Hawk War (1832–37), where Scott was to have faced the Kickapoo. However, as Alekna reminds us, this "War ended before his arrival."[87]

A vital connection between Scott and Smith—a connection that Poe scholars have ignored[88]—is that Scott's Indian campaigns and the forced removal of the Cherokee that he commanded, like Smith's "Late Bugaboo and Kickapoo Campaign," were very much in the news in the late 1830s. Critics who want to read Poe's 1839 story as a "satire of the virility of the brevet generals lionized by title-happy society" (Curran 19) forget that the brevet general most closely connected with Indian warfare in the late 1830s was anything but "the all-admired hero of the day."[89]

The year 1836 was one of Winfield Scott's longest. In January, at the time Scott assumed command of U.S. forces in the Second Seminole War, the general "ranked among the greatest military leaders in America."[90] However, by the end of the year he would appear at a military court of inquiry, charged by Brevet Major General Edmund Pendleton Gaines as "the second United States general officer who has ever dared to aid and assist the open enemy."[91] That the War Department ordered Scott to take charge in Florida illustrated the severity of the situation in the Everglades. Hostilities between the United States and the Seminole officially began in December 1835, "when the Seminole committed a series of widely separated assaults upon the whites throughout Florida, actions so well timed that they could not have been happenstance."[92] However, the Second Seminole War must be seen as one episode of an ongoing history of conflict between the United States and the Seminole. Other important episodes in this history include Andrew Jackson's infamous 1819 foray into Spanish Florida, ostensibly to chastise the Seminole for their continued alliances with the English and escaped U.S. slaves—an event that came to be known as the First Seminole War. Jackson, who believed that President Monroe's orders "included driving Spain out of Florida, burned Indian villages, captured and executed two British citizens, and occupied the Spanish settlements of St. Marks and Pensacola."[93] The United States quickly began to accumulate Seminole land: in the Treaty of Moultrie Creek (1823), for example, the Seminole "ceded over twenty-eight million acres to the United States while retaining only four million for themselves."[94] The 1830s saw a new approach to the Indian problem, and encouraged by Jackson's Indian removal policies, the Seminole signed the controversial Treaty of Fort Gibson in 1833. According to this treaty, which some of the Seminole chiefs later denied signing, the Seminole agreed to migrate to Arkansas where they would become part of the Creek Nation.[95] Over the next two years, resistance to removal began to grow among the Seminole; the well-orchestrated Seminole attacks that initiated the Second Seminole War made clear what the United States had feared for many years: the Seminole would physically resist removal to Indian territory.

Winfield Scott was ordered to take over command in Florida after the War Department heard about the four U.S. soldiers killed and the fifty-seven wounded at the Battle of Withlacoochee.[96] Scott, who "was thoroughly steeped in European methods of warfare,"[97] decided to attack the Seminole with "the standard three-prong pincer movement that the old army always seemed to favor. Although the movement was highly efficient when everything operated like clockwork and the Indians fought like white men, unfortunately this rarely if ever occurred."[98] Scott's plans failed largely because, as Mahon notes, the "theater of conflict, the Territory of Florida, was itself a mystery.... Aside from a few points along the coast and fewer still in the interior, it was scarcely better known than Africa. No white man had seen the greater part of its 58,560 square miles, nor did anyone then know its area."[99] In addition to this vague and troubling topography, Scott's military rival, General Gaines, took it upon himself to venture to Florida with his own troops and, in so doing, disrupted Scott's plans. Instead of forcing the Seminole into the grip of their pincers, Scott's forces—hungry and plagued with mumps and measles—lunged erratically at their enemy. The net result, as Scott's report to the adjutant general made clear, was that the three wings of his attack "had converged . . . not because of instructions but because they had run out of supplies. The grand campaign had not resulted in the death of as many as sixty Indians, he admitted, and now the hostiles were split up into bands, none larger than two hundred persons."[100]

The failure of this campaign set the scene for the remainder of the war. The Seminoles retreated into the swamp and waged a guerrilla war that would end up costing the United States more than $40 million—approximately ten times the amount that had originally been set aside for Indian removal. "Of about 600 commissioned officers in the army at the start of the War in 1835," Walton notes, "sixty-four died during the conflict and many times that number resigned."[101] Not surprisingly, Scott was attacked in many newspapers and even burned in effigy by angry Floridians:[102]

> Army failures made the conflict "a disgraceful war to the american character," Jackson wrote after he left office. . . . He complained that General Scott's "combined operations [tried] to encompass a wolf in the hammocks without knowing first where her den and whelps were."[103]

But what effect did this have on the consciousness of the emerging nation? Once again, the nation's Indian removal policies could proceed only to the extent that the populace was willing to exercise its capacity to forget: "In 1835 a mere handful in the Congress opposed the Florida conflict as a war of aggression.... As the War continued, as the cost in dollars and men soared, more and more... reversed their positions. When the War ended, few of our political leaders would admit that they had once supported the conflict."[104]

In "The Man That Was Used Up," Poe shows how these failures of national memory—how these forgetful hiatuses and myopic occlusions—literally give voice to the emerging U.S. nation and its colonial politics of expansion. With the savage cachinnations of Pompey, Poe brings forward the mutual processes of dispossession and appearance—of rearticulation and disarticulation—that lend the general and his "prodigies of valor" such a distinguished voice.[105] As if commenting on the detached narrator of Andrew Jackson's first speech to Congress, Poe's Pompey reminds us that such a position of enunciation, of colonial articulation is itself articulated and put together by the sound of *another* voice. If the general has come to embody the detached objectivity of the colonial voice, then Pompey is a slave to the immanent materiality—the fleshy cachinnations—of a voice indistinguishable from his body, of a voice that speaks *him*.

Cachinnations are immodest outbursts that find their etymological roots in the Greek "katakorê," a word with overtones of excessiveness and surfeit. Hence, in Aristotle's *Rhetoric*, we find the word used to warn us against the excessive use of epithets in prose:

> A third cause [of the frigidity of style] arises from the use of epithets that are either long or unseasonable or too crowded; thus, in poetry it is appropriate to speak of white milk, but in prose it is less so; and if epithets are employed to excess [*katakorê*], they reveal the art and make it evident that it is poetry.[106]

Here, as in Poe's story, the excessiveness of katakorê is not to be thought of as another *kind* of language or a different mode of speech but is, rather, what is excessive within language and speech itself—an excess that both establishes and threatens to lay bare, to disarticulate the conventions of the voice.[107] There are not two kinds of speech in Poe's text—Pompey's cachinnations and the general's remarkable voice. Cachinnation is the immanent, savage sound produced within speech that, when occluded, helps to establish the illusion of a voice that can separate itself from itself, take itself as an object, and speak articulately about its own articulation. Like Rip Van Winkle's slumber and Catlin's "nation's Park," Pompey's savage cachinnations should be read as inclusive exceptions that help to establish the distinctive timbre of the colonial voice, just as the "dismembered branch" of the Catskills and the live wreck of the Indian make manifest the spatial form and temporal destiny of the emerging U.S. nation.

5

NO THING IN COMMON

In stories like "The Man That Was Used Up," we have seen how Poe exposes the spectral special effects demanded by modern forms of national, racial, and colonial community. Like Sterne, Brockden Brown, and Montgomery Bird before him, Poe shows us how the literature of romance helps to conjure some of the peculiar common things—such as the "air distingué" of the general's voice—around which modern forms of belonging were beginning to gravitate. But Poe's engagement with the aesthetics of community is not limited to the mode of critique. As we'll see at the conclusion of this chapter, in addition to interrogating the thingifying logic of the modern commonplace, Poe is equally committed to exploring different ways of being-in-common. As such, I argue that he is following in the footsteps of the first English writer to identify his work as a form of romance: Horace Walpole.

STUDIES IN UNIQUITY: HORACE WALPOLE'S SINGULAR COLLECTION

How can the singular be collected? What kind of multiple, and what modality of the common, can blend singularities without sacrificing their uniqueness? In a 1789 letter to his bluestocking friend Hannah More, Horace Walpole describes a package he had prepared for delivery containing copies of her poem "Bishop Bonner's Ghost," printed at his own private press:

> Tomorrow departs for London, to be delivered to the Bristol coach at the White Horse Cellar in Piccadilly, a parcel containing sixty-four

Ghosts, one of which is printed on brown for your own eating. There is but one more such, so you may preserve it like a relic. I know these two are not so good as the white: but, as rarities, a collector would give ten times more for them; and *uniquity* will make them valued more than the charming poetry.[1]

In a literary and political age that celebrated the unifying force of the symbol, Walpole's fascination with the economy of "uniquity" is arresting indeed. While antiquarians, historians, and poets plumbed the annals of human experience for the signs and symbols of a shared national destiny or a common spiritual identity, Walpole dedicated his life to collecting the inessentially singular relic. Such a life is preserved through a poetic diet that finds sustenance not simply in the words, the lexical content of More's work, but also in the style of its saying. The nutritional "value" that Walpole ascribes to More's "Ghost"—the principle through which its uniquity materializes as an edible relic—is not achieved through the poem's circulation in any symbolic economy of transcendent significance. On the contrary, singularity shines through the *inessential brownness* of the poem's manner. Whereas the antique attains value through its commodification of temporality, wearing authenticity as if the flow of time inheres essentially in its form, Walpole's "unique" participates in a wholly different system of exchange. At stake in his work is the idea of an inessential value—an uncanny relic that can be collected by a community without blending its singularity into a total multiplicity of the same. Walpole's famous rehabilitation of the Gothic imagines precisely such a dwelling in the commonplaces of uniquity, and in this essay I show how the heterogeneous fragments of his literary, architectural, and historical work help to animate this inessential community of the singular.

HOSPITALIZING THE UNIQUE

In order to accommodate the strenuous demands of the singular, Walpole transformed his home by the Thames into what would become one of the most famous eighteenth-century examples of the Gothic Revival: Strawberry Hill (figure 3). While Walpole was busy at work gothicizing his villa, he published a collection of his work that includes his most

FIGURE 3. *Front of Strawberry Hill before and after Alterations.* Courtesy of The Lewis Walpole Library, Yale University. In *A Description of the Villa of Mr. Horace Walpole: Youngest Son of Sir Robert Walpole Earl of Orford at Strawberry-Hill at Twickenham, Middlesex. With an Inventory of the Furniture, Pictures, Curiosities, &c. Strawberry Hill* (Thomas Kirgate, printer, 1784).

explicit exploration of the economy of uniquity. Addressed to the editorial "Keeper" of the short-lived periodical the *Museum*, "A Scheme for Raising a Large Sum of Money for the Use of the Government, by Laying a Tax on Message-Cards and Notes" outlines Walpole's own contribution to the journal's "repository" of "literary *Curiosities.*"[2] "The notion I have of a *Museum*," he informs us,

> is an hospital for every thing that is *Singular*; whether the thing have acquired singularity, from having escaped the rage of Time; from any natural oddness in itself, or from being so insignificant, that nobody ever thought it worth their while to produce any more of the same sort. Intrinsic value has little or no property in the merit of *curiosities*. Misers, though the most intense of all *collectors*, are never allowed to be *virtuosoes*, because guineas, dollars, ducats, &c. are too common to deserve the title of *rarities*; and unless one man could attain to the possession of the whole specie, he would never be said to have a fine *collection* of money. ("SR," 47–48)

In the same way that Walpole's diet savors the brownness of a poem's flavor more than its shared symbolic content, so too his "hospital" for the unique rescues the inessential "merit" of the curiosity from its neglect at the "common" hands of commodity exchange. The virtuosity of collection here renounces any "Intrinsic" value to rarity: money relates to uniquity outside the idea of exchange value, such that the only way to collect "specie" is to amass (and therefore annul) the entirety of its symbolic power, evaporating any inherent value it might claim within systems of exchange.

Walpole's philosophy of collection proceeds by outlining three kinds of unique, all notable for their nonparticipation in the creation and commodification of authenticity. In order to help us grasp the first kind of unique, Walpole imagines the discovery of "a *Roman*'s old shoe (provided that the Literati were agreed it were a shoe, and not a leathern casque, a drinking vessel, a ballotting box, or an Empresses head-attire)" ("SR," 48). Such a shoe, he avers, "would immediately have the *entreé* into any collection in Europe; even though it appeared to be the shoe of the most vulgar artizan in Rome, and not to have belonged to any beau of Classic memory. And the reason is plain; not that there is any intrinsic value in an old shoe, but because an old Roman shoe would be a *Unique*" ("SR," 49). The unique involves the play of both particularity (the shoe must be identified as a "shoe" and not a "drinking vessel") and an inessential universality through which it attains a "value" independent of any "intrinsic" merit it might have possessed *for* someone (it is just *a* shoe, not a "beau's" shoe). Walpole's second kind of unique furthers these observations by declaring that "Monstrous births, hermaphrodites, petrifactions, &c. are all true members of a collection" ("SR," 49). "A man perfectly virtuous," he continues, "might be laid up in a *Museum*, not for any intrinsic worth, but for being a *rarity*" ("SR," 49). Again, the economy of uniquity operates here outside of traditional value judgments—judgments that are made possible, for example, by the circulation of "intrinsic" moral essences shared by the "virtuous." If we are to locate the monstrous "being" of Walpole's "*rarity*," we must ascribe its singularity to the inessential particularity of the peculiar. Walpole's third and final example of uniquity—"things become *rare* from their insignificance"—similarly evokes the language of exchange as it defamiliarizes Walpole's readers with the strange economy of the unique:

> So modern a thing as a Queen Anne's Farthing has risen to the dignity of a curiosity, merely because there were but a few of them struck. Some industrious artists who would have the greatest scruple of counterfeiting the current coin of the kingdom, have been so blinded by their love of *virtù*, as to imitate these rare farthings, looking upon them solely as

curiosities. I just mention this for the sake of those laborious medallists; because the present honorable Attorney-General, though a very learned man, is no *Antiquarian*, and might possibly be of an opinion, that those admirable copies would come under the penalties of the statute against clipping and coining. ("SR," 50)

Walpole's point is consistent throughout these three examples: the economy of curiosity operates outside of any "statute" of commodity exchange. Within his philosophy of uniquity, objects participate in a dual circulation of value: though the rare might fetch a monetary value in certain systems of exchange, its "*virtù*" as a unique emerges as a profoundly non-"intrinsic" quality of its being. The uniquity of "an object" is thus connected with the peculiar grammatical modality of the indefinite article. Both utterly particular and completely inessential, the unique relates to "*an* object" rather than to its apprehension as "an *object*" for some*one* or of some *thing*.

A TAXING PRESENCE

The nature of Walpole's "Scheme" further differentiates the structure of uniquity's value from that of the commodity. After describing the singular "*virtù*" of the "Queen Anne's Farthing," Walpole once again returns his attention to the "Keeper" of the *Museum*:

> But to come to my point. It is under this last denomination, Sir, that I apply to you for a place in your *Museum*. A scheme for raising money may (as I fear the age is too obstinate in their luxury to suffer their follies to be taxed) be admitted into a *collection*.... One of the latest and most accepted fashions is the *Sending Cards* and *Notes*: A custom that might perhaps escape the knowledge of posterity, if you and I, Sir, did not jointly transmit an account of it down to them. No business, that is no business, is now carried on in this great city, but by this expedient.... [A]ll those fatal mistakes and irreparable quarrels that formerly happened in the polite world, by Ladies trusting long messages to the faithless memory of servants, are now remedied by their giving themselves the trouble to transmit their commands to cards and paper; at once improving themselves in spelling, and adjusting the whole ceremonial of engagements, without the possibility of errors. Not to

mention the great encouragement given to the Stationary trade, by the large demands for crow-quills, paper, wafer, &c. commodities that are all the natural produce of this country. ("SR," 50–52)

Couched firmly in the language of commerce, Walpole's analysis of the "*Sending Card*" brings forward its status as "polite" cultural currency. Not only does such a custom register the "ceremonial" transactions of the everyday, it also supports the national economy by fostering consumer demand for distinctively British "commodities." Furthermore, Walpole's "account" opens up the possibility that such cards might produce additional revenue if a tax of "one penny *per card*" were to be levied on them ("SR," 57). His detailed economic analysis of such a tax proceeds as follows:

> [S]upposing a lady has but one assembly a month, to which she invites four hundred persons.... Now she must send cards to invite all these people,... and allowing her to send but twenty private messages every morning, in howd'ye's, appointments, disappointments, &c. and to make but ten visits every *night* before she settles for the *evening*, at each of which she must leave her name on a card, the account will stand thus:
>
> | | |
> |---|---|
> | Messages to 400 people | 400 |
> | 20 Messages a day, will be *per* month | 560 |
> | 10 Visits a night, will be *per* month | 280 |
> | Total | 1240 |
>
> ... I think the lowest computations make the inhabitants of this great metropolis to be eight hundred thousand. I will be so very moderate as to suppose that not above twenty thousand of these are obliged to *send cards*, because I really have not heard that this fashion has spread much among the lower sort of people; at least I know, that my own Fishmonger's wife was extremely surprized last week at receiving an invitation to an assembly at Billingsgate, written on a very dirty queen of clubs.... I shall recur to my former computation of a lady's sending 1240 *cards per* month, or 16120 *per annum*, which multiplied by 20,000, and reduced to pounds *sterling*, fixes the product of the duty at £1343333 6s. 8d. a year for the cities of London and Westminster only. ("SR," 54–58)

In addition to providing significant revenue for the nation, Walpole's humorous scheme also possesses significant historical value. "A friend of mine," notes Walpole, "was of the opinion, that where-ever the duty was collected, the office would be a court of record, because as I propose that all engagements should be registered, it would be an easy matter to compile a diary of a Lady of Quality's whole life" ("SR," 59). Swelling the economies of commerce and taxation, and registering the historical intricacies of eighteenth-century cultural transactions, Walpole's "denomination" is fecund currency indeed.

But the joke is ultimately on us: Walpole's scheme takes our account so completely that it reduces both history and the human to mere marks in his ledger book. After noting that many women, in order to avoid the duty on blank, stamped cards, purchase "pipless" playing cards on which to write their messages, Walpole proposes abolishing handwritten notes and extending his tax to "printed *cards*" ("SR," 59). He even suggests how such cards might best be configured by the printer in order to register the full scope of possible transactions:

> The most of a *message card* that I ever have seen printed, was as follows:
> "Lady M. M. or N. N.'s ————to————and
> "————the————of————company on
> "————to————."

I shall add two other cards with these blanks filled up, to shew that the rest of the message cannot be certain enough to be left to the printer.

> "*Lady* M. M. or N. N.'s *humble service* to *her*
> "*Grace the Duchess of* T. and *begs* the
> "*honour* of *her company* on *Monday five*
> "*weeks to drink Tea*."

> "Lady M. M. or N. N.'s company to Mrs. B.
> "and desires the favour of her company
> "tomorrow to play at Whist." ("SR," 60)

Here we witness the thingification of personhood within the scheme's economy: the act of registering oneself publicly for another is equated with nothing more than "*play*[ing] *at* Whist," although in Walpole's account of the game's economy, *we* are the blank cards being played, interchangeable pips that appear only to be exchanged, stamped, and taxed. Walpole's delightful scheme thus alerts us to the truly Gothic structure of values such as the "Quality" of a "Lady" or "the lower sort of people," values that seem to inhere essentially in the commodified object.

But everywhere in this text another economy circulates value of a different "denomination." For it is not simply the content of his "Scheme"—the tax on message cards—that Walpole offers to the *Museum* as a "literary" curiosity, but rather the form, the manner of the proposal itself. Like the inessential rarity of the "Queen Anne's Farthing" under which Walpole applies "for a place" in the *Museum*, we must also consider the text itself as bizarre currency, a unique "*Sending Card*" with no "Intrinsic" value that the author leaves to circulate his presence in the British periodicals. Its uniqity, he argues, possesses "a double title to a rarity. First, from never having been thought of by any other person; and secondly, as it will give posterity some light into the customs of the present age" ("SR," 50). More than any other historian in this, the age of great national histories, Walpole understands the vital historiographical function of the frivolous: "It is this merit," he points out later in the "Scheme,"

> that has preserved the works of the elder Pliny, an author who in his own time, I suppose, was upon a little better foot than the editors of the *Daily Advertisers*, the *Vade-Mecums*, and the *Magazines*. We are glad to know now how much a luxurious Roman laid out on a supper, a slave or a villa, a mistress or a tame carp; how much Pompey expended on a public show; or to read the order of a procession. But though this author now elbows Virgil and Horace, . . . I am persuaded that his works at Rome were never advanced above being read in the Steward's parlour. But hereafter I expect, that Mr. Salmon, Sylvanus Urban, and myself, shall be as good classics as Mr. Pope and Mr. Prior. ("SR," 50–51)

Though it is hard to take Pliny's history of the "tame carp" as seriously as the classicism of Virgil or Alexander Pope, the fact that Walpole was at this time establishing his own museum for the singular—the renovated Strawberry Hill—only a few yards from "Mr. Pope's" Twickenham home should stop us from simply dismissing these comments as playful bombast. Walpole's work will continue to make a home for the inessentially particular, discovering a space in which history and personhood can be registered and exchanged without reducing their "value" to some *thing* that inheres in subjects or objects, without blending the singularities of existence into a blandly essential common mixture. Sharing the modality of the indefinite object, Walpole's "hospital for every thing that is *Singular*" imagines a new home for language, a rehabilitated dwelling in the word and the world. From the intricate social life of "Lad[ies] of Quality" to readily exploitable eighteenth-century tax loopholes, this language collects vivid traces of lived time without sacrificing their uniqueness to any totalizing or thingifying economy of the sign.

ANTIQUING THE EVENT

If histories collect the unique event, what kind of narrative—and what kind of historiographical practice of collection—could assemble and make present these singular moments while preserving the finitude of their happening? Though Walpole is often dismissed as an erratic and effete dallier in eighteenth-century culture, his commitment to the philosophy of uniquity remained remarkably consistent throughout his life and work.[3] His desire to rehabilitate the inessentially singular, to revalue and accommodate the unique, not only fueled his numerous architectural, artistic, and literary projects but also led to his participation in key eighteenth-century historiographical debates.[4] At the heart of Walpole's distinction between the antique and the unique lies a philosophy of collection radically opposed to the antiquarianism of his age. Literary historians miss these nuances when they simply equate him with the revival of literary and architectural romance forms, revivals that share an antiquarian fascination with the prehistories of the modern nation.[5] Though deeply interested in memorable moments of architectural, national, artistic, and political history, Walpole's work vigorously resists their synthesis into seamless narratives of continuity. For in the same way that he hospitalizes the relic in an inessential economy of the unique, so too Walpole historicizes the singular event into a frivolous and always-preliminary engagement with the temporal.

Brimming with Enlightenment confidence, the grand historical narratives of the eighteenth century harness the symbolic force of the antique in their economies of the event. Monumental works such as David Hume's *The History of England* (1754–62) and William Robertson's *History of Scotland* (1759) synthesize these events into potent national myths of origin and emergence, myths that presume the continuity of an essential being-in-common that persists and triumphs through time.[6] What makes such histories peculiarly modern, as Michel de Certeau argues, is that they furnish "the frame of a linear succession which formally answers to questions on *beginnings* and to the need for *order*. It is thus less the result obtained from research than its condition: the web woven a priori by the two threads with which the historical loom moves forward in the single gesture of filling holes."[7] "Modern Western history," he continues,

> begins with differentiation between the *present* and the *past*.... [It takes] for granted a rift between *discourse* and the *body* (the social body). It forces the silent body to speak. It assumes a gap to exist between the silent opacity of the "reality" that it seeks to express and the place where it produces its own speech, protected by the distance established between itself and its object (*Gegen-stand*). The violence of the body reaches the written page only through absence, through the intermediary of documents that the historian has been able to see on the sands from which a presence has since been washed away, and through a murmur that lets us hear—but from afar—the unknown immensity that seduces and menaces our knowledge.[8]

Such a violent seduction is made possible by the "antiquing" of the historical event and its subsequent circulation within a truly Gothic economy of absent presence, a "labour of death."[9] The "documents" of the modern historian thus commodify and thingify temporality: events are valued only to the extent that they participate in a "frame of linear succession," only insofar as they already fill the "holes" between present and past in which history longs ceaselessly to ensnare itself. Instead of signaling a wholly new irruption in "reality"—what Alain Badiou would call a "*hole in sense*"— the event now congeals itself within the antiqued document, moving the familiar "historical loom" forward as if the murmur of temporality were vibrating palpably at its core.[10] Within this economy of the event, a "pure flow of time," as Jean-Luc Nancy observes, "could not be 'ours.' The appropriation that the 'our' indicates ... is something like an immobilization— or, better, it indicates that some aspect of time, without stopping time, or without stopping to be time, ... becomes something like a certain *space*, a certain field, which could be for us the domain, in a very strange fashion, of property."[11] Walpole's rich histories of the unique expose the queerness of this "property" and reopen the fugitive experience of time's passing.

On 18 August 1757, the "Printing-Office at Strawberry Hill" published the first work of its proud new owner. Addressed "To Cloe," an allusion to the pastoral innocence of Longus's prose romance *Daphnis and Chloe*, Walpole's poem reads as follows:

> In vain with deadly trifles arm'd
>   To murder Time you try;
> Your toil derides the Foe unharm'd,
>   Tho He affects to fly.
> A thousand lilly hands, like yours,
>   The selfsame plot we see in;
> They may indeed abridge his hours,
>   But cannot touch his being.
> Tremble, dear Nymph, at such a Foe,
>   Who, if he stays or flies,
> Ensures revenge, or swift or slow;
>   Shall dim or close those eyes.[12]

Strange words from one of the most innovative historians and prolific collectors of the eighteenth century. The central theme of this poem—the vanity and violence of human attempts to arrest time—are echoed in the many subsequent histories, dramas, and catalogues that were printed at Strawberry Hill. And its sentiment also anticipates *The Castle of Otranto* (1764), Walpole's "Gothic Story" in which a father's "vain" sins against time haunt the fate of his son and ensure a "slow" and visceral revenge in the name of the temporal and its proper, natural progression.[13]

Published in the same collection as his "Scheme" for taxing message cards, "*Numb. X.*" of Walpole's fictitious journal the *World* further explores the relationship between the human and the temporal. Dated "Thursday, March 8, 1753," this article addresses the Gregorian reform of the Julian calendar, a change that had taken effect the previous year in Britain on 2 September 1752 (which, at midnight, became 14 September in the new calendar). Walpole begins his history of the calendar by pointing out that neither Catholic supporters nor Protestant opponents of the new calendar eliminate superstition from their respective temporal practices. "The Fanatics in the reign of Charles the First," Walpole notes,

> were such successful preachers, as to procure obedience to the doctrines they taught; that is, they infused greater bigotry into their Congregations against rules, than the warmest enthusiasts of former times had

been able to propagate for the observation of times and seasons. But as most contradictions run into extremes, it must be allowed that the Presbyterians soon grew as superstitious as the most high-flown zealots of the established Church. King James the First had endeavoured to turn Sunday into a weekly wake by the book of Sports: The Presbyterians used it often for a Fast-day. In the court of king Charles, Christmas was a season of masques and revels: Under the Covenant it was still a masquerading time; for devotion may be as much disguised by hypocritic sorrow and sackcloth, as by painted vizors and harlequin jackets.[14]

Ideologies of superstition, so it would seem, inflect all human endeavors to "abridge" time, as Walpole puts it in "To Cleo." However, Walpole concludes his humorous history by drawing our attention to a "standing miracle" that challenges such an "Enlightened" ideological approach to the registration of temporality ("N," 97). Whereas much of the modern majority understood the dates of religious festivals to be "merely imaginary" and therefore unaffected by Gregorian reform, Walpole argues that something more than imagination and ideology is at work in the interface between the human and the temporal—"that the observation of certain festivals is something more than a mere political institution" ("N," 96). In defense of his position, Walpole offers the example of the "wonderful thorn of Glastonbury," a "most protestant plant" that, in spite of the recent Gregorian alterations, still continues to bloom on its "old anniversary" in the Julian calendar, Christmas Day ("N," 98). He even goes so far as to suggest "regulat[ing] the new year by the infallible Somersetshire thorn," claiming that, unlike the inflexible human calendars, it is better synchronized with the astronomical events that had rendered Julian dates so problematic in the first place ("N," 99). Like his "Scheme" for taxing "*Sending Cards*," Walpole's history of the British calendar concludes by satirizing the hubris of human attempts to collect, register, and "abridge" the singular moment. After all, what happens to April Fools' Day after the Gregorian reform? "If the clergy come to be divided about Folly's anniversary," Walpole warns, "we may well expect all the mischiefs attendant on religious wars" ("N," 101). Instead of regulating and differentiating time more precisely, Walpole's proposal threatens to collapse the "frame of linear succession" into pure madness. Hoping to restore a sense of sanity, he entreats his "readers and admirers to be very particular in their observations on that holiday, both according to the new and old reckoning . . . [and]

transmit to me or my secretary Mr. Dodsley, a faithful and attested account of... how often and in what manner they make or are made fools" ("N," 104). By opening his readers to the contingency of calendarization, such "account[s]" of madness seem the only sane way to register, to spend time.

A TRIFLING HISTORY

In the same way that Walpole's economy of uniquity bestows a nonintrinsic, inessential value on singularity, so too his philosophy of time circulates the singular event in a fluid and frivolous calendar, a temporal community that eschews the seductive, linear violence of the "historical loom." Whereas the great historians of the age look for "holes" to fill in—beginnings and ends woven together by grand narrative threads—Walpole seeks out "Serendipity," a word he coined himself in order to describe the peculiar nature of his relationship to the temporal. In a 1754 letter to his friend Horace Mann, Walpole reveals the historiographical method that has recently resulted in a "critical discovery":

> [I]n an old book of Venetian arms, there are two coats of Capello, who from their *name* bear a *hat*; on one of them is added a flower-de-luce on a blue ball, which I am persuaded was given to the family by the Great Duke, in consideration of this alliance; the Medicis, you know, bore such a badge at the top of their own arms; this discovery I made by a talisman, which Mr. Chute calls the *sortes Walpolianæ*, by which I find every thing I want, *à pointe nommée*, whenever I dip for it. This discovery, indeed, is almost of that kind which I call *serendipity*, a very expressive word, which, as I have nothing better to tell you, I shall endeavour to explain to you: you will understand it better by the derivation than by the definition. I once read a silly fairy tale, called *The Three Princes of Serendip*: as their highnesses travelled, they were always making discoveries, by accidents and sagacity, of things which they were not in quest of: for instance, one of them discovered that a mule blind of the right eye had travelled the same road lately, because the grass was eaten only on the left side, where it was worse than on the right—now do you understand *serendipity*?[15]

If, as Certeau holds, enlightened "Western history" is animated by an overdetermined search to reunite the "*present*" with its always distant "*past*,"

Walpole is guided instead by talismanic "sagacity," favoring an accidental "dip" into the temporal where he might find what he didn't know he was looking for.[16]

Nowhere is Walpole's opposition to the pregiven instrumentality of Enlightenment historiography more palpable than in his *Historic Doubts on the Life and Reign of King Richard the Third* (1768). Though often described as an impassioned defense of Richard's character, Walpole's text should be read as an intervention in eighteenth-century historical practice.[17] "So incompetent has the generality of historians been," Walpole seethes in his preface, "that it is almost a question, whether, if the dead of past ages could revive, they would be able to reconnoitre the events of their own times, as transmitted to us by ignorance and misrepresentation."[18] What is so violently Gothic about modern histories, Walpole argues, is how dead the past has become in its hands, how it *immobilizes* our relationship to temporality. Anticipating Walter Benjamin's lament for the lost art of storytelling, Walpole insists that "[i]f we take a survey of our own history, and examine it with any attention, what an unsatisfactory picture does it present to us! How dry, how superficial, how void of information! How little is recorded besides battles, plagues, and religious foundations" (*HD*, ix). The problem with modern history is that it collects the historical event as if it were, to quote Nancy again, a "strange ... property," an antiqued moment of singularity essentially marked by the temporal. "[W]hen an author has compiled our annals," writes Walpole in the "Supplement" to *Historic Doubts*, "I find he looks on the whole history of England as his property."[19] In order to counter the hubris of these "annals," Walpole performs a pointed ideological critique that opens history back up to contingency:

> The vanquished inflicted eternal wounds on their conquerors—but who knows, if Pompey had succeeded, whether Julius Cæsar would not have been decorated as a martyr to publick liberty? At some periods the suffering criminal captivates all hearts; at others, the triumphant tyrant. Augustus, drenched in the blood of his fellow-citizens, and Charles Stuart, falling in his own blood, are held up to admiration. Truth is left out of the discussion; and odes and anniversary sermons give the law to history and credulity. (*HD*, iv–v)

Just as Walpole alerts us to ideologies of superstition that inflect our celebration of the temporal, here too he uncovers the biases of histories that circulate events as if they held a fixed and timeless value. By insisting on the pastness of the past—by establishing a comfortable viewing distance from which the observer can reincorporate and recirculate the antiqued event—historians such as Hume gothicize our haunted dwelling in the temporal. "[A]dvancing like a lively crab in retrograde argumentation," according to Walpole, Hume's history registers the ghostly murmurs of an absent presence ("Supp.," 208). Meanwhile, Walpole channels "the living works of dead authors, not the dead works of living authors" ("Supp.," 188).

At stake in Walpole's intervention in the historiography of the nation is the very structure of historical registration, the manner in which singular temporal events are best collected. Whereas histories such as Hume's fill in historical holes in order to preserve a static and definitive collection of events, Walpole's method proceeds by punching doubtful "*hole[s] in sense.*" As Hannah Arendt argues, Enlightenment historians such as Hume bestow "upon mere time sequence an importance and dignity it never had before."[20] Or, as Walpole wonders, "Must [Hume] have an unbroken chain of history reposited in his head, be that history what it will, true or false, marvellous or rational?" ("Supp.," 196). Walpole's unique collections exhibit no such pretensions to totality. Responding to the harsh reception of the *Historic Doubts* (to which Hume and Edward Gibbon, among others, lent their considerable weight), the author reminds us that he "proposed [his] sentiments but as *doubts*—and yet have been told that I have not *proved* my hypothesis. If I had *proved* it, I should not have *doubted*" ("Supp.," 194). The point here is not that Walpole is uninterested in the details of history or that his methodology is intentionally imprecise. On the contrary, and as his pioneering work in the development of the footnote demonstrates, Walpole is fascinated with the ways in which historical narratives are gleaned from their sources and goes so far as to chastise Hume for his lack of documentation.[21] Without a dedication to methodological transparency, the process of gleaning can often mask spectacular violence. For example, Walpole questions Hume's gloss "[o]n the inhuman murder of the young and simple earl of Warwick": "Is it possible to palliate a shocking murder by smoother terms?" ("Supp.," 203). "How many general persecutions does the church record, of which there is not the smallest trace?" asks Walpole (*HD*, vii). "What donations and charters were forged, for which those holy persons would lose their ears, if they were in this age to present them in the most common court of judicature? Yet how long were these impostors the only persons who attempted to write history!" (*HD*, vii).

Walpole thus rehabilitates the doubt as an important historiographical method and vital dwelling space within time: it is the question mark that constitutes the central grammatical gesture of the *Historic Doubts*. Signaling not only the possibility of doubt itself, such a grammar reconceives history writing as an ongoing dialogue rather than a final declaration or an exhaustive accounting—a necessarily preliminary and structurally doubtful *process* that opens history out into a community of debate. "How little must we know of those times," Walpole reminds us, "when those land-marks to certainty . . . do not serve even that purpose!" (*HD*, vi). In the place of Hume's "unbroken chain of history," Walpole offers instead a discourse that refuses to attribute "Intrinsic" value to the event, an utterly particular and inessentially frivolous history-as-doubting. "I wished to see a foolish and absurd tale removed from the pages of gravest historians," Walpole insists, continuing:

> [A]nd [I] flattered myself, that not only the ridiculous and incoherent parts of the legend would be given up by men of sense, but that some able writer would deign to state the whole matter in so clear and consistent a manner, that not only my doubts (which indeed are of little importance to any body) would be removed, but that the history of that period would receive such satisfactory, at least probable, lights, as would prevent the reign of Richard from disgracing our annals by an intrusion of mob-stories and childish improbabilities, which at present in our best historians place that reign on a level with the story of Jack the giant-killer. ("Supp.," 185–86)

The uniquity of Walpole's practice rests in the humility of its gesture, in its refusal to participate in definitive historical economies of "importance"— economies that effectively close the temporal account from all improbability and doubt. This same methodology will be deployed in later works against specific antiquarian myths, but in *Historic Doubts* Walpole works to revivify history itself.[22] When he says that he is obsessed with the "mysterious and fugitive nature of truth," Walpole does not simply mean that "truth" exists essentially in some distant thing or at some elusive place; rather, Walpolian truth names an inessential and fugitive process.[23] His "trifling writings" do not simply collect "trifling" events as nouns but, more importantly, enact "trifling" on the level of the verb: history as trifling ("Supp.," 188).

THE CABINET OF WONDER

What kind of museum could collect this fugitive gift? Under what architectural and aesthetic principles is uniquity to be viewed and exhibited? In 1774, twenty-five years after he first began remodeling his Georgian Twickenham home, Walpole's Strawberry Hill Press published an illustrated compendium, *A Description of the Villa of Mr. Horace Walpole*. In an echo of the structure of *The Castle of Otranto*, Walpole begins this text with an apologetic preface: "It will look," he warns his readers, "a little like arrogance in a private Man to give a printed Description of his Villa and Collection, in which almost everything is diminutive. It is not, however, intended for public sale, and originally was meant only to assist those who should visit the place."[24] Much more than a simple tourist's aid, Walpole's *Description* constitutes his most thorough exploration of the architecture and aesthetics of uniquity. "A farther view succeeded," Walpole continues:

> that of exhibiting specimens of Gothic architecture, as collected from standards in cathedrals and chapel-tombs, and shewing how they may be applied to chimney-pieces, ceilings, windows, ballustrades, loggias, &c. The general disuse of Gothic architecture, and the decay and alterations so frequently made in churches, give prints a chance of being the sole preservatives of that style. (*DV*, i)

But there is much more to Strawberry Hill—the first, and most important, example of an eighteenth-century Gothic Revival home—and to its representation in the pages of the *Description*. For Walpole's project involves the ontic status of these "prints" and the "printed-ness" of historical preservation: he will give "prints a chance" to serve, to watch over, history. And, as Walpole goes on to elaborate, the "history" that these prints are charged with serving is far from a simple homage to Gothic architecture; sharing the desire expressed in the preface to *The Castle of Otranto* to blend "ancient and modern" sensibilities, the preface to his *Description of the Villa* makes a similar nod to the confusing heterogeneity of his Gothic collection:[25]

> In a house affecting not only obsolete architecture, but pretending to an observation of the *costume* even in the furniture, the mixture of modern portraits, and French porcelaine, and Greek and Roman Sculpture, may seem heterogeneous. In truth, I did not mean to make my house so Gothic as to exclude convenience, and modern refinements in luxury. (*DV*, iii)

Like Jane Austen's Northanger Abbey, modernization is an integral part of Walpole's Gothic, not an embarrassing oversight.[26] And the campy costumery that György Lukàcs will later trivialize in Walpole's work is here announced, unapologetically, up front.[27] More puzzling still is the status of his *Wunderkammer*'s blend of past and present, French and Greek, neoclassical and Gothic.[28] In one of the *Description*'s many fascinating and interlocking footnotes, Walpole tells us that his "mixture may be denominated, in some words of Pope, *A Gothic Vatican of Greece and Rome*" (*DV*, iii). Walpole's Gothic collection refuses to neatly synthesize these historical and aesthetic oppositions, insisting instead on the possibility of an uncanny "mixture" that dresses the "ancient" in the convenient costume of the "modern": a Gothic Rome, a Roman Gothic.

"Gothic" names the style, the manner of Walpole's collecting; it does not delimit a particular and essential *content to be collected*. In the eighteenth century, one of the many valences of the word "Gothic" involved its association with England's pre-Norman, Anglo-Saxon past. Whiggish Parliamentarians constructed a political and historical mythology around the Goths, claiming that the ancestry of Parliament could be traced back to England's Gothic-Saxon past.[29] But rather than legitimating a specific, Whiggish, "Gothic" history of descent that, in W. S. Lewis's words, could substitute for "the lack of a family castle," Walpole's "mixture" of interesting objects in his *Villa* demonstrates a flagrant disregard for all linear and static visions of temporality:[30]

> Far from such visions of self-love, the following account of pictures and rarities is given with a view to their future dispersion. . . . The following collection was made out of the spoils of many renowned cabinets, as Dr. Meade's, lady Elizabeth Germaine's, lord Oxford's, the duchess of Portland's, and of about forty more of celebrity. Such well-attested descent is the genealogy of the objects of virtù—not so noble as those of the peerage, but on a par with those of race-horses. In all three, especially,

the pedigrees of peers and rarities, the line is often continued by many insignificant names. (*DV*, ii)

Structured around a fecund plundering of "objects of virtù" rather than a noble genealogy of descent, Walpole's "mixture" is always in motion, always interbreeding with a view to its "future dispersion," its inevitable unfolding.[31] Strawberry Hill is thus grounded in a historical vision that eschews stasis, finds its meaning from the blending of noble "pedigrees" and "insignificant names," and refuses to reduce its contents to a univocal, historical essence—a history *that refuses to be merely Gothic*.[32] Indeed, as Eve Kosofsky Sedgwick has noted, such spaces are obsessed with surfaces, and with the promiscuity, the infectiousness, of their interbreeding.[33] It is this principle of convertibility that, above all else, registers the presence of a Gothic unique— the possibility that its presence may soon absent itself, may soon apologize for itself, in order to maintain the line and motion of the "race." If the antique is valued for its peculiar ability to materialize temporality—for its passive reception of time's stamp—Strawberry Hill's unique participates in a quite different value structure. Worth here is established not as an inherent property of an object of "virtù" but rather as a function of its fugitivity, its propensity to take flight, to disperse, and to open onto other objects.[34] It is true that Walpole quite literally slept with the Magna Charta and other fetishes of Whiggish Parliamentarianism. *A Description of the Villa*, for example, mentions "Prints, of the house and commons and warrant for beheading Charles 1st. inscribed with a pen, *Major Charta*" in its inventory of Walpole's bedroom (*DV*, 41). However, in the "Plaid Bedchamber" a quite different vein of Walpole's and England's history is singled out for display:

> In the Plaid Bedchamber . . . is the portrait of Henry Walpole the jesuit, who was executed for attempting to poison queen Elizabeth. He is crowned with glory and holds a palm-branch, the emblem of martyrdom; the arms of the family in one corner. This picture came from Mr. Walpole's of Lincolnshire, the last of the Roman catholic branch of the family, who died about the year 1748. (*DV*, 41–42)

No aesthetics of essences, Whig or other, can capture Strawberry Hill's inessential and insignificant pedigree.

Refusing to be seduced by the Enlightenment's "frame of linear succession," Walpole instead focuses our attention on unique objects that, like the "wonderful thorn of Glastonbury," reveal the hubris of such political and antiquarian romanticism. One of Walpole's favorite uniques inventoried in the *Description* is described as follows (figure 4):

> An aritical silver medal struck in Holland. On the obverse, the head of Oliver Cromwell laureated in armour. On the reverse he is kneeling in the lap of Britannia, with his breeches down; the French and Spanish ambassadors are contending which shall kiss first; the former says to the latter, *Retire toy, l'honneur apparitent au Roi mon maitre Louis le Grand*. (*DV*, 39)

Entitled "The Naked Truth," this rare coin is noteworthy both for its surprisingly bawdy vision of Cromwellian politics (very few early-eighteenth-century engravings were this explicit) and its Walpolian vision of history's "daily reel." "The history of the 'Gothic,'" writes Samuel Kliger in *The Goths in England*,

> begins not in the eighteenth but in the seventeenth century, not in aesthetic but in political discussion.... The term "Gothic" came into extensive use ... as an epithet employed by the Parliamentary leaders to defend the prerogatives of Parliament against the pretensions of the King to absolute right to govern England. To this end, the Parliamentarians searched the ancient records of English civilization for precedent and authority against the principle of monarchical absolutism. An antiquarian movement flowered, and in the ancient records the Parliamentarians discovered that the original forebears of the English were the Germanic invaders of Rome whom they called not Germans but Goths, [whom they thought] founded the institutions of public assemblies which ... the Stuarts were seeking to destroy.[35]

This mythical vision of the Goths thus made possible a Whig aesthetics, an aesthetics that "showed the triumph of Gothic humanity, honor, and simplicity over invertebrate Roman urbanism, effiminacy, and luxury. The Gothicists pictured, that is, a world of rejuvination or rebirth due to the triumph of Gothic energy and moral purity over Roman torpor and depravity."[36] It is no wonder why this coin was one of Walpole's favorites: instead of a linear, Protestant progression of "Gothic humanity, honor, and simplicity," the coin instead deflates Cromwell, the very icon of Whiggish Parliamentarianism, by associating him with "Roman torpor and depravity."

FIGURE 4. "The Naked Truth." Courtesy of The Lewis Walpole Library, Yale University. [London]: Published according to an act of Parlt. the 23rd day of June 1739, f.i.c. by John Brett [23 June 1739]. Call Number: 739.06.23.01.

The poem attached to the print offers a nice reading of the coin's philosophy of time:

> Britannia's Isle, like Fortune's Wheel,
> In *Politicks* does daily reel—
> What's up to day, to morrow's down;
> And from a smile ensues a frown.

Instead of participating in Whig aesthetics, the "Naked Truth" insists on the essential convertibility and capriciousness of history. Here, historical progression is reconceived as cyclical repetition within the erratic spatiality of national and sexual politics: the coin redraws the essential historical binary—"heads or tails"—in terms of a fluid, sexual copresence.

The Victorian critic Thomas Macaulay is both an extremely reluctant and very observant reader of the Strawberry Hill unique. "In [Walpole's] villa," he writes, every apartment is a museum; every piece of furniture is a curiosity; there is something strange in the form of the shovel; there is a long story belonging to the bell-rope. We wander among a profusion of rarities, of trifling intrinsic value, but so quaint in fashion, or connected with such remarkable names and events, that they may well detain our attention for a moment. A moment is enough. Some new relic, some new unique, some new carved work, some new enamel, is forthcoming in an instant. One cabinet of trinkets is no sooner closed than another is opened.[37]

Since the notion of taste involves essentializing aesthetics, creating a bizarre concept that somehow inheres in objects and registers their worth, it is understandable that Macaulay's *"sixth sense"* cannot come to terms with the Walpolian "unique." For if these "rarities" share any commonality, it can be only their potential for openness and connectivity. And it is precisely this constitutive motility that so perplexes Macaulay and infects his own language as it "wanders" among the "profusion" of moments that threaten to fractalize into vivid narrative before his eyes. In "The Genesis of Strawberry Hill," Lewis shares Macaulay's discomfort with Walpole's sense of taste. Himself an avid collector whose Connecticut museum now makes quite a different home for Walpolian uniquity, Lewis is simultaneously astonished by and disgusted with Strawberry Hill's aesthetic sensibility. Walpole "committed every architectural sin," he insists, "but produced something with vitality enough to affect the taste of two continents (however deplorably) for a hundred and fifty years. Modern professionals have repeated history and continued the long 'revival' with 'Collegiate Gothic.'"[38] Lewis is left powerless to describe Strawberry Hill's aesthetic effect precisely because its architecture blends high and low taste, because it insists on the originality of revival. Writing about Walpole's "Committee on Taste"—a wonderfully imprecise vehicle for aesthetic precision, comprised of Walpole and his friends John Chute and Richard Bentley—Lewis remarks:

> Strawberry Hill may be said to have been assembled rather than built, for Walpole's method was, briefly, to copy admired details of Gothic buildings (especially tombs) and translate them into whatever was required at the moment. He did this by going back to the buildings themselves or to prints of them, thus eliminating all question of the genuineness of his

"Gothic." The Committee on Taste had little conception of structural significance in what they copied and they did not bother with the intentions of the original builders.... "Gothic" was primarily a pictorial affair which exceeded anything that had yet been introduced at Covent Garden or Drury Lane. Strawberry Hill was an assemblage of historic examples of Gothic art fitted into a Georgian frame.[39]

Here the chaos, the "harmonious confusion" of Walpole's cabinet of wonder is due to its continual improvisation, to the preliminariness of its audacious and always-excessive claim to originality. It is not just the copies that exist in Strawberry Hill that trouble Lewis; rather, it is the total irrelevance of original, artistic intention—the reproduction (and reproducibility) that eliminates the possibility of modern aesthetic judgment.

In a 1753 letter to Mann, Walpole vividly describes some of the Gothic wallpapers he was using to decorate Strawberry Hill: "It is impossible at first sight," he insists,

> not to conclude that they contain the history of Attila or Tottila, done about the very era.... [T]he hall and the staircase [are] the chief beauty of the castle. Imagine the walls covered with (I call it paper, but it is really paper painted in perspective to represent) Gothic fretwork: the lightest Gothic balustrade to the staircase, adorned with antelopes... bearing shields; lean windows fattened with rich saints in painted glass, and a vestibule open with three arches on the landing place and niches full of trophies of old coats of mail, Indian shields made of rhinoceros's hides, broadswords, quivers, long bows, arrows, and spears—all *supposed* to be taken by Sir Terry Robsart in the holy wars.[40]

Walpole's *Wunderkammer* revels in its conflation of originality and repetition, creation and copy.[41] In collecting the unique event, Strawberry Hill neither clings to an essentialized spirit of "ancient" days, nor empties out history in order to play freely among the ghosts of the past. Within this space, the historicity of Strawberry Hill is experienced as a force both vividly particular and ecstatically preliminary. The logic of such space is never to measure its proximity to an authentic temporal event that has already happened, thereby reaffirming an essential difference between past and present. Rather, Walpole's work relinquishes the security of a distant and authentic past so that it can open up the experience of temporality to the present. Whether Sir Terry Robsart actually took these Indian shields and broadswords—or whether the Gothic wallpaper constitutes real fretwork—are questions that simply do not matter at Strawberry Hill. Refusing the reduction of transcendence, Walpolian camp, if we are looking to name the structure of Walpole's nontaste, brings forward the copresence of original and revival, ancient and modern. And it is this same uncanny copresence that explains the thrill that Walpole finds in *supposing* that the "broadswords" and "spears" were taken by Sir Terry Robsart: in this Gothic game, all resolution—all synthesis of past and present—is held in deferral, in potential, so that time and history remain open and motile. This is a game, a camp aesthetics, that is propelled by the continual postponement of aesthetic judgment.

Within this aesthetic vision, the wallpaper's Gothic "fretwork" can be compared with the vaulted ceilings in the Gallery of Strawberry Hill (figure 5), ceilings that seem to spring organically, like the limbs of a tree, from the trunks of the neoclassical columns that support them (figure 6). The extravagant Gothic lines refuse to invoke a static vision of history, and any attempt to reduce Walpole's Gothic to the frivolous, the unnatural, or the ahistorical ignores the fact that these lines are also, and quite literally, rooted in the neoclassical, the natural, the historical. The *View of the Chapel in the Garden at Strawberry Hill* (figure 7) makes this same point by bringing its viewers outside to the grounds of the manor. Here we witness the copresence of the natural world, the Gothic fretwork and arches of the chapel, and the neoclassical columns supporting the plants that guide us to its door. In *Garden Gate* (figure 8), the viewer again perceives an organic connectivity between the Gothic and the natural world. In the foreground, the columns of the gate are juxtaposed, on each side, with tree trunks, and the latticed gate spans these columns much as the branches of the larger tree reach across to its smaller neighbor. What the image presents is thus a dual perspective that is neither framed by the Gothic nor dominated by nature; instead we are privy to a view of the English landscape in which the very excesses of the Gothic—its intricate fretwork and extravagant lines—point to an inescapable connectivity between the Gothic and the natural world. Far from perpetuating an aesthetics of fancy, of pastiche, this image suggests that the Gothic can also guide us back to nature: instead of resting in front of the gate, daunted by its excessive and extravagant materiality, in the background two trees

FIGURE 5. *Gallery at Strawberry Hill.* Courtesy of The Lewis Walpole Library, Yale University. In *A Description of the Villa of Horace Walpole, 1784* (Walpole's extra-illustrated copy). Strawberry Hill Press. Creator, Edward Edwards.

form another gate-like structure and encourage us to open up the latticed doors in the foreground.

"My house," Walpole wrote in a 1788 letter, "is but a sketch by beginners," and it is the figurative and literal openness of the lines he draws that render his home so unhomely.[42] "Wherever the kitchen was from 1748 to 1761," Lewis notes, "it was now removed and placed at the western end of the house in the Round Tower.... It was not only as far as possible from what in ordinary houses is called the dining room, but it was impossible to reach it without going outside or up to the principal floor and down again. This of course meant that the front door must not be locked.... [Engravings in the *Description*] indicate that the outside method was a usual one."[43] Strawberry Hill thus blends one of the most fundamental architectural oppositions, inside and out—an effect of which Walpole was especially proud.[44] In another letter to Mann, Walpole refuses to reduce Strawberry Hill's architectural effect to inside or out, mansion or grounds, insisting that "there is a solemnity in the house, of which the cuts will give you an

FIGURE 6. *The Cabinet.* Courtesy of The Lewis Walpole Library, Yale University. In *A Description of the Villa of Horace Walpole, 1784* (Extra-illustrated copy, owned by Richard Bull). Strawberry Hill Press. Creator, T. Morris. Call Number: 33 30.

FIGURE 7. *View of the Chapel in the Garden at Strawberry Hill.* Courtesy of The Lewis Walpole Library, Yale University. In *A Description of the Villa of Horace Walpole, 1784* (Extra-illustrated copy, owned by Richard Bull). Strawberry Hill Press. Creator, Godfrey Pars Del. Call Number: 33 30.

FIGURE 8. *Garden Gate*. Courtesy of The Lewis Walpole Library, Yale University. In *A Description of the Villa of Horace Walpole*, *1784* (Extra-illustrated copy, owned by Richard Bull). Strawberry Hill Press. Creator, T. Morris. Call Number: 33 30.

idea, [but] they cannot add the gay variety of the scene without, which is very different from every side, and almost from every chamber, and makes a most agreeable contrast."[45] The architecture of Strawberry Hill—its insistence on an "agreeable contrast" that varies according to time and place—cannot be reduced to static aesthetic categories.

AN OPEN BOOK

When reading the *Description* and its pages of interrelated lists, anecdotes, and engravings, we are invited into a textual space that continuously threatens to open and exceed itself as the viewer approaches each object in the cabinet of wonder: inventory and iteration are the primary methodologies of this, Walpole's most formally ambitious counterhistory. Watch as we close in on the portrait of Bianca Capello in the Gallery at Strawberry Hill:

> Bianca Capello; by Vafari; brought out of the Vitelli palace at Florence by sir Horace Mann, and sent to Mr. Walpole, the hands never finished. Her story is thus written in a cartouche on the frame. *Bianca Capello, a Venetian lady, who having disobliged her family by marrying a Florentine banker, was reduced to maintain him by washing linen; Francis the great duke, saw, fell in love with, and made her his mistress, and her husband the minister: but the latter, after numberless tyrannies, for which she obtained his pardon, and after repeated ill usage of her, for which she pardoned him, having murdered a man, and being again protected by her, the great duke told her, that though he would remit her husband's punishment, he would pardon whoever should kill him. The relations of the deceased murdered the assassin, and Francis married his widow Bianca, who was poisoned with him at a banquet by cardinal Ferdinand, afterwards called the Great brother and successor of duke Francis.* (DV, 54)

In a footnote to this passage, Walpole writes that "Montaigne, in his Travels . . . gives a description of Bianca, which corresponds much with this portrait. . . . The small portrait of her in the cabinet of enamels here, p. 59, is younger and much handsomer" (*DV*, 54). And on page 59 of the *Description*, the narrative voice refers us back to the discussion of her portrait in the gallery on page 54: "Bianca Capello, great duchess of Tuscany. . . . *See her history, p.54*" (*DV*, 59). Valued for its fecund and inessential connective potentiality, Walpole's inventory of Capello's portrait epitomizes the fugitivity of his Gothic collections. Echoing the dialectic of enclosure and openness that inheres within and without the architecture of Strawberry Hill, Capello's portrait opens the reader onto an interlocking, ever-expanding nexus of image, history, and text. It is as if each object in the *Wunderkammer* ineluctably unfolds its own history, a history that is tied to other images, other places in the text. No genealogy of univocal, linear historical descent, the architectural spaces of Strawberry Hill and the structure of its unique relics bespeak a different view of temporality and spatiality, a different model of history and historiography. Indeed, the ontic status of these objects, each imbued with its own promiscuous architecture and textuality, refuses to distinguish between text, object, and architecture. Within this vision of time and space, surfaces open up interrelational historical depths that elude the Enlightenment's sterile and immobile "frame of succession."

Origination is as impossible as termination in such an ever-expanding space. The closer we get to the end of Walpole's inventory, the more insistently it refuses to come to closure. The text of *A Description of the Villa* appears to end with "Additions," a section in which Walpole lists the objects that Strawberry Hill has accumulated between the composition of the text and its publication by Walpole's own Strawberry Hill Press. Not content to conclude with this open ending, the text then tries to close with "Strawberry-Hill, A Ballad, by William Pulteney Earl of Bath" (*DV*, 85). But this ballad also attests to the fecundity, the expansiveness, of Strawberry Hill's architectural and textual boundaries. Described as a ballad that should be sung "*To the tune of a former song written by* George Bubb Doddington"—a song that, in a footnote in the text, is identified as being "written in praise of Mrs. Strawbridge, a lady with whom Mr. Doddington was in love"—the text again asserts its structural and historical expansiveness (*DV*, 86). The text next lists a description of the "Books Printed at Strawberry-Hill" and prints the "Directions to the Bookbinder" (*DV*, 87). As a text perfectly aware of its own textuality—and aware of the inevitable interrelationships of textuality and reproduction—the *Description* tries to end by signaling its own death—a death that always brings the promise of new life, other "Books." Next follows another "APPENDIX" that lists further additions to Strawberry Hill since the completion of the "Additions" section, the assertion of "THE END," another section entitled "Curiosities added since this Book was compleated," and then, finally, "More Additions" (*DV*, 95).

The unique relics of Walpole's Gothic collection are thus patterned by *the open*. This whimsical expansiveness of uniqueness is not, however, to be understood as a specifiable arrangement of spatiality, where "open" stands for a particular content of that space. On the contrary, Walpole's open is a verb, and it is this *in*essential potentiality of his texts, his architecture, and his objects of virtù—their potentiality to mobilize narrative and open history for "future dispersion"—that is held in common at Strawberry Hill.

CODA: POE'S ALLEGORIES OF BELONGING

In his 1845 story "Mystification," Edgar Allan Poe inherits both the spirit and the vocabulary of Walpole's studies in the singular. As Walpole's popular letters were enjoying their first print serialization in the United States, Poe resurrected the term "uniquity" in order to further explore the play of authenticity and fakery at work in the unique.[46] Originally published in 1837 as "Von Jung, the Mystific" in the *American Monthly Magazine*, Poe's story revolves around the enigmatic Baron Ritzner Von Jung, a man who, like General A. B. C. Smith in "The Man That Was Used Up," is "pronounced by all parties at first sight 'the most remarkable man in the world,'" even if "no person made any attempt at accounting for this opinion."[47] "That he was *unique*," continues Poe, "appeared so undeniable, that it was deemed impertinent to inquire wherein the uniquity consisted" (253). Von Jung's uniquity is, like Walpole's, both vague and puissant, inessential and yet utterly specific. "From the first moment of his setting foot within the limits of the university," observes Poe,

> he began to exercise over the habits, manners, persons, purses, and propensities of the whole community which surrounded him, an influence the most extensive and despotic, yet at the same time the most indefinitive and altogether unaccountable. Thus the brief period of his residence at the university forms an era in its annals, and is characterized by all classes of people appertainting to it ... as "that very extraordinary epoch forming the domination of the Baron Ritzner Von Jung." (254)

No common thing, Von Jung's uniquity names a mode of "community" that can "unnacountab[ly]" collect "all classes of people" and assemble "an era" that gathers passing moments into the "annals" of an "extraordinary epoch." Like Walpole's serious engagement with the frivolous as a method of historiographical and aesthetic practice, in "Mystification" Poe will attribute Von Jung's "indefinitive" yet "despotic" power to his "atmosphere of whim":

> The beauty, if I may so call it, of his *art mystifique*, lay in that consummate ability ... by means of which he never failed to make it appear

that the drolleries he was occupied in bringing to a point, arose partly in spite, and partly in consequence of the laudable efforts he was making for their prevention, and for the preservation of the good order and dignity of Alma Mater. The deep, the poignant, the overwhelming mortification which, upon each such failure of his praiseworthy endeavors, would suffuse every lineament of his countenance, left not the slightest room for doubt of his sincerity in the bosoms of even his most sceptical companions.... Continually enveloped in an atmosphere of whim, my friend appeared to live only for the severities of society; and not even his own household have for a moment associated other ideas than those of the rigid and august with the memory of the Baron Ritzner Von Jung. (254–55)

The powerful "beauty" of Von Jung's "*art mystifique*" is generated by an aesthetic program in which whimsy and severity form copresent, rather than simply antagonistic, forces.[48] We have seen this same "harmonious confusion" at work in the Walpolian *Wunderkammer*, and with Poe such inessential and ethereal modes of communion stand in stark contrast to the thingified forms of modern sociality and belonging that he so frequently satirizes. As Jonathan Elmer has argued, Poe's fiction brings to light the Gothic coordinates of mass culture by exploring the vexed position of the individual within its logic. For example, Elmer connects Poe's interest in mesmerism—and with the mesmeric "'nervo-vital fluid'" thought to tie us together in "'magnetic sympathy'"—with modern theories of sentimental community.[49] Stories such as "Mesmeric Revelation" thus transform the implicit engine of sentimental modes of belonging—feeling as a common *thing* that somehow glues us together—into a horrific vision that always also exceeds the social limit: Poe's work "tarr[ies] with the truth of sentiment *as* substance" by describing "the substantialization of a sentiment that cannot be regulated."[50] In what follows, I continue to explore the aesthetics of belonging in Poe's fiction—paying particular attention to his most extensive reflection on the form of the commonplace, *Eureka*. In addition to registering this text's pointed critique of various modern forms of national, racial, political, and imperial community, I will also adumbrate the "*art mystifique*" of another kind of "good order and dignity" at work in its pages—an aesthetic practice that, in refusing to congeal community or gravitate textual meaning around some symbolic substance or essentialized thing, promises a different mode of relationship between the unique and the common.

EUREKA'S INESSENTIAL "BROTHERHOOD AMONG THE ATOMS"

"Never was necessity less obvious," insists Poe in *Eureka* (1848), "than that of supposing Matter imbued with an ineradicable *quality* forming part of its material nature—a quality, or instinct, *forever* inseparable from it, and by dint of which inalienable principle every atom is *perpetually* impelled to seek its fellow."[51] What is most remarkable about Poe's "Essay on the Material and the Spiritual Universe" is the way in which it attends to the immanent "uniqueness" (1261) of the world without reinforcing either an Enlightenment "fellow[ship]" of essences or a "Frogpondian" transcendence of "Matter."[52] Indeed, as Colin Dayan so powerfully argues, "[m]ost of Poe's fiction can be read as his struggle to reclaim matter before the surrender to the unspeakable."[53] But what kind of materialism is possible without "Matter?" And what kind of language can register its "unspeakable" uniquity?[54]

At the conclusion of *Eureka*—a text the author felt finalized his life's work ("I have no desire to live since I have done 'Eureka,'" he claimed months before his death)[55]—Poe will answer the first of these questions by urging us to consider "Matter as a Means—not as an End" (1354)—a conclusion for which he has prepared his readers as early as the text's preface. "I offer this Book of Truths," Poe tells us, "not in its character of Truth-Teller, but for the Beauty that abounds in its Truth; constituting it true. To these I present the composition as an Art-Product alone:—let us say as a Romance; or, if I be not urging to lofty a claim, as a Poem" (1259). Above all, Poe implores us, we should not search for the "Truths" of this "Art-Product" as if they exist as a content of its "character" to be told—or, as he puts it, as a "*thing*" or a "theorum" awaiting "demonstration" (1261). To be sure, Poe will tell truths and demonstrate theorums in the pages that follow, but from the outset of *Eureka* he urges us to focus on the *manner* of his presentation—to think about the way its beauty emerges as "a Means" in the process of its truth-telling rather than "as an End," as informational content that is simply told.[56] "Truth" is not some pregiven beautiful thing, and "Beauty" not some essential character or material attribute that signals truth's presence: on the contrary, "Beauty" names the "constituting" and constellating processes through which truth "abounds."

When Walter Benjamin attempts his own "demonstration" of allegory's beautiful force in *The Origins of German Tragic Drama*, his work draws inspiration from both genre studies and cosmology. In the same way that "Beauty" is, for Poe, an idea that emerges immanently through singular expressions of "Truth," for Benjamin we have seen how genre names an active, gravitational process—a "timeless constellation ... within which the unique and extreme stands alongside its counterpart."[57] No simple content to be collected or definitive "End" to be reached, Benjamin's idea of genre is an energetic process, a "Means" through which the critic engages with and breathes life into his material. As such, the truth of genre's idea comes to life only "in a comprehensive explanation of ... its form, the metaphysical substance of which should not simply be found within, but should appear in action, like the blood coursing through the body."[58] Throughout Poe's *Eureka* we are also witness to the respiratory movement of ideas. These ideas attempt their own "explanation" of the "form" of the universe—a "form" that is better described by vectorized forces of exhalation and inhalation, of "Repulsion" and "Attraction," than it is explained by linear narratives of temporal origination or axial maps of spatialized growth.[59] Rather than read his text as providing a generalized and objective cosmological theory, Poe warns us again and again to focus on the immanent and beautiful movement of "Truth" in both the universe and in his "Poem." As we will see, the author offers us an astrology rather than a cosmology if, by the former term, we are to understand a rigorously mundane science that approaches the stars solely in terms of their singular relation to our finite human experience.

When it comes to the "Universe," Poe wants to express the "uniqueness of [our] prospect" rather than deduce some transcendental order that represses the singularities of experience and perspective (1261). This is why he immediately clarifies his use of "the expression, 'Universe,'" by replacing it with a "phrase of limitation—'the Universe of Stars'" (1262). As much as he admires Alexander Von Humbolt (*Eureka* is dedicated "With Very Profound Respect" to his work), Poe is also quick to distance his own limited "Universe of Stars" from the "Cosmos" of the famous German naturalist. Von Humbolt's approach to the universe, argues Poe,

> presents the subject ... *not* in its individuality but in its generality. His theme, in its last result, is the law of *each* portion of the merely physical Universe, as this law is related to the laws of *every other* portion of this

merely physical Universe.... In a word, he discusses the universality of material relation.... But however admirable be the succinctness with which he has treated each particular point of his topic, the mere multiplicity of these points occasions, necessarily, an amount of detail, and thus an involution of idea, which preclude all *individuality* of impression. (1262)

Poe practices a methodology that attends to the "*individuality* of impression" rather than the "universality of material relation." Where Von Humbolt extracts static, universal laws that appear to transcend and govern experience from afar, Poe is concerned with the calculus of an infinite series of singular relationships and immanent, unique forces. Indeed, *Eureka* will go on to critique the "rectilinearity" of Von Humboldt's technique for mapping experience:

While the *merely general direction* of each atom—of each moon, planet, star, or cluster—would [be] absolutely rectilinear,... it is clear, nevertheless, that this general rectilinearity would be compounded of what, with scarcely an exaggeration, we may term an infinity of particular curves—an infinity of local deviations from rectilinearity—the result of continuous differences of relative position among the multitudinous masses, as each proceeds on its own proper journey to the End. (1347)

As Colin Dayan observes, "Poe begins his own journey by locating us at the confines of a perceptible universe. Instead of carrying us away into the unseen, Poe first dares to measure the supposed sublime. Insistently positioning us under, in, and between things, he thus makes marvels materially credible instead of ideal."[60] We will now turn to the material credibility of these "local deviations" in order to further adumbrate the "proper" path that *Eureka* urges us to journey.

In an echo of Benjamin's rejection of inductive and deductive methodological approaches to genre theory, Poe begins *Eureka* by attacking the "pompous and infatuate proscription of all *other* roads to Truth than the two narrow and crooked paths [of induction and deduction] to which [philosophers] dared to confine the Soul—the Soul which loves nothing so well as to soar in those regions of illimitable intuition which are utterly incognizant of '*path*'" (1268–69). In travelling the pathless path of "intuitive *leaps*," the methodology of *Eureka* revives the spirit of Walpolian serendipity (1264). For example, when Poe discusses the concept of infinity, what is most important for him is the singularity and intensity of our effort to think —thought's ability to *leap*—*not* the proof of some ultimate, impersonal and universal solution. A true thinker, Poe insists, will simply "direct his mental vision toward . . . the intellectual firmament, where lies a nebula never to be solved. To solve it, indeed, he makes no effort; for with a rapid instinct he comprehends . . . the *inessentiality* . . . of its solution" (1275). After all, a concept that attempts to approach the infinite, continues Poe,

> is by no means the expression of an idea—but of an effort at one. It stands for the possible attempt at an impossible conception. Man needed a term by which to point out the *direction* of this effort—the cloud behind which lay, forever invisible, the *object* of this attempt. A word, in fine, was demanded, by means of which one human being might put himself in relation at once with another human being and with a certain *tendency* of the human intellect. Out of this demand arose the word "Infinity"; which is thus the representative but of the *thought of a thought*. (1272)

Notice how Poe here imagines community in terms of the "*inessentiality*" of pure "relation"—as unique, vectorized "effort" and singular, directional "tendency"—rather than as the collection of some essential quality in some pregiven space and time. And so where the question mark provides Walpole with the appropriate grammatical gesture with which to open up our doubtful dwelling in the temporal, it is the dash that becomes, as Dayan points out, "Poe's most aggressive device" in his attempt to register the unique tendencies of the universe.[61] This is because the dash—like Walpole's question mark—initiates intensive movement rather than symbolizes static, extensive content. "Turning our attention away from words to the space *in-between*," Dayan continues, "Poe dramatizes a pulsing world . . . . As a force of division and dynamism, the dash proves most effectively Poe's equation between his science and his language."[62] As such, "'hypothesis'" does not so much name a stage in *Eureka*'s proof as it does describe the movement of all its ideas—the ever-adjusting modesty of speculation that, for Poe, always directs the effort of true thinking (1301). Where Walpole celebrates rather than defends his dedication to doubtfulness in the practice of history writing, so too Poe unabashedly declares the mereness of his methodological assumptions. "As a starting point," he informs us, "I have taken it for granted, simply, that the Beginning had nothing behind it or before it.... —in short that this Beginning was — *that which it was.* If this be a 'mere assumption' then a 'mere assumption' let it be" (1304).[63]

In order to foment Poe's vision of an inessential community—and in order to approach its impossible conception—"we require," Poe continues,

> something like a mental gyration on the heel. We need so rapid a revolution of all things about the central point of sight that, while the minutiae vanish altogether, even the more conspicuous objects become blended into one. Among the vanishing minutiae, in a survey of this kind, would be all exclusively terrestrial matters. The Earth would be considered in its planetary relations alone. A man, in this view, becomes Mankind; Mankind a member of the cosmical family of Intelligences. (1262)

With the help of a wonderful pun, Poe connects this "revolution" of astrological perspective with his philosophy of "Matter." For what matters least when the mind gyrates so rapidly—what vanishes from sight into a blur of vector forces—are precisely the isolated, essentialized points of matter thought to inhabit the axes of our "terrestrial" space. Rejecting the notion that matter contains some common *thing*, some "ineradicable *quality* forming part of its material nature," Poe instead thinks materiality in terms of inessential vectors of respirating differences. "Matter *exists* only as Attraction and Repulsion," as a pulsating dialectical process that vibrates the unique gaps "*in-between*" men—a blur of community uniting the "cosmic family" of "Mankind" in the gyration of its effort (1283). Matter exists not as a noun, as an isolated, singular "quality;" matter matter*s* as a verb: it names the movement of differential forces of relation. "For the effectual completion of the general design," Poe argues,

> we thus see the necessity for a repulsion of limited capacity—a separative *something* which, on withdrawal of the diffusive Volition, shall at the same time allow the approach, and forbid the junction, of the atoms; suffering them infinitely to approximate, while denying them positive contact. (1280)

The "*something*" toward which *Eureka* leaps is not an object or an "End" but, rather, a force, a "Means"—a "separative *something*" that activates and enables relations of difference. What is primary here is not the solitary punctuality of the atom but, rather, the effort and direction of oppositional intensities which, in their dance of "withdrawal" and "approach," enable these atoms to maintain their precarious self-identity. From this perspective, matter's atoms do not possess common qualities; what they share is their capacity to be differentiated and singularized by these universal forces: "it would be supererogatory, and consequently unphilosophical," Poe cautions us, "to predicate of the atoms, in view of their purposes, any thing more than *difference of form* at their dispersion, with particular inequidistance after it—all other differences arising out of these" (1279). If matter names a community of atoms, then what Poe attempts to think is community as a vibrating assemblage of intensive differences rather than as a totalizing collection of common, essential things: "All existing bodies . . . are composed of these atoms in proximate contact, and are therefore to be considered as mere assemblages of more or fewer differences" (1282).

Working in tandem with the "separative *something*" of *Eureka* is the force of attraction—the "tendency of the diffused atoms to return into Unity"—that Poe calls "Gravity" (1281)[64]. When discussing gravitational force, Poe is always quick to warn us away from thinking this "Unity" as a specific, solitary point. Unity, he argues,

> is merely the *condition* and not the point or locality at which this condition took its rise . . . . "But they seek a centre," it will be said, "and a centre is a point." True; but they seek this point not in its character of point . . . but because it so happens, on account of the form in which they collectively exist—(that of the sphere)—that only *through* the point in question—the sphere's centre—they can attain their true object, Unity. In the direction of the centre each atom perceives more atoms than in any other direction. Each atom is impelled towards the centre because along the straight line joining it and the centre and passing on the surface beyond, there lie a greater number of atoms than along any other straight line—joining it, the atom, with . . . a greater number of tendencies to Unity—a greater number of satisfactions for its own tendency to Unity. (1298–99)

What does it mean to think the "Unity" of community as a "condition" or a "tendency" rather than as a "locality" or a "point?" Again, Poe asks us to think of unity's "centre"—like the "Means" of matter—in terms of an intensive force seeking satisfaction, rather than as a discrete endpoint to be reached.

It is this common desire, this "tendency to Unity" that provides the gravitational glue for what Poe will call a "brotherhood among the atoms" (1286)—a collective "form" that constellates these unique sympathies into an assemblage of pure relation: not a brotherhood *of* discrete atoms, but a community of relation *among* them. "[E]ach atom attracts—sympathizes with the most delicate movements of every other atom," observes Poe in shimmering and breathless incantation,

> and with each and with all at the same time, and forever, and according to a determinate law of which the complexity, even considered by itself solely, is utterly beyond the grasp of the imagination. If I propose to ascertain the influence of one mote in a sunbeam on its neighboring mote, I cannot accomplish my purpose without first counting and weighing all the atoms in the Universe and defining the precise positions of all at one particular moment. If I venture to displace, by even the billionth part of an inch, the microscopical speck of dust which lies now on the point of my finger, what is the character of the act upon which I have adventured? I have done a deed which shakes the Moon in her path, which causes the Sun to be no longer the Sun, and which alters forever the destiny of the multitudinous myriads of stars that roll and glow in the majestic presence of their Creator. (1286)

If, as W. C. Harris has noted, *Eureka* critiques U.S. forms of political "brotherhood" by associating "the abstract philosophical problem of *the one and the many* [with the] concrete, particular form [of] the federal enigma (*e pluribus unum*),"[65] then passages such as these remind us that Poe's vision of common "Unity" offers no simple blend of the unique, no definitive "theorum" of the singular's place in the plural. Harris argues that Poe "takes the not unheard of and characteristically American stance that endorses political equality at the same time that it eschews social equality in favor of social hierarchy."[66] "*Eureka*," he concludes, tells "us to accept about constitution what Constitution is uncomfortable with . . . : the necessity of anomaly, of hierarchy."[67] But Poe is not simply imagining "brotherhood" as a particular distribution of the common—be that distribution democratic, aristocratic or a "characteristically American" blend of the two. In the same way that *Eureka* opens by celebrating its mode of aesthetic presentation—the "Beauty that abounds in its Truth"—rather than boasting of its capacity to carry "Truth" as if it were a mere content of its "character," so too when Poe pronounces the tendency for atoms to "sympathize . . . with the most delicate movements of every other atom," we should approach his articulation of being-in-common as *itself* vibrating the beauty of "Unity" rather than simply outlining a solution to the "abstract philosophical problem" of the commonplace. At stake in the respiratory force of such a vision is an aesthetics of belonging dedicated to what Kant so famously calls a "universal communicability that is . . . not based on a concept."[68] The "majestic" beauty of *Eureka*'s "multitudinous myriads," like the fugitive openness of Walpole's inessential collection, performs the promise of being-in-common even as it critiques the thinghood of generic "Matter" thought to congeal our modern systems of community.

NOTES

INTRODUCTION

1. Available online at: www.armellecaron.fr/art/index.php?page=plans_de_berlin.

2. Jean-Luc Nancy, *The Inoperative Community*, trans. Peter Connor, Lisa Garbus, Michael Holland, and Simona Sawhney (Minneapolis: U of Minnesota P, 1991), 3.

3. Benedict Anderson's *Imagined Communities: Reflections on the Origins and Spread of Nationalism* (New York: Verso, 1983), first published in 1983, has had a lasting influence on the scholarship of eighteenth- and nineteenth-century British and American literature. In *Common Things*, I extend the debate on the "imagined" community by exploring not only the content of the national imagination but also its form—the way that it imagines *being-in-common*.

4. In *Dissensus: On Politics and Aesthetics* (New York: Continuum, 2010), Rancière claims that the "essence [of politics] lies in a certain way of dividing up the sensible. I call 'distribution of the sensible' a generally implicit law that defines the forms of partaking by first defining the modes of perception in which they are inscribed.... A partition of the sensible refers to the manner in which a relation between a shared common (*un commun partagé*) and the distribution of exclusive parts is determined in sensory experience" (36).

5. Angus Fletcher, "Allegory without Ideas," *boundary 2* 33.1 (2006): 88.

6. In *The Statesman's Manual*, Coleridge famously contrasts the power of the symbol with the "empty echoes" of allegory (33) (see *The Statesman's Manual*, vol. 1, *Lay Sermons*, 2 vols., ed. Derwent Coleridge, 3rd ed. (London: Edward Moxon, 1852).

7. See Hans-Georg Gadamer, *Truth and Method*, trans. Joel Weinsheimer and Donald G. Marshall (New York: Continuum, 2004), 42–81.

8. In chapter 1, I discuss Benjamin's theory of allegory and his critique of Romanticism in *The Origin of German Tragic Drama*, trans. John Osborne (New York: Verso, 1998).

9. Other work, not otherwise cited in this text, that has influenced my approach to these systems of belonging includes a collection of essays by the Miami Theory Collective, *Community at Loose Ends* (Minnesota: U of Minneapolis P, 1991); and Alphonso Lingis's *The Community of Those Who Have Nothing in Common* (Bloomington and Indianopolis: Indiana University Press, 1994). For a fascinating survey of Lingis's contributions to the question of, and potentialities for, community, see Alexander E. Hooke's review essay, "Alphonso Lingis's We: A Collage, Not a Collective," *Diacritics* 31.4 (2001): 11–21.

10. Rancière, *Dissensus*, 35.

11. See, for example, José David Saldívar's *Border Matters: Remapping American Cultural Studies* (Berkeley: U of California P, 1997) and *Criticism in the Borderlands: Studies in Chicano Literature, Culture, and Ideology*, ed. Héctor Calderón and José David Saldívar (Durham, NC: Duke UP, 1991). For a critique of "border studies," see the essays in *Border Theory: The Limits of Cultural Politics*, ed. Scott Michaelsen and David E. Johnson (Minneapolis: U of Minnesota P, 1997); and my "The Short Way of Saying 'Mexicano': Patrolling the Borders of Mario Suárez's Fiction," *MELUS* 26.2 (2001).

12. For other critical approaches to this problem, see Aijaz Ahmad's "The Politics of Literary Postcoloniality," in *Contemporary Postcolonial Theory: A Reader*, ed. Padmini Mongia (London: Arnold, 1996), 276–93; and Arif Dirlik's "The Postcolonial Aura: Third World Criticism in the Age of Global Capitalism," in *Critical Inquiry* 20 (1994): 328–56.

13. Winfried Fluck, "A New Beginning? Transnationalisms," *New Literary History* 42.3 (2011): 376.

14. Ibid., 365.

15. Ibid., 379.

16. Ibid., 380.

17. Ibid.

18. Robyn Wiegman, "The Ends of New Americanism," *New Literary History* 42.3 (2011):392.

19. Ibid.

20. Giorgio Agamben, *Means without End: Notes on Politics*, trans. Vincenzo Binetti and Cesare Casarino (Minneapolis: U of Minnesota P, 2000), 19.

21. For a detailed critique of the logic of "human rights," see Aihwa Ong's "Experiments with Freedom: Milieus of the Human," *American Literary History* 18.2 (2006): 229–44. See also the essays collected by Eduardo Cadava and Ian Belfour in "The Claims of Human Rights," special issue, *South Atlantic Quarterly* 103.2–3 (2004).

22. Étienne Balibar, *We, the People of Europe? Reflections on Transnational Citizenship*, trans. James Swenson (Princeton: Princeton UP, 2004), 67.

23. Jonathan Culler, "Literary History, Allegory, and Semiology," *New Literary History* 7.2 (1976): 260.

24. Werner Hamacher, "One 2 Many Multiculturalisms," in *Violence, Identity, and Self-Determination*, ed. Hent de Vries and Samuel Weber (Stanford: Stanford UP, 1997), 298.

25. See the introduction to David Kazanjian, *The Colonizing Trick: National Culture and Imperial Citizenship in Early America* (Minneapolis: U of Minnesota P, 2003).

26. "Eureka: An Essay on the Material and Spiritual Universe," in *Edgar Allan Poe: Poetry, Tales, and Selected Essays* (New York: Library of America, 1996), 1286.

27. *The Sketch-Book of Geoffrey Crayon, Gent.*, ed. Susan Manning (Oxford: Oxford UP, 1996), 47.

28. Horace Walpole, *Fugitive Pieces in Verse and Prose* (Twickenham: Strawberry-Hill Press, 1763), 47.

1. GENRE

1. Horace Walpole, *The Castle of Otranto* (Oxford: Oxford UP, 1996), 9; hereafter cited in the text.

2. Ian Duncan, *Modern Romance and Transformations of the Novel: The Gothic, Scott, Dickens* (Cambridge: Cambridge UP, 1992), 20.

3. See my final chapter for a detailed discussion of Walpolian uniquity.

4. Bertrand Russell quoted in Claire Ortiz Hill's *Rethinking Identity and Metaphysics: On the Foundations of Analytic Philosophy* (New Haven: Yale UP, 1997), 87.

5. In "Literary Genres and Textual Genericity," Jean-Marie Shaeffer claims that the "way literary studies have used the term 'literary genre' . . . is closer to magic thought than to rational investigation. In magic thought, the word creates the thing. . . . [T]he very fact of using the term has led us to think we ought to find a corresponding entity which would be added to the texts and would be the cause of the relationship" (in *The Future of Literary Theory*, ed. Ralph Cohen [London: Routledge, 1989], 167–68).

6. See Ortiz Hill and Michael D. Potter's *Set Theory and Its Philosophy: A Critical Introduction* (Oxford: Oxford UP, 2004) for an introduction to the philosophy of set theory.

7. Gottlob Frege, "On Concept and Object," trans. P. T. Geach, translation revised by Max Black, *Mind* 60.238 (1951): 172.

8. Walter Benjamin, *The Origin of German Tragic Drama*, trans. John Osborne (New York: Verso, 1998), 42; hereafter cited in the text.

9. As Samuel Weber puts it, "what is articulated in the Idea is a relation of singularities among themselves, in which they are not subsumed under a general concept . . . but rather assembled in terms of their singularizing differences, of their irreducibility to one another" ("Genealogy of Modernity: History, Myth and Allegory in Benjamin's Origin of the German Mourning Play," *MLN* 106.3 [1991]: 472).

10. In a similar move, Gilbert Simondon refuses to limit the forces of "invention" inherent in individuation to either inductive or deductive processes. "In the area of knowledge," he argues, "[the preindividual] maps out the actual course that invention follows, which is neither inductive nor deductive but rather transductive, meaning that it corresponds to a discovery of the dimensions according to which a problematic can be defined" (see "The Genesis of the Individual," in *Incorporations*, trans. Mark Cohen and Sanford Kwinter, ed. Jonathan Crary [New York: Zone, 1992], 313). I would like to thank Bernard Stiegler for bringing my attention to the work of Simondon.

11. My work on Benjamin and allegory has been especially influenced by Jim Hansen's "Formalism and Its Malcontents: Benjamin and de Man on the Function of Allegory," *New Literary History* 35.4 (2004): 663–83; Kyoo Lee's "A Calligraphy of Time: Allegory (Dis)orders in the Materialist Aesthetics of Walter Benjamin and Paul de Man," *parallax* 10.3 (2004): 6–19; Henry Sussman's "Between the Registers: The Allegory of Space in Walter Benjamin's Arcades Project," *boundary 2* 30.1 (2003): 169–90; Doris Sommer's "Allegory and Dialectics: A Match Made in Romance," *boundary 2* 18.1 (1991): 61–82; Bainard Cowan's "Walter Benjamin's Theory of Allegory," *New German Critique* 22 (Winter 1981): 109–22; and Matthew Wilken's "Toward a Benjaminian Theory of Dialectical Allegory," *New Literary History* 37 (2006): 285–98.

12. Compare Angus Fletcher's concept of an "allegory without ideas" discussed in the introduction to this volume.

13. Gilles Deleuze, *The Logic of Sense*, trans. Mark Lester, ed. Constantin V. Boundas (New York: Columbia UP, 1990), 1–2.

14. For a fascinating discussion of the relationship between the vernacular and Latin, see chapter 3 of Agamben's *The End of the Poem*, trans. Daniel Heller-Roazen (Stanford: Stanford UP, 1999).

15. Michael McKeon, *The Origins of the English Novel, 1600–1740* (Baltimore: Johns Hopkins UP, 2002), 36; hereafter cited in the text.

16. See McCormick's superb account of the relationship between Schmitt's and Lukács's ideas in his "Transcending Weber's Categories of Modernity? Left and Right 'Weberians' on the Rationalization Thesis in Interwar Central Europe," *New German Critique* 75 (Fall 1998): 133–77.

17. See Barrett Kalter's dissertation, "Modern Antiques: Imagination, Scholarship, and the Material Past," (Rutgers University, 2004) for an interesting discussion of Walpole, authenticity, and the effects of commodification on the antique.

18. Susan Stewart, "Notes on Distressed Genres," *Journal of American Folklore* 104.411 (1991): 6.

19. Nancy, *The Inoperative Community*, 45.

20. Jacques Rancière, *The Flesh of Words*, trans. Charlotte Mandell (Stanford: Stanford UP, 2004), 11; hereafter cited in the text.

21. For a more detailed discussion of potentiality and poeisis, see chapters 11–14 of Giorgio Agamben's *Potentialities: Collected Essays in Philosophy*, trans. Daniel Heller-Roazen (Stanford: Stanford UP, 199).

22. In a 2003 issue of *New Literary History* dedicated to genre studies, Michael B. Prince explores what I have called the genericity of genre in the eighteenth century, as it loses its neoclassical foundation and attempts to reground itself in eighteenth-century discourses of taste and beauty (see his "Mauvis Genres," *New Literary History* 34.3 [2003]: 452–79).

23. Frederic Jameson, "Magic Narratives: Romance as Genre," *New Literary History* 7 (1975/76): 151; hereafter cited in the text.

24. For a fascinating and detailed account of such work, see Michael Gamer's *Romanticism and the Gothic: Genre, Reception, and Canon-Formation* (Cambridge: Cambridge UP, 2006).

25. Clery and Miles collect a variety of different approaches to the Gothic—both primary and secondary—in their *Gothic Documents* (Manchester, UK: Manchester UP, 2000). See section 4.4 for a discussion of "Terrorist Novel Writing."

26. Jerrold E. Hogle, "The Gothic Ghost of the Counterfeit and the Progress of Abjection," in *A Companion to the Gothic*, ed. David Punter (Oxford: Blackwell, 2000): 296–97.

27. Erich Auerbach, *Mimesis: The Representation of Reality in Western Literature*, trans. Willard R. Trask (Princeton: Princeton UP, 2003), xiii.

28. William Warner, "Realist Literary History: McKeon's New Origins of the Novel," *Diacritics* 19.1 (1989): 71.

29. Ibid., 78.

30. Jacques Rancière, *The Names of History: On the Poetics of Knowledge*, trans. Hassan Melehy (Minneapolis: U of Minnesota P, 1994), 32.

31. Sigmund Freud, "The Uncanny," in *On Creativity and the Unconscious: Papers on the Psychology of Art, Literature, Love, Religion* (New York: Harper Colophon, 1958), 124; hereafter cited in the text.

32. My discussion of Gothic "convertibility" is indebted to the mentorship and scholarship of Colin Dayan, in particular her essay "Amorous Bondage: Poe, Ladies, and Slaves," *American Literature* 66.2 (1994): 239–73.

33. Sigmund Freud, *Beyond the Pleasure Principle*, trans. James Strachey (New York: Norton, 1961), 46–47.

34. Ibid.. 47.

35. Quoted in Peter Sabor's *Horace Walpole: A Reference Guide* (Boston: G. K. Hall, 1984), 68–69.

36. Ibid., 69.

37. Ibid., 71.

38. Ibid., 67.

39. Ibid.

40. Derrida describes a similarly uncanny generic process in "The Law of Genre": "The law and the counter-law serve each other citations summoning each other to appear, and each recites the other in this proceeding (*procès*)" (*Critical Inquiry* 7.1 [1980]: 58).

41. Samuel Weber, "Genealogy of Modernity: History, Myth and Allegory in Benjamin's *Origin of the German Mourning Play*," 468.

42. Duncan, *Modern Romance and Transformations of the Novel*, 22–23; hereafter cited in the text.

43. Walter Benjamin, "Theses on the Philosophy of History," in *Illuminations*, ed. Hannah Arendt (New York: Schocken, 1969), 261.

44. Abigail Coykendall discusses the nuances of Walpolian historiography in her wonderful dissertation, "Conjuring Inherited Empire: Gothic Real Estate and the Eighteenth-Century British Novel." (SUNY Buffalo, 2002)

45. Henry George Liddell and Robert Scott, *A Greek-English Lexicon* (Oxford: Oxford UP, 1940), 206.

46. Ibid., 192.

47. In *Inescapable Romance*, Patricia Parker argues that the genre "is characterized primarily as a form which simulataneously quests for and postpones a particular end" (see *Inescapable Romance: Studies in the Poetics of a Mode* [Princeton: Princeton UP, 1979], 4).

48. Quoted in Richard Schlatter's *Hobbes's Thucydides* (New Brunswick, NJ: Rutgers UP, 1975), 546.

2. FEELING

1. Karl Marx, *Capital: A Critique of Political Economy* (London: Penguin Classics, 1990), 1: 205; hereafter cited in text.

2. In *Mixed Feelings: Feminism, Mass Culture, and Victorian Sensationalism* (New Brunswick, NJ: Rutgers University Press, 1992), Ann Cvetkovich reads *Capital* as a "sensation narrative," arguing that Marx deploys the tropes of sentimental fiction in order to humanize the worker and to spotlight the exploitation of his body.

3. Perhaps this is why Marx was so enamored with the literature of romance, a fact that is relayed with obvious delight by his daughter Eleanor:

> And [he] would also read to his children. Thus to me, as to my sisters before me, he read the whole of Homer, the whole *Nibelungen Lied, Gudrun, Don Quixote*, the *Arabian Nights*, etc. . . . Scott was an author to whom Marx again and again returned, whom he admired and knew as well as he did Balzac and Fielding. And while he talked about these and many other books he would . . . show his little girl where to look for all that was finest and best in the works, teach her — though she never thought she was being taught, to that she would have objected — to try and think, to try and understand for herself.

See "Recollections of Mohr," in *Marx and Engels on Literature and Art*, ed. Lee Baxandall and Stephen Morawski (New York: International, 1974), 150.

4. Frederic Jameson, "Magic Narratives: Romance as Genre," *New Literary History* 7 (1975/76): 142.

5. Anthony, Third Earl of Shaftesbury, "Sensus Communis: An Essay on the Freedom of Wit and Humour in a Letter to a Friend," *Characteristics of Men, Manners, Opinions, Times*. ed. Lawrence E. Klein (Cambridge: Cambridge UP): 51–52.

6. Henry Mackenzie, *The Man of Feeling* (New York: Oxford University Press, 2001), 18; hereafter cited in text.

7. *The Mirror*, in *The Miscellaneous Works of Henry Mackenzie, Esq*. (New York: Harper and Brothers, 1836), 498; hereafter cited in the text.

8. William Godwin, *Fleetwood: or, the New Man of Feeling* (Peterborough, Ontario: Broadview Press, 2001), 56.

9. For a fascinating discussion of the it-narrative, see Jonathan Lamb "Modern Metamorphoses and Disgraceful Tales," *Critical Inquiry* 28.1 (2001): 133–66. See also *The Secret Life of Things*, ed. Mark Blackwell (Cranberry, NJ: Rosemont, 2007); and Christina Lupton's "The Knowing Book: Authors, It-Narratives, and Objectification in the Eighteenth Century," *Novel* 39.3 (2006): 402–20.

10. Henry Mackenzie, *Julia de Roubigné*, ed. Susan Manning (East Linton: Tuckwell Press, 1999), 116; hereafter cited in the text.

11. Carl Schmitt, *Political Romanticism* (Cambridge: MIT P, 1986), 84.

12. In a footnote to page 113 of *Julia de Roubigné*, Manning observes that "Mackenzie's essay for *The Mirror*, No. 30 (8 May 1779), raises the same question, and treats it as indisputable that 'whether or not there be a sex in the soul . . . there is one in manners'" (113). Similar language is also present in the *Lounger*, No. 32 (10 September 1785): "There is something . . . in the circumstance of sex, that mixes a degree of tenderness with our duty to a female" (in *The Miscellaneous Works of Henry Mackenzie, Esq*. [New York: Harper and Brothers, 1836]: 114).

13. Laurence Sterne, *A Sentimental Journey* (London: Penguin Classics, 1986), 138.

14. My discussion of sentimental servitude is influenced by Dayan's "Amorous Bondage: Poe, Ladies, and Slaves."

15. See Giorgio Agamben, "The Logic of Sovereignty" in *Homo Sacer*, trans. Daniel Heller-Roazen (Stanford: Stanford UP, 1998), 15–29.

16. Over the past decade, there has been an explosion of scholarly interest in the relationships between the politics of nation building, the ideologies of race, and the aesthetics of sentimentality. The texts that have influenced this work the most include Ezra Tawil's *The Making of Racial Sentiment: Slavery and the Birth of the Frontier Romance* (New York: Cambridge University Press, 2006); Marianne Noble's *The Masochistic Pleasures of Sentimental Literature* (Princeton: Princeton UP, 2000); Julia Ellison's *Cato's Tears and the Making of Anglo-American Emotion* (Chicago: U of Chicago P,

1999); Julia A. Stern's *The Plight of Feeling: Sympathy and Dissent in the Early American Novel* (Chicago: U of Chicago P, 1997); Saidiya V. Hartman, *Scenes of Subjection: Terror, Slavery, and Self-Making in Nineteenth-Century America* (New York: Oxford UP, 1997); and Sianne Ngai, *Ugly Feelings* (Cambridge: Harvard UP, 2005).

17. Markman Ellis, *The Politics of Sensibility: Race, Commerce, and Gender in the Sentimental Novel* (New York: Cambridge University Press, 1996), 55.

18. Kazanjian, *The Colonizing Trick*, 7.

19. See also Maja-Lisa von Sneidern, "'Monk Lewis's Journals and the Discipline of Discourse," *Nineteenth-Century Contexts* 23 (2001): 59–68.

20. Matthew Lewis, *Journal of a West India Proprietor* (Oxford: Oxford University Press, 1999), 62.

21. Quoted in Kevin Hayes's *The Road to Monticello: The Life and Mind of Thomas Jefferson* (New York: Oxford UP, 2008), 136.

22. Ibid., 134.

23. Susan Manning, "Why Does It Matter That Ossian Was Thomas Jefferson's Favorite Poet?," *Symbiosis* 1.2 (1997): 220.

24. Thomas Jefferson, *Notes on the State of Virginia* in *Thomas Jefferson: Writings* (New York: Library of America, 1984), 264–65.

25. Quoted in *"The Castle of Otranto" and "The Man of Feeling": A Longman Cultural Edition*, ed. Laura Mandell (New York: Longman, 2006), 252.

26. See chapters 25 and 27 of *The Man of Feeling* (London: Cassel, 1886).

27. Ibid. Thanks to my colleague Mike Hill for bringing this index to my attention.

28. Thomas Jefferson, *Notes on the State of Virginia* (Boston: H. Sprague, 1802), 322–23.

29. See Keith Thomas, "Jefferson, Buffon, and the Moose," *American Scientist* 96.3 (2008): 200.

30. *The Speech of Logan* (New York: Elliot and Hunt, 1803), 4.

31. Jonathan Elmer, *On Lingering and Being Last: Race and Sovereignty in the New World* (New York: Fordham UP, 2008), 135; hereafter cited in the text. Elmer's argument is that such a position of ruined isolation is a necessary corollary of modern systems of sovereignty—systems that, like Savillon's abolitionism, create their expansive political communities only at the same time that they produce devastating racial ruins at their liberal or pluralistic cores.

3. PROPERTY/PERSONHOOD

1. *Charles Brockden Brown: Three Gothic Novels* (New York: Library of America, 1998), 347; hereafter cited in the text.

2. See, for example, Ronald Paulson's "Gothic Fiction and the French Revolution," *ELH* 48.3 (1981); chapter 1 of Ian Duncan's *Modern Romance and*

Transformations of the Novel; the introduction to Gamer's *Romanticism and the Gothic*; Jerrold E. Hogle's "Hyper-Reality and the Gothic Affect: The Sublimation of Fear from Burke and Walpole to *The Ring*," *English Language Notes* 48.1 (2010): 163–76; and David B. Morris's "Gothic Sublimity," *New Literary History* 16.2 (1985): 299–319.

3. For two recent examples, see Bridget M. Marshall's *The Transatlantic Gothic Novel and the Law, 1790–1860* (Farnham, UK: Ashgate, 2011); and Leonard Tennenhouse's *The Importance of Feeling English: American Literature and the British Diaspora* (Princeton, NJ: Princeton UP, 2007).

4. Siân Silyn Roberts opens her essay "Gothic Enlightenment: Contagion and Community in Charles Brockden Brown's *Arthur Mervyn*" by similarly invoking Fiedler's "legacy to the field of gothic criticism" (*Early American Literature* 44.2 [2009]: 307). Rather than contributing to the kind of "psychologically inflected readings" that Fiedler has inspired, Roberts instead establishes rich historical contexts that explain the "enduring appeal" of the Gothic in America (307).

5. *Charles Brockden Brown: Three Gothic Novels* (New York: Library of America, 1998), 641.

6. Quoted in Theresa Goddu's *Gothic America: Narrative, History, and Nation* (New York: Columbia UP, 1997), 57.

7. Leslie Fiedler, *Love and Death in the American Novel* (New York: Critereon, 1960), 143.

8. Susan Scheckel, *The Insistence of the Indian* (Princeton, NJ: Princeton UP, 1998), 12.

9. Benedict Anderson's *Imagined Communities: Reflections on the Origin and Spread of Nationalism* (New York: Verso, 1983) continues to influence scholarship on the emerging U.S. nation.

10. Berlant develops her idea of the "National Symbol" in *The Anatomy of National Fantasy: Hawthorne, Utopia, and Everyday Life* (Chicago: U of Chicago P, 1991).

11. In *The Parallax View* (Cambridge: MIT P, 2006), Žižek quotes the following footnote from *The Interpretation of Dreams* in order to highlight this common error:

> Formerly I found it extraordinarily difficult to accustom my readers to the distinction between the manifest dream-content and the latent dream-thoughts. Over and over again arguments and objections were adduced from the un-interpreted dream as it was retained in the memory, and the necessity of interpreting the dream was ignored. But now, when the analysts have at last become reconciled to substituting for the manifest dream its meaning as found by interpretation, many of them are guilty of another mistake, to which they adhere just as stubbornly. They look for the essence of the dream in this latent content, and thereby overlook the distinction between latent dream-thoughts

and the dream-work. The dream is fundamentally nothing more than a special form of our thinking, which is made possible by the conditions of the sleeping state. It is the dream-work which produces this form, and it alone is the essence of dreaming—the only explanation of its singularity. (55)

12. See chapter 1, "The Seven Veils of Fantasy," in Žižek's *The Plague of Fantasies* (London: Verso, 1997), for example.

13. See, for example, chapter 3 of Andy Doolen's *Fugitive Empire: Locating Early American Imperialism* (Minneapolis: U of Minnesota P, 2005); chapter 1 of Shirley Samuels's *Romances of the Republic: Women, the Family, and Violence in the Literature of the Early American Nation* (New York: Oxford UP, 1996); and chapter 5 of Sean X. Goudie's *Creole America: The West Indies and the Formation of Literature and Culture in the New Republic* (Philadelphia: U of Pennsylvania P, 2006).

14. Online at http://wesley.nnu.edu/fileadmin/imported_site/biblical_studies/wycliffe/Mat.txt.

15. Geoffrey Chaucer, "The Prioress' Prologue and Tale," in *The Canterbury Tales* (New York: Penguin Classics, 2005), 498.

16. Roberto Esposito, *Bios*, trans. Timothy Campbell (Minneapolis: U of Minnesota P, 2008).

17. Robert Esposito, *Immunitas: The Protection and Negation of Life*, trans. Zakiya Hanafi (Cambridge, UK: Polity Press, 2011), 159 and 7.

18. For another account of the relationship between immunity and sovereignty, see Jacques Derrida's *Rogues: Two Essays on Reason*, trans. Pascale-Anne Brault and Michael Nass (Stanford: Stanford UP, 2005). Here Derrida is interested in exploring the "autoimmunity of sovereignty in general," and—in particular—describes how the logic of autoimmunity operates in the United States, when this nation "come[s] to resemble [its] enemies, to corrupt itself and threaten itself in order to protect itself against their threats" (80, 40).

19. Robert Esposito, *Communitas: The Origin and Destiny of Community*, trans. Timothy Campbell (Stanford: Stanford UP, 2010), 139.

20. Esposito, *Bios*, 61; hereafter cited in the text.

21. John Locke, *Second Treatise of Civil Government*, ed. C. B. Macpherson (Indianapolis: Hackett, 1980), 29; hereafter cited in the text by section number.

22. See chapter 2 of Donald McNutt's *Urban Revelations: Images of Ruin in the American City, 1790–1860* (New York: Routledge, 2006) for another exploration of architecture and urban space in *Arthur Mervyn*.

23. For another detailed discussion of the "thing" of Lockean personhood, see chapter 2 of Esposito's recently published *Third Person: Politics of Life and Philosophy of the Impersonal*, trans. Zakiya Hanafi (Cambridge, UK: Polity Press, 2012).

24. See chapter 1 of *Capital: Volume 1: A Critique of Political Economy* (New York: Penguin Classics, 1992).

25. Mervyn's negotiations of these "perilous precincts of private property"—and their relationship to early national republican values—are the subject of chapter 3 of Elizabeth Jane Wall Hinds's *Private Property: Charles Brockden Brown's Gendered Economies of Virtue* (Cranberry, NJ: Associated UP, 1997); and Sarah Wood's "Private Properties, Public Nuisance: *Arthur Mervyn* and the Rise and Fall of a Republican Machine," *U.S. Studies Online* 2 (2001).

26. Goudie, *Creole America* 188.

27. For a fascinating dicussion of Benjamin, Poe, and the role of the detective in modernity, see Carlo Salzani's "The City as Crime Scene: Walter Benjamin and the Traces of the Detective," *New German Critique* 100 (2007): 165–89.

28. "One-Way Street," in *Walter Benjamin: Selected Writings* (Cambridge: Harvard UP, 2004), 1: 446.

29. In *The Culture and Commerce of the Early American Novel: Reading the Atlantic World-System* (University Park: Pennsylvania State UP, 2008), Stephen Shapiro uncovers a rich "counterhegemonic practice" in the mysterious "narrative architecture" of *Arthur Mervyn*, a "tactic [that] points to alternative social practices but often in highly inferential ways" (263).

30. Many thanks to Ed White for suggesting that I look at this text in connection with *Arthur Mervyn*'s immunitary logic.

31. Charles Brockden Brown, "The Man at Home–No. I," *Weekly Magazine* 1.1 (1798): 2.

32. Charles Brockden Brown, "The Man at Home–No. XII." *Weekly Magazine* 1.12 (1798): 354.

33. Ibid.

34. Charles Brockden Brown, "The Man at Home–No. XI," *Weekly Magazine* 1.11 (1798): 322.

35. Ibid., 322–23.

36. Shapiro, *The Culture and Commerce of the Early American Novel*, 282

37. Goudie, *Creole America*, 21.

38. Ibid., 194.

39. Shapiro, *The Culture and Commerce of the Early American Novel*, 286.

40. Laurence Sterne, *A Sentimental Journey through France and Italy* (London: Penguin Classics, 1986), 92; hereafter cited in the text.

41. See Danielle Bobker's "Carriages, Conversation, and *A Sentimental Journey*," *Studies in Eighteenth Century Culture* 35 (2006): 243–66.

42. In "Voltaire's Parrot; or, How to Do Things with Birds," Thomas DiPiero notes that by "the eighteenth century talking parrots had allowed philosophers and naturalists to interrogate the place of the human in existing taxonomies" (*Modern Language Quarterly* 70.3 [2009]: 362).

43. John Locke, *An Essay Concerning Human Understanding*, ed. Peter H. Nidditch (Oxford: Oxford UP, 1975), 335; hereafter cited in the text by page and section.

44. Quoted in DiPiero, "Voltaire's Parrot," 360.

45. Goudie, *Creole America*, 191.

46. Robert Montgomery Bird, *Sheppard Lee: Written by Himself* (New York: New York Review of Books, 2008), 405; hereafter cited in the text.

47. "United We Scam," *Nation*, January 28, 2008, available online at: www.thenation.com/article/united-we-scam.

48. G. W. F. Hegel, *Phenomenology of Spirit*, trans. A. V. Miller (New York: Oxford UP, 1977), 111.

49. Edgar Allan Poe, review of *Sheppard Lee*, by Robert Montgomery Bird, Southern *Literary Messenger* 2.10 (1836): 666.

50. Chris Looby, introduction to *Sheppard Lee*, by Bird, xxxiv–xxxv.

51. Ibid., xxxv.

52. Ibid.

53. Looby and Justine Murison, in "Hypochondria and Racial Interiority in Robert Montgomery Bird's *Sheppard Lee*" (*Arizona Quarterly* 64.1 [2008]), also explore mechanisms of thingification in the novel.

54. James Fenimore Cooper, *Autobiography of a Pocket-Handkerchief*, ed. Walter Lee Brown (Evanston, IL: Golden Booke Press, 1897), 142; hereafter cited in the text.

55. For a fascinating discussion of the dialectics of taste, see chapter 3 of Giorgio Agamben's *The Man without Content* (Stanford: Stanford UP, 1999).

56. See Reginald Horsman's *Race and Manifest Destiny: Origins of Racial Anglo-Saxonism* (Cambridge: Harvard UP, 1981).

57. The term "species" appears nine times in the text.

58. In *Reading at the Social Limit: Affect, Mass Culture, and Edgar Allan Poe* (Stanford: Stanford UP, 1995), Jonathan Elmer powerfully connects the science of mesmerism with emerging models of sentimental community. After all, he argues, "mesmeric phenomena were understood to tap into a fundamental social sympathy, to be peculiarly exacerbated instantiations of the fluid links between all social beings" (117). Quoting John Bovee Dods, Elmer points to the "nervo-vital fluid" that "affects another, and that still another, till the whole assembly are brought into magical sympathy with the speaker" (118).

4. EVENT/HIATUS

1. James Tully, *An Approach to Political Philosophy: Locke in Contexts* (Cambridge: Cambridge UP, 1993), 139. See also Kathy Squadrito's "Locke and the Dispossession of the American Indian," in *Philosophers on Race: Critical Essays*, ed. Julie K. Ward and Tommy L. Lott (Oxford: Blackwell, 2002) and Herman Lebovics's "The Uses of America in Locke's Second Treatise of Government," *Journal of the History of Ideas* 47.4 (1986): 67–81.

2. "The Fundamental Constitutions of Carolina," in *The Works of John Locke*, 10 vols. (Darmstadt, Germany: Scientia Verlag Aalen, 1963).

3. Quoted in Tully, *An Approach to Political Philosophy*, 168.

4. *De la démocratie en Amérique*, I, ed. Jean-Marie Tremblay, 25. Available online at: http://classiques.uqac.ca/classiques/De_tocqueville_alexis/democratie_1/dem ocratie_t1_1.pdf.

5. *Democracy in America and Two Essays on America*, trans. Gerald Bevan (London: Penguin, 2003), 36.

6. As early as 1395, we find John Wycliffe articulating a primordial idleness in his translation of Genesis 1:2. There he describes the "erthe [as] idel and voide" even before any distinctions between light and dark, land and water, heaven and earth, and day and night have been made.

7. I thank Jennifer Greiman for her help with the original French source of Bevan's translation.

8. Charles Brockden Brown, review of *Continuation of the History of the Province of Massachusetts Bay, from the Year 1748. With an Introductory Sketch of Events from its Original Settlement*, by George Richards Minot, Fellow of the American Academy of Arts and Sciences, and Member of the Massachusetts Historical Society, 8 vols. (Boston: Manning and Loring, 1798), 1: 304, in *American Review and Literary Journal* 1.1 (1801): 2.

9. I do not mean to suggest that this is Brockden Brown's lone blueprint for "the historian of the United States." Throughout his fiction and, especially, in the fragmented and fascinating *Historical Sketches*, Brockden Brown explored a number of different visions of temporality and experimented with alternative modes of history writing. As Ed White notes, in the *Historical Sketches* "Brown virtually inaugurated the tradition of the alternative history by abandoning his national setting for an unexpected plunge into the Mediterranean past." See his "The Ends of Republicanism," *Journal of the Early Republic* 30 (Summer 2010): 196. For other readings of Brockden Brown's historical methodology in the *Sketches*, see Philip Barnard's "Culture and Authority in Brown's Historical Sketches," in *Revising Brockden Brown: Culture, Politics, and Sexuality in the Early Republic* (Knoxville: U of Tennessee P, 2004), 310–31; and Robert Battistini's "'Not to Forsake . . . but to Restore': Usable Pasts and Generic Play in Brown's Historical Sketches," in *Literature in the Early American Republic: Annual Studies on Cooper and His Contemporaries* 3 (2011): 41–60.

10. Jeffrey Insko, "Diedrich Knickerbocker, Regular Bred Historian," *Early American Literature* 43.3 (2008): 610.

11. Robert Ferguson, "'Hunting down a Nation': Irving's *A History of New-York*," *Nineteenth-Century Fiction* 36.1 (1981): 32.

12. Christopher Looby, *Voicing America: Language, Literary Form, and the Origins of the United States* (Chicago: U of Chicago P, 1996), 93.

13. Insko, "Diedrich Knickerbocker, Regular Bred Historian," 609.

14. Ibid.

15. William Hedges, "Knickerbocker, Bolingbroke, and the Fiction of History," *Journal of the History of Ideas* 20.3 (1959): 326.

16. Ibid., 320.

17. Ibid., 317.

18. See note 61 of this chapter for a detailed discussion of Laura J. Murray's wonderful "The Aesthetic of Dispossession: Washington Irving and Ideologies of (De)Colonization in the Early Republic," *American Literary History* 8.2 (1996): 205–31.

19. Jeffrey Rubin-Dorsky, "The Value of Storytelling: *Rip Van Winkle* and *The Legend of Sleepy Hollow* in the Context of *The Sketch Book*," *Modern Philology* 82.4 (1985): 398.

20. Ibid.

21. Michael Warner, "Irving's Posterity," *ELH* 67 (2000): 776.

22. Ibid., 776–77.

23. Ibid., 790.

24. Ibid.

25. Washington Irving, *The Sketch-Book of Geoffrey Crayon, Gent*, ed. Susan Manning (Oxford: Oxford UP, 1996), 47; hereafter cited in the text.

26. Giorgio Agamben, *Homo Sacer: Sovereign Power and Bare Life*, trans. Daniel Heller-Roazen (Stanford: Stanford UP, 1998), 28. For Nancy's discussion of the ban, see "Abandoned Being" in *The Birth to Presence* (Stanford: Stanford UP, 1993), 36–47.

27. See note 61 of this chapter.

28. For a more detailed discussion of the place of trauma in *The Sketch-Book*, see Robert Hughes's "Sleepy Hollow: Fearful Pleasures and the Nightmare of History," *Arizona Quarterly* 61.3 (2005): 1–26.

29. "Where'er I roam, whatever realms to see,/My heart untravell'd fondly turns to thee;/Still to my brother turns, with ceaseless pain,/And drags at each remove a lengthening chain," in Oliver Goldsmith, *The Traveller; or, a Prospect of Society* (London: J. Newberry, 1765), 2.

30. *Julia de Roubigné*, ed. Susan Manning (East Linton: Tuckwell Press, 1999), 116.

31. Irving may also have in mind Euphrasia's comment concerning the popularity of "Novels" in Clara Reeve's *Progress of Romance*: "The press groaned under the weight of Novels, which sprung up like Mushrooms every year" (qtd. in Gamer, *Romanticism and the Gothic*, 63).

32. *An Essay on the Principle of Population*, 2 vols., 4th ed. (London: J.Johnson, 1807).

33. Quoted in Malthus, *An Essay on the Principle of Population; or, a View of Its Past and Present Effects on Human Happiness; with an Inquiry into our Prospects*

Respecting the Future Removal of the Evils which it Occasions, 2 vols. (London: J. Johnson, 1807), 1:400.

34. For other examples of the lastness of race (and its relationship to modern forms of power), see Jonathan Elmer's *On Lingering and Being Last: Race and Sovereignty in the New World* (New York: Fordham UP, 2008).

35. See, for example, William Apess's *Eulogy on King Philip, as Pronounced at the Odeon, in Federal Street, Boston* in *On Our Own Ground: The Complete Writings of William Apess, a Pequot*, ed. Barry O'Connell (Amherst: U of Massachusetts P, 1992).

36. This is how we should read the traces of Indian legend in Knickerbocker's postscript to "Rip Van Winkle." Rip's hiatus makes possible the pastness of the Indian past—the "Once upon a time" of their "abode of spirits"—at the same time as it paves the way for the new nation to emerge by forgetting ongoing indigenous resistance to U.S. colonial violence (49, 48).

37. Quoted in Goddu, *Gothic America*, 57.

38. See Kai von Fintel and Anthony S. Gillies, "Epistemic Modality for Dummies," available online at: http://rci.rutgers.edu/~thony/fintel-gillies.ose2–final.pdf. In this paper, von Fintel and Gillies explain and develop Kripke's ideas concerning the semantics of modals. See, for example, his "Semantical Analysis of Modal Logic I: Normal Modal Propositional Calculi," *Zeitschrift für mathematische Logik und Grundlagen der Mathematik* 9 (1963): 67–96.

39. For more on the inherent latency of traumatic experience, see Cathy Caruth's *Unclaimed Experience: Trauma, Narrative, and History* (Baltimore: Johns Hopkins UP, 1996); hereafter cited parenthetically.

40. See chapter 2 for a discussion of the function of the ruined woman—often named Maria—in eighteenth-century communities of feeling.

41. Sarah Wood, "Refusing to R.I.P.; or, Return of the Dispossessed: The Transatlantic Revivals of Irving's Rip Van Winkle," *Symbiosis: A Journal of Anglo-American Literary Relations* 10.1 (2007): 3.

42. Wood's details of historical performances come from William Winter's *Life and Art of Joseph Jefferson* (New York: Macmillan, 1894), 177–78; and Montrose J. Moses, *Representative Plays by American Dramatists* (London: Blom, 1964), 18–22.

43. John Kerr, *Rip Van Winkle; or Demons of the Catskill Mountains!!! A National Drama*, 6.

44. Ibid., 8. "After drinking and eating with the natives," Wood continues, "he lavishes looks of love on an Indian maid, and leaves with the promise to return but never does. Delivered in Act Two, by a character called Sophia, the song is clumsily inserted into the drama; it bears no relation to the rest of the action, and in this sense is just as dismembered and as fragmentary as Washington Irving's postscript" (8).

45. See, for example, Frederick E. Hoxie's *Native Americans and the Early Republic* (Charlottesville: U of Virginia P, 1999).

46. "Andrew Jackson," ed. James D. Richardson, *A Compilation of Messages and Papers of the Presidents, 1789–1902*, 10 vols. (Washington, DC: U.S. Government Printing Office, 1902), 2: 457–58.

47. See George Catlin's *North American Indians*, ed. Peter Matthiessen (New York, Penguin 1989). For discussions of Catlin's work, see, for example, Kate Flint's *The Transatlantic Indian, 1775–1930* (Princeton, NJ.: Princeton UP, 2009); Mildred Goosman's *Exploration in the West: Catlin, Bodmer, Miller* (Omaha: Joslyn Art Museum, 1967); Steven Conn's *History's Shadow: Native Americans and Historical Consciousness in the Nineteenth Century* (Chicago: U of Chicago P, 2006); and Mark D. Spence's *Dispossessing the Wilderness: Indian Removal and the Making of the National Parks* (New York: Oxford UP, 2000).

48. Drawing on the language of phrenological science, Irving describes Black Hawk as follows: "old man upwards of seventy with aquiline nose—finely formed head—organs of benevolence—his two sons—oldest a fine-looking young man.... They are all chained arms and ankles with cannon, but are allowed to walk about escorted by soldier" (from *The Journals of Washington Irving*, ed. William P. Trent and George S. Hellman [New York: Haskell House, 1970], 1: 113).

49. Quoted in Benjamin Drake's *The Life and Adventures of Black Hawk: With Sketches of Keokuk, the Sac and Fox Indians, and the Late Black Hawk War*, 7th ed. (Cincinnati: George Conclin, 1849), 202–3; see also Kendall Johnson's "Peace, Friendship, and Financial Panic: Reading the Mark of Black Hawk in Life of Ma-Ka-Tai-Me-She-Kia-Kiak," *American Literary History* 19.4 (Winter 2007): 771–99.

50. See my discussion of *Beyond the Pleasure Principle* in chapter 1.

51. Quoted in David Mazel's "'A Beautiful and Thrilling Specimen': George Catlin, the Death of Wilderness, and the Birth of the National Subject," in *Reading the Earth: New Directions in the Study of Literature and Environment*, ed. Michael P. Branch, Rochelle Johnson, Daniel Patterson, and Scott Slovic (Moscow: U of Idaho P, 1998), 129.

52. Wilderness Act, PL 88–577, 3 September 1964.

53. Richard Batman, foreword to *A Tour on the Prairies*, by Washington Irving (Norman: U of Oklahoma P, 1956), xiv.

54. Stanley T. Williams, *The Life of Washington Irving*, 2 vols. (New York: Octagon, 1971), 2: 30.

55. Ibid., 2: 32.

56. Quoted in John Francis McDermott's introduction to *A Tour on the Prairies* (Norman: U of Oklahoma P, 1985), xxiii.

57. Stanley T Williams and Barbara D. Simison, introduction to *Washington Irving on the Prairie: or, A Narrative of the Tour of the Southwest in the Year 1832*, by

Henry Leavitt Ellsworth, ed.Williams and Simison (New York: American Book Company, 1937), xi.

58. Ibid., 71; hereafter cited in the text.

59. Michael Paul Rogin, *Fathers and Children: Andrew Jackson and the Subjugation of the American Indian* (New Brunswick: Transaction, 1991), 206.

60. Washington Irving, *A Tour on the Prairies*, ed. John Francis McDermott (Norman: U of Oklahoma P, 1956), 3; hereafter cited in the text.

61. Given the nature of Irving's relationship with Ellsworth, it is surprising that critics have ignored how *A Tour on the Prairies*—the much-anticipated literary product of Irving's adventures in Indian Territory—interacts with the complex sociocultural and literary discourses and debates surrounding Indian removal. This silence is even more puzzling given Irving's own literary preoccupation with fictions of possession and dispossession. In "The Aesthetic of Dispossession: Washington Irving and Ideologies of (De)Colonization in the Early Republic," Laura J. Murray looks at how Irving's representations of Native Americans and his depictions of the artist in *The Sketch-Book* form an aesthetic that romanticizes dispossession and thereby reconfigures the violence attending colonial expansion in the early republic. "This aesthetic," Murray avers, "operated through romanticization of the ideas of dispossession, homelessness, and loss. . . . On the one hand, Irving nurtured a sense of dispossession from an English heritage, which became in his writing a poetic and poignant loss; on the other, he also dwelt with romantic fascination on the Native Americans' loss of land and life and lifeways, removing Native Americans from history and positioning them in the realm of romance" (212). Murray points out how Irving's rhetorical strategies in *The Sketch-Book* enable him to distance himself and his readership from their complicity in colonial violence. For example, Irving begins one of its central stories, "Stratford-on-Avon," by recoding dispossession in terms of a positive aesthetic and "territorial" gain: "To a homeless man, who has no spot on this wide world which he can truly call his own, there is a momentary feeling of something like independence and territorial consequence, when, after a weary day's travel, he kicks off his boots, thrusts his feet into slippers, and stretches himself before an inn fire" (224). As the story develops, Irving invokes the legend that "Shakespeare was ordered to leave Stratford for poaching, a punishment that initiated his theater career" (215). Again, Murray notes, Irving here develops the intimate connection between material dispossession and aesthetic production. The two Indian sketches that follow "Stratford-on-Avon"—"Traits of Indian Character" and "Philip of Pokanoket"—further develop this rhetorical strategy through their depictions of Native Americans. In these two stories, Murray argues, "the discourse of noble savagery smoothes out the Native American path to extinction: Irving predicts that, 'driven to madness and despair,' Indians will 'vanish like a vapour from the face of the earth'" (233). Coupled with "the discourse of noble savagery," Murray argues,

Irving's "aesthetic of dispossession" effectively distances his readership in the early republic from the violence attending colonial expansion.

62. Irving makes it clear that his extended removal in Europe was anything but voluntary. Although he had originally planned "to visit the fairest scenes of Europe, with the prospect of returning home in a couple of years" (3), "a reversal in fortune ... cast [Irving] down in spirit" (4): "I turned to my pen for solace and support. I had hitherto exercised it for amusement; I now looked to it as my main dependence, resolving, if successful, never to ... return to my friends, until, by my literary exertions, I had placed myself above their pity, or assistance" (4). Dispossessed of wealth and his native land, Irving returns to the U.S. an independent artist, free to convey the "simple narrative" of his tour "into the wilderness of the Far West" (9).

63. Mark K. Burns, "'Ineffectual Chase': Indians, Prairies, Buffalo, and the Quest for the Authentic West in Washington Irving's *A Tour on the Prairies*," *Western American Literature* 42.1 (2007): 58.

64. Quoted in Martha Dula's "Audience Response to *A Tour on the Prairies* in 1835," *Western American Literature* 8 (1973): 68.

65. Ibid., 58.

66. Williams, *The Life of Washington Irving*, 2:43.

67. Ibid., 344.

68. Richard Slotkin, *Gunfighter Nation: The Myth of the Frontier in Twentieth Century America* (New York: Athenaeum, 1992), 13.

69. Quoted in Francis Paul Prucha's *Documents of United States Indian Policy* (Lincoln: U of Nebraska P, 1976), 61.

70. In contrast, Ellsworth's account of the prairie dog village makes no mention of dispossession (127).

71. In "The Winning of the West: Washington Irving's *A Tour on the Prairies*," *The Yearbook of English Studies* 34 (2004), Guy Reynolds argues that Irving "writes his own [Mandevillian] 'fable of the bees'" (92). "Irving," he continues, "presents a benign process of settlement, even though other commentators had noted that the Indians feared the bees, since they were a signal of the white man's relentless advance" (93).

72. Edgar Allan Poe, review of *Astoria*, by Washington Irving, "Astoria: Or, Anecdotes of an Enterprise beyond the Rocky Mountains. By Washington Irving. Philadelphia: Carey, Lea and Blanchard." *Southern Literary Messenger* 3.1 (1837): 59.

73. Ibid., 64.

74. "Instinct vs. Reason—A Black Cat," in *Edgar Allan Poe: Poetry, Tales, and Selected Essays* (New York: Library of America, 1996), 370; all Poe stories from this collection hereafter cited in the text.

75. Roy Harvey Pearce explores the discourses of civility and savagism—and how these discourses inflected U.S. colonial expansion and U.S. literary production—in his *Savagism and Civilization: A Study of the Indian and the American Mind* (Baltimore: Johns Hopkins UP, 1967).

76. Edgar Allan Poe, "The Journal of Julius Rodman," 1227–28; emphasis added.

77. Edgar Allan Poe, "The Man That Was Used Up: A Tale of the Late Bugaboo and Kickapoo Campaign" *Burton's Gentleman's Magazine and American Monthly Review* 5.2 (August 1839): 66–67; hereafter cited in the text.

78. Joan Tyler Mead, "Poe's 'The Man That Was Used Up': Another Bugaboo Campaign," *Studies in Short Fiction* 23.3 (1986): 281; hereafter cited in the text.

79. Ronald Curran, "The Fashionable Thirties: Poe's Satire in 'The Man That Was Used Up.'" *Markham Review* 8 (1978): 14; hereafter cited in the text.

80. Poe edited this passage out of later versions of this story.

81. Colin Dayan, "Amorous Bondage: Poe, Ladies, and Slaves," *American Literature* 66.2 (1994): 257.

82. Ortwin de Graef, "The Eye of the Text: Two Short Stories by Edgar Allan Poe," *Modern Language Notes* 104 (1989): 1104.

83. In "A Folklore Source for 'The Man That Was Used Up,'" *Poe Studies* 8 (1975), Elmer R. Pry argues that Poe's story was influenced by "popular American folk traditions about Indians" (46). Pry notes that such traditions "both oral and written, persisted from the Colonial American period deep into the nineteenth-century era of Western expansion, recounting over and over the duping of ignorant Indians by clever white men" (46). Pry cites folklorist Richard Dorson's account of this tradition:

> A chronicle of 1675 relates how Captain Mosely with sixty men faced three hundred Indians in battle; the captain plucked off his periwig and tucked it into his breeches, preparatory to fighting, whereupon the red men turned tail and fled, crying out "Umh, Umh, me no stay more fight Engismon, Engismon got two head, if me cut off un head he got noder a put on beder as dis." This theme persisted across the frontier, and we hear of a Yankee on the western plains, confronted by hostile Indians, pulling out his false teeth and unstrapping his cork leg, then making a move as if to unscrew his head, the while informing the braves he could similarly dismember them; they fled in terror. (quoted in Pry 46)

Pry's research reinforces my contention that "The Man That Was Used Up" was influenced by U.S. attitudes toward Indian removal and Indian warfare.

84. At the beginning of the Second Seminole War, when Scott arrived at Fort Dane, he was described as "one of nature's finest specimens of the genus homo" (qtd. in John K. Mahon's *History of the Second Seminole War: 1835–42*, rev. ed. [Gainesville: U of Florida P, 1991], 140).

85. Richard A. Alekna, "'The Man That Was Used Up': Further Notes on Poe's Satirical Targets," *Poe Studies* 12 (1979): 36.

86. Quoted ibid.

87. Ibid., 36.

88. Curran briefly mentions in a footnote that "two well-known Indian wars took place during this period: the Black Hawk War of 1832 and the Second Seminole War, 1835–42" (19). However, Curran does not explore in any detail how these wars might have influenced the text's production, choosing instead to analyze Poe's satire of the "Fashionable Thirties" in "The Man That Was Used Up."

89. *Poe Poe Poe Poe Poe Poe Poe* (New York: Doubleday, 1972), 97.

90. George Walton, *Fearless and Free: The Seminole Indian War 1835–42* (Indianapolis: Bobbs-Merrill, 1977), 103.

91. Quoted in Mahon, *History of the Second Seminole War*, 165.

92. George E. Buker, *Swamp Sailors: Riverine Warfare in the Everglades 1835–1842* (Gainesville: U of Florida P, 1975), 13.

93. Ibid., 8.

94. Ibid.

95. See Mahon, *History of the Second Seminole War*, 82–85; and Buker, *Swamp Sailors*, 9, for further discussion of this treaty and the controversy surrounding its signing.

96. See Mahon, *History of the Second Seminole War*, 108–12, for further discussion of the Battle of Withlacoochee.

97. Ibid., 140

98. Walton, *Fearless and Free*, 106.

99. Ibid., 129.

100. Mahon, *History of the Second Seminole War*, 157.

101. Walton, *Fearless and Free*, 239.

102. Mahon, *History of the Second Seminole War*, 161.

103. Rogin, *Fathers and Children*, 239.

104. Walton, *Fearless and Free*, 241.

105. See the introduction to *The Colonizing Trick: National Culture and Imperial Citizenship in Early America* for David Kazanjian's fascinating discussion of "articulation" in early American literature, politics, and culture.

106. Aristotle, *The "Art" of Rhetoric*, trans. John Henry Freese (Cambridge: Harvard UP, 1939), 363, sec. 3.3.1.

107. In *A Voice and Nothing More* (Cambridge: MIT P, 2006), Mladen Dolar defines the voice as "the material element recalcitrant to meaning, and if we speak in order to say something, then the voice is precisely that which cannot be said. It is there, in the very act of saying, but it eludes any pinning down, to the point where we could maintain that it is the non-linguistic, the extralinguistic element which enables speech phenomena, but cannot itself be discerned by linguistics" (15).

5. NO THING IN COMMON

I would like to thank Eduardo Cadava, Colin Dayan, Ruth Mack, Claudia L. Johnson, Kir Kuiken, and Evan Horowitz for their help with this chapter. Much of the research for the Walpole section was conducted while I was a Fletcher Jones Foundation Fellow at the Huntington Library; and I am also indebted to Anna Chalcraft and the Friends of Strawberry Hill for their private tour of Walpole's villa.

1. Horace Walpole to Miss Hannah More, 20 July 1789, in *The Yale Edition of Horace Walpole's Correspondence*, ed. W. S. Lewis (Yale: Yale UP), 31: 312–14; available online courtesy of the Lewis Walpole Library at http://images.library.yale.edu/hwcorrespondence/.

2. Horace Walpole, "A Scheme for Raising a Large Sum of Money for the Use of the Government, by Laying a Tax on Message-Cards and Notes," in *Fugitive Pieces in Verse and Prose* (Twickenham: Strawberry-Hill Press, 1763), 47; hereafter cited parenthetically as "SR," followed by page number.

3. Edmund Burke sees him, more generously, as a learned loiterer—the "best of *that* kind." Quoted in Abigail Lynn Coykendall, "Conjuring Inherited Empire: Gothic Real Estate and the Eighteenth-Century British Novel" (Ph.D. diss., State University of New York at Buffalo, 2002), 40.

4. In *Literary Historicity: Literature and Historical Experience in Eighteenth-Century Britain* (Stanford: Stanford UP, 2009), Ruth Mack argues that Wapole's work—in particular his famous Gothic novel *The Castle of Otranto*—offers a powerful critique of Enlightenment historiography: "[*Otranto*] uses imagination—ultimately the supernatural itself—to what we might still think of as realist ends. Far from simply opposing realist truth [as in the standard reading of the Gothic], it is deeply invested in interrogating the terms for that truth in order to support the possibility of real historical representation on grounds other than those empiricist philosophy was willing to offer outright" (128). Mack's book uncovers a richly interdisciplinary vein of Counter-Enlightenment thinking in eighteenth-century Britain, and she contextualizes *Otranto*'s skepticism within debates concerning the nature of historical truth. In what follows, I show how this critique is mobilized in a number of Walpole's other texts, and I read his philosophy of uniquity as an important intervention in and alternative to these same debates. For other recent critical attempts to take Walpole's historiography seriously, see Coykendall, "Conjuring Inherited Empire"; Sean Silver, "Visiting Strawberry Hill: Horace Walpole's Gothic Historiography," *Eighteenth-Century Fiction* 21.4 (2009): 535–64; Barrett Kalter, "DIY Gothic: Thomas Gray and the Medieval Revival," *ELH* 70 (2003): 989–1019; and Susan Bernstein, *Housing Problems: Writing and Architecture in Goethe, Walpole, Freud, and Heidegger* (Stanford: Stanford UP, 2008).

5. For a fascinating assessment of the place of the Gothic in romance revivals, see Duncan, *Modern Romance and Transformations of the Novel*, 20–50.

6. Chapter 1 of Coykendall's dissertation, "Conjuring Inherited Empire," further explores the relationship between Walpole and David Hume.

7. Michel de Certeau, *The Writing of History*, trans. Tom Conley (New York: Columbia UP, 1988), 12.

8. Ibid., 2–3.

9. Ibid., 5.

10. Alain Badiou, *Infinite Thought: Truth and the Return to Philosophy*, ed. and trans. Oliver Feltham and Justin Clemens (London: Continuum, 2003), 102.

11. Jean-Luc Nancy, *The Birth to Presence*, trans. Brian Holmes and others (Stanford: Stanford UP, 1993), 150.

12. Horace Walpole, "To Cloe," in *Journal of the Printing-Office at Strawberry Hill, Now First Printed From the Ms. of Horace Walpole* (London: Chiswick Press, 1923), 3–4.

13. Horace Walpole, *The Castle of Otranto* (Oxford: Oxford UP, 1996). The second edition of *Otranto* (1765) was subtitled "A Gothic Story."

14. Horace Walpole, *World*, "Numb. X.," in *Fugitive Pieces*, 95–96. Hereafter cited parenthetically as "N," followed by page number.

15. Horace Walpole to Horace Mann, 28 January 1754, in *Correspondence*, 20: 407–11.

16. Silver is an astute reader of serendipity as a historiographical methodology in *The Castle of Otranto* and *The Historic Doubts on the Life and Reign of King Richard III*. For Silver, *Otranto* "dramatizes a series of scenes of ... serendipitous illumination: helmet, glove, suit of armour, sword, and so forth, each serially come to light in Otranto, in spite of the fact—or even because of the fact—that nobody was looking for them, and nobody particularly wanted them when they had got them" (551).

17. Coykendall also discusses the *Doubts* in her dissertation, "Conjuring Inherited Empire," 25–102.

18. Horace Walpole, *Historic Doubts on the Life and Reign of King Richard the Third* (London: J. Dodsley, 1767), iii; hereafter cited parenthetically as *HD*, followed by page number.

19. Horace Walpole, "Supplement to the Historic Doubts on the Life and Reign of King Richard III," in *The Works of Horatio Walpole, Earl of Orford*, 5 vols. (London: G. G. and J. Robinson, 1798), 2:188; hereafter cited parenthetically as "Supp.," followed by page number.

20. Hannah Arendt, "The Concept of History," in *The Portable Hannah Arendt*, ed. Peter Baehr (London: Penguin, 2000), 297.

21. For further discussion of the Walpole-Hume correspondence regarding citations and footnotes, see Coykendall, "Conjuring Inherited Empire," 42.

22. For example, Walpole voiced his doubts over James Macpherson's translation of Ossian's *Fingal* (1762)—an ostensibly ancient Gaelic poem that Macpherson claimed to have recovered from the Scottish Highlands. Though initially taken by the "beautiful images [and] shining ideas" contained in the poem, Walpole quickly began to share the growing suspicion of its authenticity (Walpole to Sir David Dalrymple, 14 April 1761, in *Correspondence*, 15: 71–72). On 8 December 1761, Walpole aired his doubts in a letter to George Montagu:

> *Fingal* is come out—I have not yet got through it . . . but it is very fine—yet I cannot at once compass an epic poem now. It tires me to death to read how many ways a warrior is like the moon, or the sun, or a rock, or a lion, or the ocean. *Fingal* is a brave collection of similes, and will serve all the boys at Eton and Westminster for these twenty years. I will trust you with a secret, but you must not disclose it, I should be ruined with my Scotch friends—in short, I cannot believe it genuine—I cannot believe a regular poem of six books has been preserved, uncorrupted, by oral tradition, from times before Christianity was introduced into the island. What! Preserved unadulterated by savages dispersed among mountains, and so often driven from their dens, so wasted by wars civil and foreign! Has one man ever got all by heart? I doubt it. Were parts preserved by some, other parts by others? Mighty lucky, that the tradition was never interrupted, nor any part lost—not a verse, not a measure, not the sense! Luckier and luckier—I have been extremely qualified myself lately for this Scotch memory; we have had nothing but a coagulation of rains, fogs, and frosts, and though they have clouded all understanding, I suppose if I had tried, I should have found that they thickened and gave great consistence to my remembrance. (*Correspondence*, 9: 407–8)

Mired in a "coagulation of rains, fogs, and frosts," Walpole finds his suspicions aroused by *Fingal*'s cloying and savage "similes" and can effect only qualified admiration. Walpole will later voice similar doubts over the authenticity of Thomas Chatterton's *Rowley* poems, accusations that were thought by many to have contributed to Chatterton's suicide. Walpole, however, attributed more blame to the nation's thirst for the antique, claiming in a 1777 letter that "Macpherson's success with Ossian was more the ruin of Chatterton than I" (Walpole to the Reverend William Cole, 19 June 1777, in *Correspondence*, 2: 51–53).

23. Walpole to the Countess of Ossory, 5 January 1772, in *Correspondence*, 32: 78–83; quoted in Coykendall, "Conjuring Inherited Empire," 98.

24. Horace Walpole, *A Description of the Villa of Mr. Horace Walpole* (Twickenham: Thomas Kirgate, 1784), i; hereafter cited parenthetically as *DV*, followed by page number. Walpole frequently gave tours of Strawberry Hill and took great pleasure in printing his own admission tickets.

25. *Otranto*, 9.

26. Compare the "convenience" of Walpole's modern Gothic with Catherine Morland's description of Northanger Abbey:

> The furniture was all in the profusion and elegance of modern taste.... The windows, to which she looked with peculiar dependence, from having heard the General talk of his preserving them in Gothic form with reverential care, were yet less what her fancy had portrayed. To be sure, the pointed arch was preserved—the form of them was Gothic—they might be even casements—but every pane was so large, so clear, so light! ... The General ... began to talk of the smallness of the room and simplicity of the furniture, where every thing being for daily use, pretended only to comfort.

(Jane Austen, *Northanger Abbey, Lady Susan, The Watsons, Sanditon*, ed. James Kinsley and John Davie [New York: Oxford World's Classics, 2003], 118).

27. *See* György Lukàcs, *The Historical Novel* (Boston: Beacon Press, 1983), 19.

28. In *The Man without Content*, trans. Georgia Albert (Stanford: Stanford UP, 1999), Giorgio Agamben observes:

> [I]n the countries of continental Europe, princes and learned men used to collect the most disparate objects in a *Wunderkammer* (cabinet of wonder), which contained, promiscuously, rocks of an unusual shape, coins, stuffed animals, manuscript volumes, ostrich eggs, and unicorn horns. Statues and paintings stood side by side with curios and exemplars of natural history in these cabinets of wonders when people started collecting art objects. ... Only seemingly does chaos reign in the *Wunderkammer*, however: to the mind of the medieval scholar, it was a sort of microcosm that reproduced, in its harmonious confusion, the animal, vegetable, and mineral macrocosm. This is why the individual objects seem to find their meaning only side by side with others, between the walls of a room in which the scholar could measure at every moment the boundaries of the universe. (30)

The boundaries of Walpole's universe are measured by a similar "chaos" of "harmonious confusion." In the same way that his economy of uniquity attributes a nonintrinsic value to the inessential relic, so too Strawberry Hill, his promiscuous *Wunderkammer*, collects "disparate objects" without sacrificing their singularity to a total and tasteful collectivity.

29. For selections of Gothic-Saxonist materials, see E. J. Clery and Robert Miles, eds., *Gothic Documents: A Sourcebook, 1700–1820* (Manchester: Manchester UP, 2000). The first four chapters of Reginald Horsman, *Race and Manifest Destiny: The Origins of American Racial Anglo-Saxonism* (Cambridge: Harvard UP, 1981) explore the rise of Gothic-Saxon mythology in Europe and its relationship to nationalism and theories of racial difference.

30. W. S. Lewis, "The Genesis of Strawberry Hill," *Metropolitan Museum Studies* 5.1 (1934): 57. In *Visiting Strawberry Hill* (AquatintBSC: Wimbledon, 2005), Anna

Chalcraft and Judith Viscardi frequently note the "asymmetrical arrangement" of Walpole's villa. "This false symmetry," they conclude, "must have been deliberately designed to surprise" (31).

31. In "Paper Castle, Paper Collection: Walpole's Extra-Illustrated Copy of the *Description of... Strawberry* Hill," Ruth Mack shows how Walpole understood even the objects of his collection to be temporary, rather than permanent, possessions: "For Walpole, then, the formal process of memorialization in the *Description* is double-edged: even as it preserves the objects through listing them individually, it makes plain the very conditions for their eventual dispersal and redistribution" (in *Horace Walpole's Strawberry Hill*, ed. Michal Snodin [New Haven: Yale UP, 2009], 109).

32. In *Housing Problems*, Susan Bernstein describes Strawberry Hill's relationship to originality and history as follows: "The mansion presents a peculiar mélange of authenticity and phoniness. Its materials and proportions do not resemble Gothic buildings, but rather reinforce the cottage origins and recall the process of imitation and revival they show off. Historical reference is thus established and demolished in the same gesture" (46).

33. See Eve Kosofsky Sedgwick, "The Character in the Veil Imagery of the Surface in the Gothic Novel," *PMLA* 96.2 (1981): 255–70.

34. Both Mack and Silver read the Walpolian object as an antiquarian response to the linearity of Enlightenment and empiricist historiography. "Each of these objects," argues Silver, "is less interesting for what it can teach us about a type or a series of things than as a unique object with its own historical associations" (541). My analysis of fugitivity shows how, for Walpole, these excessive "associations"—rather than the static, material object itself—constitute the vital movement of an effective engagement with history. I am, therefore, less interested than Mack and Silver in recovering a subversive antiquarian practice in Walpole's work. Walpole himself referred to those "boobies" at the Society of Antiquaries (Walpole to Reverend William Cole, 14 December 1775, in *Correspondence*, 1: 383–85), and, in a May 1774 letter to Cole, he describes the vanity of their attitude toward history as follows:

> The Society of Antiquaries put me in mind of what the old Lord Pembroke said to Anstis the herald: "Thou silly fellow! thou dost not know thy own silly business." If they went behind taste by poking into barbarous ages when there was no taste, one could forgive them—but they catch at the first ugly thing they see, and take it for old, because it is new to them, and then usher it pompously into the world as if they had made a discovery; though they have not yet cleared up a single point that is of the least importance, or that tends to settle any obscure passage in history. (*Correspondence*, 1: 328–31)

Rather than focus on the hubris of the material antiquarian object, it is important to foreground the sense of an ever-fractalizing and fugitive network of "historical associations" that Walpole's work opens up. For other accounts of antiquarianism and theories of collection in the eighteenth century, see John Bender and Michael Marrinan, eds., *Regimes of Description: In the Archive of the Eighteenth Century* (Stanford: Stanford UP, 2005); and Martin Myrone and Lucy Peltz, eds., *Producing the Past: Aspects of Antiquarian Culture and Practice, 1700–1850* (London: Ashgate, 1999).

35. Samuel Kliger, *The Goths in England: A Study in Seventeenth and Eighteenth Century Thought* (Cambridge: Harvard UP, 1952), 1.

36. Ibid., 3.

37. Thomas Babington Macaulay, *Critical and Historical Essays, Volume 1* (London: ElecBook, 2001), 504–5.

38. Lewis, "The Genesis of Strawberry Hill," 82–83.

39. Ibid., 64.

40. Walpole to Horace Mann, in *Correspondence*, 12 June 1753, 20: 379–84.

41. See Kalter for a discussion of Gothic wallpaper (including Walpole's) during the Medieval Revival in Britain.

42. Walpole to Thomas Barret, 5 June 1788, in *Correspondence*, 42: 220–22.

43. Lewis, "The Genesis of Strawberry Hill," 80.

44. As Chalcraft and Viscardi note, Walpole also refused to distinguish between private and public spaces during tours of Strawberry Hill: "[R]ooms may have been excluded to maintain privacy, as in modern country house tourism, and it is [Walpole's] choice of these private spaces which is the first surprise. The Blue Breakfast Room and the Green Closet, in which he wrote that he spent most of his time, and from which it could be expected that visitors would have been excluded, are both listed for viewing by a public who had applied for tickets" (7).

45. Walpole to Thomas Mann, 30 September 1784, in *Correspondence*, 25: 527–32.

46. See the *Letters of Horace Walpole, Earl of Orford, to Sir Horace Mann*, 2 vols., ed. Lord Dover (New York: George Dearborn, 1833).

47. "Mystification," in *Edgar Allan Poe: Poetry, Tales, and Selected Essays* (New York: Library of America, 1996), p. 253; hereafter cited in the text.

48. In *Fables of Mind* (Oxford: Oxford UP, 1987), Colin Dayan "attempt[s] to introduce a difficult Poe—serious in his farce and farcical in his seriousness" (8).

49. *Reading at the Social Limit*, 118.

50. Ibid., 117, 119.

51. "Eureka: An Essay on the Material and Spiritual Universe," in *Edgar Allan Poe: Poetry, Tales, and Selected Essays* (New York: Library of America, 1996), p. 1348; hereafter cited in the text.

52. "The Rationale of Verse," in *Edgar Allan Poe: Poetry, Tales, and Selected Essays* (New York: Library of America, 1996), 1430.

53. Dayan, *Fables of Mind*, 45.

54. For another approach to the paradoxes of language in "Eureka," see John T. Irwin's *American Hieroglyphics: The Symbol of the Egyptian Hieroglyphics in the American Renaissance* (Baltimore: Johns Hopkins UP, 1980), 22.

55. Qtd. in W. C. Harris, "*Eureka* and the Poetics of Constitution," *American Literary History* 12.1/2 (2000): 1.

56. Dayan claims that Poe "bases the 'true poetical effect' in *tone*—that 'mystic' or 'undercurrent' of meaning, which is not so much a mystical as a rhythmical rendering of words . . . that converts known into unknown" (70).

57. Benjamin, *The Origin of German Tragic Drama*, 34–35.

58. Ibid., 43.

59. See, for example, 1282–83.

60. Dayan, *Fables of Mind*, 25.

61. Ibid., 55.

62. Ibid.

63. See also Dayan's section "The Language of Mereness," 44–55.

64. See chapter 3 of John Limon's *The Place of Science Fiction in the Time of Science* (Cambridge: Cambridge UP, 1990) for a fasinating discussion of *Eureka*, gravity, and *Naturphilosophie*.

65. Harris, "*Eureka* and the Poetics of Constitution," 3.

66. Ibid., 31.

67. Ibid.

68. Immanuel Kant, *Critique of Judgment*, trans. Werner S. Pluhar (Indianapolis: Hackett, 1987), 79.

INDEX

aesthetics, 78, 168, 184, 186–89, 191, 207; allegory and, 4–5, 20–22, 212n11; camp, 32, 185; of the commodity, 50–51, 81–82 117; of dispossession, 140–46; and Enlightenment, 83, 102, 110–11; of idling, 12–13, 120–22, 125, 130; and memory, 129, 138, 140, 142; of pastoralism, 62; of property, 84, 87–88, 102; and politics, 143, 150–52, 159; theories of, 4–6; and the sublime, 75–76
Agamben, Giorgio, 7, 9, 13, 63, 126, 212n14, 220n55, 232n28
Anderson, Benedict, 209n3
antiquarianism, 10, 116, 134, 136, 169, 172, 176, 183, 187, 233n34
Arendt, Hannah, 7–9, 182
Austen, Jane, 55–56, 185, 232n26

Badiou, Alain, 177
Balibar, Étienne, 8
Benjamin, Walter, 5, 11, 15, 45–46, 90, 181; *The Origin of the German Tragic Drama*, 20–24, 43–44, 49, 201–2
Berlant, Lauren, 77, 217n10
Bird, Robert Montgomery, 104, 108; *Sheppard Lee*, 12, 103–13, 115, 117
Brown, Charles Brockden, 11, 123, 221n9; *Arthur Mervyn*, 11–12, 75, 78–104, 112–13, 115; *Edgar Huntly*, 76; "The Man at Home," 91–92
Buffon, Comte de, 71, 102–3
Burke, Edmund, 75, 79, 114, 119

Caron, Armelle, 1–2
Catlin, George, 144–47, 149, 167
Certeau, Michel de, 176–77, 180
Chaucer, Geoffrey, 81
Coleridge, Samuel Taylor, 209n6
community, theories of, 1–3, 6–10, 13–14, 20–21, 27. *See also* democracy
Cooper, James Fenimore, *Autobiography of a Pocket-Handkerchief*, 12, 113–19
Coykendall, Abigail, 214n44, 230n6, 230n17, 230n21
Culler, Jonathan, 9

Dayan, Colin, 162, 200, 202–3, 213n32, 234n48, 235n56, 235n63
Deleuze, Gilles, 22, 26
democracy, 9,11, 206; citizenship and, 7–9; and romance, 51, 63, 67, 76, 78, 83, 95, 103, 106, 108–14, 162
Derrida, Jacques, 214n40, 218n18
Dolar, Mladen, 228n107
Duncan, Ian, 45–46, 216n2, 230n5

Ellis, Markman, 64–65

Ellsworth, Henry Leavitt, 149–50, 157
Elmer, Jonathan, 72–74, 199, 216n31, 220n58, 223n34
Enlightenment, 11–12, 68–69, 71, 76, 82, 102–5, 110–12, 115, 117, 200; historiography and, 176–77, 181–82, 186–87, 196–97, 229n4, 233n34
Esposito, Roberto, 82–83, 85, 87–89, 218n23

Fiedler, Leslie, 76–77, 83, 217n4
Fletcher, Angus, 4–5
Fluck, Winfried, 6–7
Frege, Gottlob, 17–19
Freud, 77; *Beyond the Pleasure Principle*, 36–39, 49; the *unheimlich* and, 36–39
Frye, Northrop, 27

galvanic reanimation, 12, 104–6
Gamer, Michael, 213n24, 216n2
genericity, 21–27, 40, 49, 211n5, 213n22
Godwin, William, 55
Goldsmith, Oliver, 128
Goudie, Sean X., 89, 96–97

Hamacher, Werner, 9
Hegel, G. W. F., 107
historiography, 13, 23. See also Enlightenment and historiography
Hobbes, Thomas, 49, 82–83, 87,
Hoffman, E.T.A., 37
Hogle, Jerrold, 31, 33, 216n2
Humboldt, Alexander von, 201–2
Hume, David, 146, 176, 182–83
Hutcheson, Francis, 70

Irving, Washington, 12–13, 125, 148, 158; *A History of New-York*, 123–25; "Rip Van Winkle," 124–26, 129–32, 134–35, 137, 141–42, 148, 151, 153, 167, 223n36; *The Sketch-Book*, 125–44; *A Tour on the Prairies*, 151–58
it-narrative, 112–13, 115, 117–18

Jackson, Andrew, 142–43, 150–51, 156, 158, 162, 164–66
Jameson, Fredric, 27–29, 35, 52
Jefferson, Thomas, 11, 67–72, 88, 107, 110; *Notes on the State of Virginia*, 68–71; Ossian and, 67–68

Kant, Immanuel, 207
Kazanjian, David, 9, 63, 211n25, 228n105
Kerry, Benno, 19
Kristeva, Julia, 31

Levinas, Emmanuel, 51
Lewis, Matthew, 66
Lewis, W.S., 185–86, 189–90
Lincoln, Abraham, 144
Locke, John, 10–12, 68, 84–90, 100–105, 107, 110–11, 116, 118, 120–23, 130, 137, 218n23, 220n1
Logan's speech, 68, 71–74
Looby, Christopher, 108, 124
Lukács, Gyorgy, 24, 185

Macaulay, Thomas, 188–89
Mack, Ruth, 229n4, 233n31, 233n34
Mackenzie, Henry, 10–11, 51, 60–61; *Julia de Roubigné*, 55–67, 131; *The Man of Feeling*, 53–55, 57–58, 70, 73, 88, 131
Macpherson, James, 24
Malthus, Thomas, *An Essay on the Principle of Population*, 136–37
Manning, Susan, 64, 68, 215n12
Marx, Karl, 4, 34–35, 50–51, 53, 55, 81–82, 84, 88, 107, 118, 214n3
McKeon, Michael, 23, 27, 33–35
mesmerism, 3, 12, 78, 104, 112, 118–20, 199, 220n58

metempsychosis, 3, 12, 78, 103–4, 106, 109, 111–13, 116–18, 132
More, Hannah, 168–69
Murray, Laura J., 225n61

Nancy, Jean-Luc, 1, 13, 25, 126, 177, 181, 222n26
National Park, origins of, 146–49
Native Americans, 10, 71; Black Hawk, 144–45, 150; Cherokee, 149–50, 156–57, 164; Indian removal, 137, 142–44, 149–50, 154–58, 163–66, 225n61; King Philip and, 138–39; Seminole, 164–66. *See also* Logan, Speech of
Neal, John, 75–76, 139, 143

The Odyssey, 48
Ossian, 24, 67–68, 231n22

Parker, Patricia, 214n47
Pearce, Roy Harvey, 226n75
Percy, Thomas, 24
phrenology, 70, 224n48
Poe, Edgar Allan, 10, 14, 90, 107, 117, 159; *Eureka*, 10, 13, 200–207; "The Journal of Julius Rodman," 158–60; "The Man That Was Used Up," 160–68; "Mystification," 198–99; *The Narrative of Arthur Gordon Pym*, 159
Pope, Alexander, 175
Propp, Vladimir, 27

Rancière, Jacques, 3, 5–6, 25–26, 36, 209n4
Rip Van Winkle; or Demons of the Catskill Mountains!!! A National Drama (John Kerr), 141–42
romance, 3, 17, 20, 22–35, 50–52; Gothic, 11, 14, 15–16, 29–36, 39–47, 53, 66, 75–78, 82–84, 102, 106, 110–12, 118, 120, 139, 169–90; medieval, 22–23; poiesis of, 26–27; politics of, 6, 63–64, 75–78, 83, 139, 153–58, 163, 215n16; of race and blood, 11, 62–74, 94–103, 107–11, 115–19
Romanticism, 5, 23–25, 30, 44, 124
Russell, Bertrand, 17–19

Schmitt, Carl, 24, 59
Scott, General Winfield, 163–66
Scott, Sir Walter, 127
set theory, 16–20
Shaftesbury, Earl of, 52–53
Shapiro, Stephen, 96–97, 219n29
Silver, Sean, 230n16, 233n34
Simondon, Gilbert, 212n10
Sterne, Laurence, 72; *A Sentimental Journey*, 59, 61–62, 97–103, 119

Tocqueville, Alexis de, 121–23
transatlantic studies, 6–9

Vattel, Emeric de, 121, 130

Walpole, Horace, 13–14, 16, 168–81, 203; *The Castle of Otranto*, 10–11, 15–16, 29–36, 39–47, 49; *A Description of the Villa of Mr. Horace Walpole*, 184–98; *Historic Doubts on the Life and Reign of King Richard the Third*, 181–84
Warner, Michael, 125, 131
Warner, William, 34–35
Watt, Ian, 33
Weber, Samuel, 44, 211n9
Wiegman, Robyn, 7
Wollstonecraft, Mary, 62
Wyclif, John (John Wycliffe), 81

Žižek, Slavoj, 77–78, 217n11, 218n12

Index 239

COMMONALITIES

Timothy C. Campbell, series editor

Roberto Esposito, *Terms of the Political: Community, Immunity, Biopolitics.* Translated by Rhiannon Noel Welch. Introduction by Vanessa Lemm.

Maurizio Ferraris, *Documentality: Why It Is Necessary to Leave Traces.* Translated by Richard Davies.

Dimitris Vardoulakis, *Sovereignty and Its Other: Toward the Dejustification of Violence.*

Anne Emmanuelle Berger, *The Queer Turn in Feminism: Identities, Sexualities, and the Theater of Gender.* Translated by Catherine Porter.

James D. Lilley, *Common Things: Romance and the Aesthetics of Belonging in Atlantic Modernity.*